EERL Withdrawn
Surplus/Duplicate

Welfare or Bureaucracy?

PUBLICATION OF THE SCIENCE CENTER BERLIN
Volume 20

Editorial Board

Prof. Dr. Karl W. Deutsch
Prof. Dr. Meinolf Dierkes
Prof. Dr. Frieder Naschold
Prof. Dr. Fritz W. Scharpf

Office of the Secretary General

Welfare or Bureaucracy?

Problems of Matching Social Services
to Clients' Needs

Research on Service Delivery
Volume II

Edited by
Dieter Grunow
Friedhart Hegner

Oelgeschlager, Gunn & Hain, Publishers, Inc.
Cambridge, Massachusetts

Verlag Anton Hain
Königstein/Ts.

HV
8
W44
THE ELMER E. RASMUSON LIBRARY
UNIVERSITY OF ALASKA

Copyright © 1980 by Oelgeschlager, Gunn & Hain, Publishers, Inc., and by Verlag Anton Hain Meinsenheim GmbH., Konigstein/Ts. All rights reserved. No part of this publication may be reproduced, stored in a retrieval system, or transmitted in any form or by any means, electronic mechanical photocopy, recording or otherwise, without the prior written consent of the publishers.

International Standard Book Number: 0-89946-060-7 (U.S.A.)
3-445-12054-4 (Germany)

Library of Congress Catalog Card Number: 80-20631

Printed in the United States of America

Library of Congress Cataloging in Publication Data
Main entry under title:

Welfare or bureaucracy?

(Research on service delivery; v.2)
Bibliography: p.
1. Social service—Congresses. 2. Social policy—Congresses. I. Grunow, Dieter. II. Hegner, Friedhart. III. Series.
HV8.W44 361.3 80-20631 ISBN 0-89946-060-7

Contents

List of Figures

List of Tables

Foreword

This is the second publication of the Science Center Berlin on Research on Service Delivery. It is one of the main tasks of the Science Center Berlin to venture into new research fields relating to urgent social and political problems, and public services are such a problem area. In the Federal Republic of Germany, as in other western countries, the proportion of the service industries in the labor force as well as in the GNP is steadily increasing. Accordingly, the expansion of the service sector is becoming more and more subject to criticism and analysis. All the social criticism is primarily directed at the quantitative and qualitative expansion of services and the financial and personal resources they require. But these evident trends must be interpreted in the wider context of social changes in highly industrialized countries. The OECD report on "Policies for Innovation in the Service Sector" took up this problem and encouraged research in this field.

Within the framework of the research program of the International Institute of Management at the Science Center Berlin, a number of activities have been initiated in the past few years in the problem area of "service delivery." These soon went beyond the scope of single projects and turned out to be a research program in their own right. The scientists involved in these projects decided to unite their efforts with those of researchers at the University of Bielefeld who were working in the same field and formulated an integrated research program covering problems of health services, legal services, and social services. This integrated research concept may lead to the institutionalization of "service delivery" as a research priority at the Science Center Berlin.

As part of the initial research, and stimulated by the abovementioned OECD report, the Science Center, in cooperation with the OECD, held an international conference on Innovations in Service Delivery in the summer of 1978. I am very pleased to include these conference proceedings in the Science Center publication series. The discussion and results of this conference demonstrate the relevance of the approaches developed at the Science Center in the research field of service delivery.

Needless to say, the responsibility for the data, results, and conclusions presented rests solely with the authors.

Helmut G. Meier
Secretary General
Science Center Berlin

Preface

In 1977 the former secretary general of the Science Center Berlin, Dr. Helmut G. Meier, together with some research fellows of the International Institute of Management, developed the idea of organizing an international conference on Innovations in the Public Services. With the support of the OECD, Paris, and the Senate of Berlin this conference took place in June 1978.

The general topic of the conference, "Responsiveness of Public Services to Clients' Needs," was dealt with in three sections or work groups: Innovations in Health Services, Innovations in Legal Services, and Innovations in Social Services.

The papers presented to this conference are being published in three volumes. Anybody with personal experience of editing a reader with manuscripts coming from different countries knows how fascinating and tedious a business this can be. In the group on "Social Services" (in German *Soziale Dienstleistungen*, which constitute a field of benefits in cash, in kind, and in personal services of a more limited scope than the Anglo-Saxon term "social services" suggests), authors from six countries—France, Federal Republic of Germany, Great Britain, Israel, Norway and the United States—presented papers. All the authors agreed to go through their papers, after the conference, to fit them better to the "red line" developed by the editors.

Dorothy Sinfield, in Edinburgh, Scotland, had the difficult task of supervising the translation and undertaking the stylistic revision of these papers, assisted by Adrian Sinfield. She was supported by the excellent secretarial skills of Susan Carpenter at the University of Essex, who prepared the manuscripts for printing.

As editors we were lucky to have committed authors as well as help with technical editing. We are deeply indebted to all of them. At the same time we want to express our thanks to the former secretary general of the Science Center, Dr. Helmut G. Meier, who arranged the financial support for the editing process. Finally, we are obliged to Professor Meinolf Dierkes, who made helpful comments on the revision and arrangement of the manuscripts with a view to the general topic "Responsiveness of Social Services to Clients' Needs."

The final responsibility for any deficiencies lies with the editors.

Friedhart Hegner
Dieter Grunow

Chapter 1

Introduction: Can We Say Good-bye to the Attempt to Solve Social Problems by Expanding and Reorganizing the Social Services?

*Friedhart Hegner**

After hours of intensive discussions, one of the participants in the conference on Innovations in the Public Services emphatically made the following proposition:

> We should say good-bye to the present ways of expanding or reorganizing social services. Before planning or implementing new measures to deal with social problems, we should systematically evaluate the existing delivery systems and their outcomes. It is completely useless to take new steps before we know what kinds of positive or negative effects our former measures had or have.

This proposition was strongly opposed by the majority of the participants. They agreed that we are in urgent need of better evaluation of services as well as of delivery systems. But they also feared that a scientifically based demand for a stop to further reforms and innovations in the field of social policy and social administration would present arguments to those politicians and administrators who oppose reforms and innovations on ideological—mostly conservative—grounds. Instead of looking for better means to foster the welfare

*International Institute of Management, Science Center Berlin, and Research Group, Social Planning and Social Administration, Bielefeld, Federal Republic of Germany.

of those who are in need of benefits, these politicians and administrators would passively wait for the so-called "self-healing forces," thereby supporting the "passive bureaucracy" as a rationing mechanism for social services.

From my point of view, the speaker was as right as the discussants. It could be true that the expansion and reform of social services do not add anything valuable to the well-being of those who are in need of organized support, but only serve the vested interests of those who are members of service organizations or research institutues and planning agencies. On the other hand, it could also be true that stagnation and passivity with regard to improving the delivery of social services are not in the interest of the whole society, but only serve the vested interests of those who are in work (and not those without work) and those who enjoy a good lifestyle (and do not suffer from poverty, sickness, mental illness, and the like).

At present, scientific knowledge can neither completely reject nor absolutely prove either of the two assumptions. It seems to me that it is, and will continue to be, one of the main tasks of scientific research in the field of social services to find out

Which types of services should be expanded and improved,
Which types of social problems and individual needs could and should be met—or even abolished—with the help of new social services and innovations in the field of social policy, and
Which types of service delivery organizations, professions, and benefits (in cash, in kind, and in personal services) could and should be reduced, without aggravating the situation of those who suffer from social problems.

Ten or fifteen years ago this kind of question was not fashionable in research dealing with social problems, social policy, and social administration. The reform enthusiasm of the Johnson era in the United States and the Brandt-Scheel era in the Federal Republic of Germany focused on planning the expansion and improvement of almost every kind of public service. It seemed to be self-evident that nearly all kinds of social problems and individual needs should and could be met—or even removed—by better planning and organizing within the public sphere. Old bureaucracies were reorganized and new ones were planned and implemented. To overcome the deficiencies of former service delivery organizations, hundreds and thousands of professionals were educated in expanding universities and hired for expanding ministries of social welfare, public assistance agencies, hospitals, daycare centers, and so forth. From the beginning, there were some sophisticated critics asking whether all kinds of social problems could adequately be met by formally organized service delivery systems and whether the deficiencies of bureaucratized "help agencies" could actually be overcome by professionalized "helpers." But these critics were not listened to at that time, when the initial successes of the "new" social policy—and there were some enormous improvements in the conditions of hitherto neglected groups—legitimized bureaucratization and professionalization.

In the middle of the 1970s the "social climate" changed—and scientific priorities changed, too. Inconsistencies within political reform programs were criticized, deficiencies in program implementation became evident, dysfunctions of formally organized service delivery were rediscovered, and the optimistic assessments of professionalism were counteracted by empirical findings on "biases in professional client selection." There are at least three reasons for the rude awakening of the reformers:

1. The so-called energy crisis and its consequences made it evident that the "limits to growth" not only exist in the papers of the Club of Rome, but are inherent in the economy and in the natural environment of the modern industrial state.
2. The persistence of old social problems and the emergence of new ones made it evident that the planning, organizing, and professionalizing of social service delivery systems quickly reach built-in limits of the welfare state. These stem from characteristics of the social and economic order—that is, from the societal environment of delivery organizations.
3. Symptoms of growing dissatisfaction and waning "mass loyalty" within parts of the population as well as citizen protest against deficiencies of bureaucratism and professionalism made it evident that there can be a sharp contrast between the inner dynamics of service delivery systems, with their routinized standards of selecting or handling client problems, on the one hand, and individual claimants with their preferences for "social warmth" and encompassing assistance, on the other hand.

The disillusion emerging with this rude awakening provoked strong reactions and criticisms against some components of the established welfare state. It is interesting to see how radical protest and conservative opposition coincide with regard to calling for alternatives to the present modes of handling social problems by organized and professionalized service delivery systems. The two most prominent forms of calls for alternatives are:

1. The encouragement of radical social services, which aim at a radical change in the structure of the social order, because the

problems of groups and individuals are seen as rooted in the larger "social chaos." From this point of view, social services are thought to become organizing tools for raising consciousness and aggressively confronting the structural deficiencies of the social order.

2. The encouragement of passive social services, which limit themselves to the handling of problems that threaten public order or social peace. Social services are thought to guarantee a minimum of well-being to every member of society and to improve the conditions for those who jeopardize the ideology of the welfare state by falling below a widely accepted national minimum. All other kinds of social problems and individual needs should be met by, and left to, the "self-healing" forces of mutual aid and individual self-help.

None of the authors of this reader adheres—or adhered in 1978—to the programs of "radical" or "passive" social services. Seen as a whole, the following articles advocate a mixture of different kinds of services:

1. Radical social services concentrating on those problem areas where urgent individual needs can only be met by radical changes in working conditions, housing or environment;
2. Passive social services, leaving room for self-help, mutual aid, and private associations in those problem areas where formally and professionally organized service delivery tends to destroy or threaten individual motives to (re)gain self-esteem and self-consciousness by "doing things on behalf of myself or in close contact with my associates";
3. Supportive social services, encouraging or initiating self-help groups and citizen associations in those problem areas where individual needs can only be fulfilled by the combined efforts of social "self-healing forces" and public services (for example, in the form of community work and social action);
4. Conventional social services, producing, organizing, and distributing all kinds of benefits (in cash, in kind, in personal services) for those problem areas where the maintenance of well-being or the improvement of living conditions cannot be guaranteed—given the present social and economic order—without bureaucratically and professionally organized service delivery.

Most of the chapters in this reader focus on the latter type of services. In dealing with the biases and deficiencies of bureaucratism and professionalism, the questions considered are (1) whether there is enough room within the present structures of delivery systems to augment responsiveness to clients' needs, and (2) whether there are built-in limitations to responsiveness that make it necessary to substitute the principles of formal and professional organizations by alternative modes of service production and distribution.

It is characteristic of all the articles that they do not leave out the environment of the service delivery organizations: Individual properties of staff members and clients are taken into account as well as the psychological problems of transforming personal needs into claims and demands. The reflection and manifestation of larger social, economic, or political order in the structures and dynamics of service organizations are considered, as well as the influence of vested (professional) interests on the distribution of goods and services. The relationships between social policy formation, implementation, and evaluation are taken into account, as well as the present neglect of these relationships within large areas of the social sciences.

Parts I and IV focus on general societal (political, economic, cultural, social) conditions influencing or shaping service delivery organizations. Parts II and III aim at elaborating the structural properties and specific dynamics of formal and professional service organizations. Besides the organizational characteristics resulting from environmental influences, there are those organizational patterns of selecting and handling clients that result from communication, cooperation, conflict, and social perception within a framework of abstract formal rules and professional standards. The social mechanisms of recruiting, placing, promoting, or downgrading staff members constitute a further basis for the lack of responsiveness to clients' needs; nor must we forget the resulting perceptions, expectations, and aspirations of the personnel.

Parts I through III deal mainly with faults, biases, and deficiencies of established service delivery systems. The attempt to diagnose and explain these deficiencies consciously aims at identifying room for improvement by innovation. This attempt forms the core of the articles in Part IV. There, alternatives to present forms of service delivery are outlined. At the same time, reformulations of concepts, theories, and research tools with a view to the analysis of service delivery systems are proclaimed.

What answer can be given to the initial question, Can we say good-bye to the attempt to solve social problems by expanding and reorganizing the social services?

1. We have to say good-bye to the blinkered view that nearly all kinds of social problems and individual needs can be met by bureaucratically and professionally organized services.

2. We have to say good-bye to the one-sided focus on conventional social services, and we must search for an adequate mixture of "radical," "passive," "supportive," and "conventional" social services.
3. We have to say good-bye to the false belief that reorganization of service delivery systems can be implemented without changing some of the larger social and political conditions and some of our present scientific concepts, theories, and research tools.
4. We have to say good-bye to the ideology that improvements and innovations in the fields of social services and social science can succeed in overcoming social inequality and social problems without structural changes in some aspects of the larger economic and social order.

Neither expanding nor stopping or restricting social service delivery can function as a panacea for unacceptable forms of social inequality and social problems. Nothing else but taking the real life situations and personal needs of citizen groups as a reference point can help us to attain an adequate balance between the expansion and the restriction of service delivery organizations. Making social services more responsive to clients' needs requires detailed analysis of the dynamics of delivery systems as much as investigation of deficient life situations and corresponding needs. Therefore, the participants in the conference agreed that the analysis of "supply" had to be complemented by an analysis of "demand"—a topic for another conference.

PART I

Societal Dimensions of Delivering and Denying Social Services

At first sight it seems to be self-evident that social policy and social administration aim at the delivery of services to needy persons: "the welfare state is devoted to the well-being of the whole society; it is as much concerned with maintaining or improving conditions for those who enjoy a good life style as with raising the standard of living of those who fall below an acceptable national minimum, . . ." (Robson 1976: 174). Strictly speaking, social policy and social administration not only deliver social services but also withhold their delivery. There are several reasons for this ambivalence. One is the fact that welfare is of unlimited scope whereas the resources of the welfare state are limited. Another results from the fact that the said standards ("a good life style"; "an acceptable national minimum") have been socially defined and are subject to historical changes of values and norms. A third is rooted in the opposition between the dynamics of people having a multiplicity or variety of needs and the dynamics of bureaucratically or professionally organized delivery systems with their limited capacities and selectively structured awareness of needs.

In examining these reasons, discussion of service delivery is always accompanied by critics referring to the withholding of services. Often these critics narrowly concentrate upon deficiencies of the structure of delivery systems—for example, focusing on "bureaucratism" or "professionalism." Undoubtedly, these structural deficiencies of delivery systems form one important restriction to an adequate provision of social services; they are empirically described and theoretically analyzed in Parts II and III of this volume. At the same time, it must be clear that reforms of delivery organizations will never succeed in overcoming the withholding of social services. These reforms or innovations take place within the structural constraints of social, economic, and political conditions—that is, by society and history. Part I focuses on these societal constraints.

In Chapter 2, Rivka Bar-Yosef elaborates the idea that the definition of needs as well as their satisfaction depends not only on personal preferences and organizationally set up priorities but also on societal mechanisms. The "inventory of needs" is constituted by sociopolitical trends as well as by scientific knowledge and moral standards: the "satisfaction of needs" depends not only on individual levels of aspiration and organizational patterns of selecting and dealing with clients but also on the societal patterns of distributing goods and services on the basis of economic or fiscal priority setting and ethical or moral responsibility attribution. The structures and functions of service delivery systems result from these environmental (social, economic, cultural, political) conditions as well as from specific organizational and professional dynamics, as Rivka Bar-Yosef demonstrates.

Franz-Xaver Kaufmann's article (Chapter 3) deals with the links and interdependencies of global societal conditions and specific strategies of social policy by elaborating the relationship between "social policy and social services." It is no accident that the terms ("social policy" and "social services") have different origins and meanings in Great Britain and Germany and that there are differences in the prevailing "forms of political intervention" (by law, by money, and by personal services). To understand the prerequisites and consequences of these different forms of intervention for need satisfaction, one has to consider the process of policy formation and implementation as well as the outcome and impact of declared citizens' rights and of benefits in cash, in kind, and in personal services. Once again we become aware of the interdependencies among specific forms of service delivery organizations, services delivered, and global sociopolitical conditions or trends that hitherto have often been neglected in research—as Kaufmann demonstrates.

The development of different "strategies" (e.g., income strategy versus service strategy) and "forms of intervention" (by law, by money, and by personal services) is often said to promote the expansion of welfare benefits to the whole society—that is, to all strata and kinds of social problems. Else Øyen's article (Chapter 4)—dealing with the Norwegian Social Security system—gives many indications of the ideological mystifications of this statement. The rights of citizens to the benefits of the welfare state may—*cum grano salis*—aim at equality with regard to need satisfaction, but the modes of actualizing these rights in the process of service delivery do not. There are a lot of "rationing mechanisms," implicitly or explicitly effectuating the withholding of service delivery from certain groups of the target population. These rationing mechanisms apparently result from the proper dynamics of "red tape" and professional standards, but at the same time they are deeply rooted in the social structure of the so-called welfare society. Besides the discrimination against low income groups, there is a more or less overt conflict between those in work and those not working, leading to lack of services and to utilization barriers for the elderly, the young, housewives, the sick, and so forth.

The discrimination against those not working cannot be overcome by isolated reforms or innovations within existing service delivery organizations. Beyond this, we are in need of structural changes within society as a whole—for example, with regard to the relationship between economic position (level of income), social status (rights and duties), and sociocultural prestige (self-esteem and attributed social "value"). At this point we definitely leave the area of isolated reforms or innovations within the public services.

Chapter 2

The Social Perspective of Personal Needs and Their Satisfaction

*Rivka W. Bar-Yosef**

INTRODUCTION

The elementary prerequisite for the continuous existence of a society is the maintenance of its members. In spite of this truism, sociological theory does not provide us with satisfactory concepts, institutional models, or comparative analyses focused on the ways and means by which members of different societies satisfy their needs and wants. Functionalist theory, which until recently dominated sociology, focused attention on "societal needs." In the words of Homans, functionalists were interested in norms, roles, and the ways in which institutions fit together. The unit of analysis was not the individual but the norms of institutionalized behavior. Homans extends his criticism to the theories of Parsons and Smelser, who "separated the personality system from the social system and proposed to deal with the latter. It was the personality system that had 'needs, drives, skills, etc.' It was not part of the social system, but only conducted exchanges with it, by providing it, for instance, with disembodied motivation" (Homans 1964). The Parsonian universe, when first conceptualized, contained three subsystems—the social, the cultural, and the personality—each the legitimate

*Hebrew University, Jerusalem.

subject matter of a division of the social sciences—sociology, anthropology, and psychology, respectively. Only some three decades later did Parsons add the fourth action subsystem of the "behavioral organism" (Parsons 1970b).

Sociology, being defined as the discipline that deals with one subsystem, is interested in processes that ensure the maintenance of the social order, while the maintenance of the person has been seen as an axiomatic prerequisite. The satisfaction of personal needs and desires was at the same time studied by two other disciplines—psychology and economics. In both disciplines "need satisfaction" is one of the basic elements of the majority of current theories. The disciplinary division was reflected in conceptual differentiation. Psychology and economics tried to explain individual behavior and its aggregates, while sociology concentrated on the combined and interrelated actions of individuals. The theoretical attempt of Homans to develop a model of elementary social behavior was inspired by the simple and elegant models of behavioral psychology and of the economics of exchange. Homans indeed "brings back the person and the person's needs [values]" into the language of sociology. In spite of my reservations about some aspects of the model, it is a very useful conceptual system for the analysis of the dynamics of wants, desires, and their satisfaction (Homans 1961). Nevertheless, Homans' theory is not a satisfactory instrument for the analysis of the institutional structure that makes possible the satisfaction of personal needs. In Homans' words, his is a model of "subinstitutional" behavior which "clings to institutions as to a trellis" (Homans 1961).

The issue of person maintenance appears in a systematic way at the macrosocial level as the basis of modern social policy and at the microsocial level as the special concern of casework-oriented social work. The theoretical interest of sociologists is a late follower of these ideological-institutional developments.

The obvious welfare trend in the political orientations of the power establishment was probably the major stimulant in raising the interest of the sociological community in the institutional aspects of need satisfaction. But even now there seems to be some reluctance in recognizing the problem as one of the basic processes of any society. Among dozens of textbooks of introductory sociology there is hardly one that mentions housing, health care, social insurance, guidance and training organizations, or other personal services. Sporadic studies of these did not lead to theoretical generalizations, and their conclusions were not incorporated into a conception of the institutional structure of society. Because of these omissions, sociology today is poorly equipped for a meaningful contribution to the understanding and guiding of social policy.

Although the concepts of "institutionalized system of need satisfaction" and "social policy" are not identical, in the context of modern industrialized societies they are partially overlapping. A sociological paradigm of social policy has to be rooted in the understanding of the societal processes of need satisfaction.

THE PROBLEM OF NEEDS

The concept of need is prevalent both in the life sciences and in the social sciences. The life sciences—biology, physiology, psychology—define needs, generally speaking, as an imbalance in the functioning of the human being. For the study of the societal system of need satisfaction it is necessary that the concept of need should be seen in the social context. Hence, in contradistinction to the life sciences, the sociological concept is need as defined, recognized, and legitimized by society. It is difficult to ascertain the limits that divide the social definition of the concept from its non-social core, while it is trivial to discuss the flexibility and the relativity of human needs, whether for maintenance or for comfort and well-being. Such an endeavor is akin to the "nature-nurture" controversy and probably as barren.

The relativity of human needs was recognized early in the development of modern social thought. Adam Smith says in the *Wealth of Nations*: "By necessities I understand not only the commodities of life, but whatever the custom of the century renders it indecent for creditable people, even of the lowest order, to be without" (Smith 1776, 1976 ed.). Similar ideas are expressed by Karl Marx, who writes about the spiritual and social needs of the workers being determined by the general cultural level (*allgemeiner Kulturzustand*) (Marx 1887, 1952 ed.). Adam Smith and Marx were interested not in the idiosyncratic individual variations of the inventory of needs but in its social definition. They both assumed that in spite of the social relativity of conceptions about human needs, at a given time in a given society certain common standards will develop. The same conclusion is reached by the contemporary sociologist: "The concept of need is relative [but it] is not so relative that each individual can set his own standards. There is some consensus of opinion on what deprivation may reasonably inspire sympathy in other people . . ." (Smith 1776, 1976 ed.).

The Social Definition of "Need"

In everyday language as well as in the various social disciplines, there is much semantic confusion. Need, desire, want, interest, necessity, purpose, demand, deprivation, insufficiency, and so forth are often used interchangeably. Nevertheless, there is agreement in general that three different aspects of need can be distinguished. I shall denote these as "lack," "want," and "demand"—concepts used by economists—although the definitions that I propose for them are not identical with the economic ones. "Need" should be considered as the general concept, used for convenience when further qualifications are not desired.

Let us define lack as being a state of deprivation that impairs the proper functioning of a person; want as the subjectively felt lack, which the person desires to eliminate; and demand as the readiness to act—especially to invest resources in order to satisfy one's want. Social definition and legitimization are relevant to each of these concepts. It may well be that according to psychological logic these three should be hierarchically ranked and determined—lack causing wants, which will tend to become demands. But this is not necessarily the social logic. The relationship between these three concepts is normatively defined, and within the moral framework it is sometimes considered desirable to suffer deprivation without trying to relieve it. It is also deemed feasible that one is not aware of one's own needs, and it is the duty of the social environment to satisfy those needs without expecting "self-initiated" demand. The assumption that human beings are not always aware of their needs and the proper ways to satisfy them is most obvious in the case of categories of persons who are in general considered as unable to care for themselves, such as children, the sick and the elderly, or those who are seen as lacking moral judgement and responsibility, like addicts. Discrepancy between needs, wants, and demands is not therefore a deviant situation, but rather a characteristic of human nature. Such concepts as permissiveness, over- and underutilization of services, or conspicuous consumption are expressions of the underlying assumption about the feasibility and in certain cases the desirability of such discrepancy.

The Inventory of Needs

In modern society, a growing group of experts is engaged in establishing the inventory of human needs, while educators, moralists, ideologists, and politicians are persuading the public as to which needs are morally acceptable and which should be ignored or repressed, what is the proper priority of needs, which are those that it is not only permissible but desirable to strive toward fulfilling, and which are rightfully expected to be satisfied. The division of functions between the experts and the evaluators is not as clear-cut as formulated in the above statements. Experts are involved in evaluating statements based, presumably, on expert knowledge of the prerequisites for a well-functioning human being. They, no less than the moralists, assume that there are functionally right and wrong wants and demands. They agree that lacks, such as addiction, can be artificially created and that their satisfaction can be detrimental to the person. The changing content of the need inventory is probably as much the result of additional knowledge as of new ideas, new moral standards, and social and political trends. Social policies, educational programs, and political and economic ideologies built on assumptions about needs are reflected—albeit after some time lag—in the evaluation process of experts and moralists and in the formal and informal social response to the needs of the individual (Laslett and Runciman 1967).

There are countless examples of this kind of transaction in such disparate areas as child feeding and toilet training, drug addiction and drug policy, the attitude toward homosexuals, and job enrichment or client participation. In each of these cases policies, programs, and practices have been developed with reference to theories about needs and about the results of their deprivation or satisfaction.

The legitimation process of the need inventory provides the resolution of the ongoing tension between the individualistic perspective of needs centered on the functioning and well-being of individual persons and the collectivistic perspective when reference to the society and its institutions is dominant. Pareto distinguishes between utility of the society when society is seen as a unit and utility for the community when the individual and his satisfactions are the relevant unit (Pareto 1963). In Pareto's scheme the two do not overlap and may be inversely related. Titmuss sees these two perspectives as strongly related and not easily distinguishable:

> Needs may . . . be thought of as "social" and "individual"; as interdependent, mutually related essentials for the continued existence of the parts and the whole. No complete division between the two is conceptually possible; the shading of one into the other changes with time over the life of all societies; it changes with time over the cycle of needs of the individual and the family, and it depends on prevailing notions of what constitutes a "need" and in what circumstances; and to what extent, if at all, such needs, when recognized, should be met in the interests of the individual and/or of society. (Titmuss 1958)

The kibbutz in Israel is one of the most interesting societies for the study of the dynamics of the social definition and legitimation of needs (Meyer-Cronemeyer 1969; Spiro 1956; Weller 1974). The kibbutz community is committed to the satisfaction of the needs of its members, the ideal being "to each according to his or her needs." But the limits of the acceptable needs, the allocation of resources, and the form in which satisfaction is secured are collectively discussed and decided. Hence the visibility of the process, which can be followed much more easily than in an open market society. A historical analysis of the ideas concerning the needs of the members and the urgency of their satisfaction shows the concomitant changes of these ideas, the methods of allocation, and their connection with the economic growth of the kibbutz. The changes affect the range of legitimate needs, the standards of satisfaction, and the scope left to individual choice. The kibbutz of the early years was poor and ascetic, and it was postulated that the dominant need of the individual was self-realization through service to society (Talmon 1970).

This was a classic example of the equation proposed by Lundberg.

$$\frac{\text{wants}}{\text{satisfactions}} = \text{tension} \qquad \frac{\text{goods}}{\text{demand}} = \text{satisfaction}$$

> if the disparity between wants and the power to satisfy them is the basic tension under consideration then the tension can be reduced *either* by *increasing* men's powers of satisfying wants *or* by *decreasing wants* . . . . Which of these mechanisms will come into operation and to what degree in a given case will . . . be broadly determined by the resistance which the situation offers to the operation of each. (Lundberg 1953)

The kibbutzim of prestate Israel did not have the goods and were strongly committed to invest in the development of their collective economy. The ideology that enabled this, while it controlled the individual deprivation tension, was a secular quasi-protestant ethic of simplicity, sacrifice, work, and values of economic growth. Personal needs were recognized only as necessities for maintenance, and the slogan of "to each according to his needs" was interpreted only within this context. Thus illness, as defined by an expert, commanded full recognition and collective responsibility for its cure. Disability and old age were part of communal care for the individual and so were children. Housing standards were defined by the community and provided by it. There was very little individual freedom of choice either of the quality or the quantity of food, clothing, personal care items, hobbies, or private entertainment. Comfort and aesthetic standards were first of all reserved for the community as a whole—for public places, the common parks, communal dining halls, and the communal houses of the children.

The kibbutz of the 1970s is wealthy and more individualistic and allows a much wider range of individual wants and choices. Some legitimacy is accorded to self-expression that is not oriented toward the community. The main forces discernible as having specific function in this process of change are the growing availability of resources, stronger reliance on "need-defining experts" (among them psychologists and sociologists), increased tension created by individual wants that could no longer be managed by collectivistic ideology, and a dynamic process of institutional decisions manoeuvering between ideological constraints and the communal need for social integration.

The kibbutz is by no means an exception in techniques of deliberate need management. Wants are stimulated and dampened in all societies by means other than value pressure, advertising being the most blatant example. It was the postulate of this discussion that all three aspects of need are relative, changing, and in a very large measure socially and culturally determined. Hence the difficulty of creating a universally valid list of human needs. Nevertheless, for a proper study of the societal need satisfaction system, it is necessary to have a frame of reference of needs or need types. Nearly all the applied social sciences—social policy, industrial sociology and psychology, economy, education, quality of life studies, and others—built theories and programs on lists of needs that are partly overlapping. I shall not try to quote or to summarize the extensive literature on need inventories. Attempts to create a general typology tend to converge toward a four- or five-sector taxonomy: (1) biological, (2) psychological, (3) cultural and/or (4) spiritual, and (5) social needs (Kahn and Kamerman 1976; Ponsioen 1962). Probably one lower level of subdivision could still be defined in a sufficiently universal way to be valid in the majority of societies. Relativity of needs appears at the third level subdivision containing the operational variables.

THE SATISFACTION OF NEEDS

The discussion in this chapter has its starting point in the axiomatic statement that although needs are primarily person related, no society takes a laissez-faire attitude toward the satisfaction of the needs of its members. But societies vary in the philosophy and arrangements concerning the parameters of the process of need satisfaction. I propose to discuss three parameters—responsibility, modes of distribution, and means of satisfaction.

Responsibility

If, as I assumed, human needs and their satisfaction are not a purely personal matter but a societal topic, then it is expected that ideas and norms exist, specifying the locus of responsibility. From the viewpoint of social policy it is important to distinguish ideologies and norms, according to which the responsibility for the well-being of the people rests with some social unit or is defined as nonsocial.

The nonsocial orientations can be individualistic when satisfaction of needs is the private responsibility of the individual. The risks of a negative balance and the successful achievement of a positive balance are seen as the result of individual skills, need management, or personality traits. If there is any onus on the society it is to provide the opportunities for individual activity. Nonsocial orientation can be situational when there is no active agent to be held responsible and when it is presumed that success or failure are the result of circumstances, luck, or other impersonal processes.

The ideology of societal responsibility requires that certain social units be concerned about the specific or the diffuse well-being of their members (Parsons 1951). The communal orientation expects the primary community of family, neighborhood, or a commune to assume responsibility for the satisfaction of its members' needs. The nuclear family and the kibbutz are such examples. The welfare orientation maintains that society—through its formal legal and administrative machinery—is responsible for the well-being of the population.

Responsibility may be stated in various degrees of formality, such as the marriage contract, parents' legal responsibility for their children, the partly unwritten laws of a kibbutz, or the formal welfare policy in many modern states. Responsibility defines the expectation rights of the receiver, while accountability of the provider confers the right to blame when needs are not satisfied.

In a research study, unemployed professionals—among them new immigrants to Israel—were asked where the blame lay for their situation (Bar-Yosef, Schild, and Varsher 1974a). There was a highly significant correlation between the answers and the country of origin of the professionals. The North American immigrants tended to blame themselves—lack of knowledge of the language, lack of orientation problems of adjustment. Professionals coming from Communist states thought that the government was responsible; while the Israelis tended, more than the others, to throw the blame on neutral factors like the situation of the market or the slowdown of economic activity in general. This is a clear case of cultural influence on the notion of responsibility.

McKinlay (Chapter 8) mentions the "client culpability" attitude of service organizations as alienating the clients. I see this as an example of the individualistic ideology of the formal organization, according to which "[the organizations] lay emphasis on and identify the knowledge, skills and lifestyles that clients lack which, if present, would prevent or minimize any breakdown." It can be assumed that the same idology prompts a stigmatizing judgement of the poor as being responsible for their own plight.

Distribution

As the second parameter I suggest the modes of distribution of the means of satisfaction. The term distribution is used here rather loosely, since it refers also to psychological and social needs, which may be satisfied by such not strictly distributable intangibles as freedom from anxiety, affiliation, and the like. The topic of modes of distribution is not a new invention, and sociological and economic literature provides us with several schemes. These appear under various names and are not necessarily linked to the problem of need satisfaction, but they are suitable for our purpose of qualifying the parameters of a universal paradigm for the societal process of need satisfaction.

First let us distinguish between modes of distribution that are based on particularistic relationships as opposed to those based on universalism. In the first category are self-care (or self-help), mutual aid, and altruistic giving (Howard 1969; Peyser 1951). In the universalistic category are the "distributive institutions"—market exchange, the role structure, and various welfare-oriented agencies and organizations (Bar-Yosef 1977; Galbraith 1973; Howard 1969; Kuhn 1966).

There is a certain parallelism of interaction types in the particularistic and the universalistic modes of distribution. Self-care and market activity are self-initiated actions: resources and priorities are managed according to self-choice; there is little dependence on others, but strong dependence on the availability of resources. The role structure (the positional system) is a mutual expectation and interaction system, where even in a universalistic setting there is much particularistic involvement. Because of the two-directional commitment of any mutuality, the choice and the control of each individual is reduced, and dependence is increased. The unique advantage of this type of relationship is that once established, diffuse loyalty develops, which ensures continuity without a strictly priced resource exchange. A combination of various psychological and social reward side effects tends to result in the integration of the person in a web of social relationships, which provides a stable supply system of need satisfiers.

Altruistic giving is one-directional from the giver to the receiver. Usually the receiver has to show some criterion of eligibility and to apply for help. Modern welfare institutions are a sort of formalized altruism. In both cases the recipient is—in principle at least—saving resources. Nevertheless, there are other costs involved—for example, strong dependence on the need definition and control of the situation by the giver. Therefore, resources are needed for coping with the situation as required, and mere eligibility is not sufficient. Further, the cost involved in being the recipient of philanthropic-altruistic giving is increased by the loss of status caused by the stigma that such a situation often carries (Howard 1969).

Satisfaction

The third parameter is related to the content of distribution. It is possible to prepare lists of items that serve as means for the satisfaction of needs, and in many cases of research in policy analysis or program planning it is important to do so. For our analysis it is more appropriate to use some general classifications based on need-relevant variables. The combination of two such variables results in a fourfold typology, which covers the types customarily used (see Table 2–1). One variable denotes the need specificity of the means—namely, whether it is intended for the satisfaction of one well-defined need or to be used for a variety of different needs. The second variable concerns the distance between distribution and satisfaction, determined by the nature of the distributed means.

Services and goods are intended for the satisfaction of certain specific needs. In the case of services it is impossible to separate the situation and the act of distribution from that of satisfaction. Giving the service is the satisfaction of the need ("the principle of 'uno-actu'—the non-material good is produced and consumed in the same act" [Gross and Badura, 1977]), hence its classification as a one-step process. The service situation is a cooperative action where the recipient is actively involved in the process, usually in face-to-face interaction. Hence, like other face-to-face interactions it implies emotional sensitivity and problems of face saving, of presentation of self, and of ongoing verbal and nonverbal communication (Goffman 1959, 1961).

It is different with goods that can be separated from the giver and the giving situation, with their consumption occurring in most cases

Table 2-1. Means and Need Satisfaction

	Distribution-Satisfaction Distance	
Need Specificity	*One step*	*Two step*
Need-specific	service	in kind benefits
Not need-specific	status	cash payments

at a different time and place and with other persons. While in a service situation, the role of the recipient and that of the consumer overlap; when goods are distributed, the recipient role does not extend into the consuming situation in which any other role can be assumed—even that of the giver, when, for instance, the received goods are consumed by family and friends.

Benefits that are not need specific can be used for various purposes, and the choice of their use is in the hands of the recipient. Although in the terminology of social policy analysis only cash payment is regarded as such a generalized means, I suggest including status in this category as the one-step type, corresponding to services. The suggestion does not merely serve my sense of symmetry. It seems that omission of the status category obscures some of the important problems of our modern system of need satisfaction. It is well known from studies of both primitive and modern societies that in the giver and receiver interaction statuses are asymmetric, the receiver being of a lower status. When the mode of distribution is based on exchange—whether the market type or of mutual aid—the symmetry is restored, the same person being both giver and receiver. But altruistic gratuitous distribution, whether informal or formal, creates a permanent status of receivers.

In a modern welfare society whole groups of people are tied to several agencies and organizations in the recipient status. Their status is labeled as "the needy," "the poor," "the welfare recipients." The social position of these groups will be determined by the sum total of their recipient statuses in the major institutional areas. For example, in Israeli studies of new immigrants who are for some time after their arrival totally dependent on public agencies, we learned about the desocializing effects of such a situation (Bar-Yosef 1968). But we found also that in a community of recipients, such dependence may become a legitimate status, with its own status symbols, prestige, and status differentiation (Bar-Yosef, Schild, and Varsher 1974b).

The generality and versatility of cash has been analyzed so often that it would be redundant to do so here. In spite of its obvious advantages, there are limits to its usefulness. Some of the limits affect the satisfaction of the need, and others are the result of the policy and ideology of the dispenser. Cash is not the most effective means for the satisfaction of needs when:

1. Its utilization presupposes knowledge of the market and skills of management lacking in the recipients (Caplowitz 1963);
2. The desired means are not available in the market;
3. The price of the desired means exceeds the cash received, or cash payments do not increase at the same rate as the prices of the suitable means (Bar-Yosef 1977);
4. when "buying" cannot provide satisfaction because the need is for diffuse "uno actu" interaction and for intangibles, which lose their meaning when acquired in a two-step transaction.

The dispensers' reluctance to make cash payments stems sometimes from value considerations. Money is easily hoarded, saved, and turned into capital, which may clash with egalitarian ideologies.

Further attitudes include that personal giving is valued more than impersonal money, or that the giving and receiving of money carries stigma. The act of giving need-specific or nonmarketable service is rewarding for the giver (Titmuss 1971). Lack of consensus between the giver and the receiver on the definition of needs and their priorities creates doubts in the mind of the dispenser as to the wants of the recipient and the "proper" use of the means. The giver assumes responsibility for the satisfaction of the lacks of the recipient by providing need-specific means. The availability of resources may become a powerful constraint on the dispensation of cash payments. Formal organizations as well as private persons possess time, skills, and the like that can be used for the benefit of the recipient but cannot be easily exchanged for cash. The best known example is the time of family members, of children, of retired persons, or of employed persons who have flexible workloads or who are underemployed, but whose employment is not terminated for various reasons.

Means are provided to satisfy certain needs. Their efficient provision, distribution, and proper use is one of the important questions in a world of scarce resources. Hoarding of means, waste, and unauthorized or unintended use of them are the main threats to efficiency (Kuhn 1966). Various types of means differ in their propensity to disefficiency. Money is the most hoardable and the most tempting for unauthorized use. Nevertheless, whatever the use of money, it is very seldom wasted. Its use may not conform with the intentions of the dispenser, but it fulfills some function for the user.

Goods are often wasted because of hoarding. They deteriorate or they become outdated once the need is satiated, and often they are neither transferable nor exchangeable. Hence the hoarding of goods is more costly than the hoarding of money. Free or cheap goods tend to be used inefficiently for unauthorized purposes—such as using bread for feeding animals. While this is not a waste of resources, it increases the costs for satisfaction of high priority needs by transferring resources to the satisfaction of low priority needs. Services are equally subject to inefficient utilization. Underutilization and overutilization are parallel to hoarding and waste, and cases when the client changes the function of services are well-known phenomena.

The three parameters answer the questions of who gives what and how. These have to be complemented with a fourth question—to whom—which is answered by norms of eligibility and their implementation. The paradigm thus has four main elements: responsibility for the satisfaction of needs, modes of distribution of means, the means for satisfaction of needs, and eligibility. These seem to be the necessary and, for a macrolevel analysis, sufficient parameters. Yet I tried to show that each of them is a complex mechanism and that the system itself can be understood only by taking into account the particular complexities of each parameter.

NEED SATISFACTION IN THE WELFARE STATE

In 1948, the United Nations decided to formulate the Universal Declaration of Human Rights, which states in Article 25 (1) that

> Everyone has the right to a standard of living adequate for the health and well-being of himself and his family, including food, clothing, housing, and medical care and necessary social services, and the right to security in the event of unemployment, sickness, disability, widowhood, old age or other lack of livelihood in circumstances beyond his control.

The declaration is the global legitimation of societal responsibility for the satisfaction of personal needs. In 1948, many European states were already on their way toward extensive social security programs. Since then the programs have been extended, and the responsibility of the state for the welfare of its citizens is accepted and expected. The United States is only reluctantly recognizing the failure of the "equal opportunity" ideology and moving toward the European model.

> In the past century the welfare state has developed in every urban-industrial country. Although they vary greatly in civil liberties and civil rights, the rich countries vary little in their general strategy for constructing the floor below which no one sinks. The values invoked to defend the welfare state—social justice, political order, efficiency, or equality—depend on the group articulating the defence. But the action in the end has produced one of the major structural uniformities of modern societies. The richer countries become, the more likely they are to broaden the coverage of both population and risks—that is, they will insure more people against seven or eight risks of modern life:—risks of injury on the job, sickness or maternity or both, old age, invalidity and death, reduced standard of living because of increased family size (offset by family allowances), and unemployment. However reluctant the government or the more affluent citizens may be, they are moved toward the welfare state by needs for political order (under conditions of the push for equality) and stable economic incentives. (Wilensky 1975).

The principal structural characteristic of the welfare state is the proliferation of a conglomerate of organizations and agencies engaged in the distribution of utilities outside the commercial market and the regular positional system. The activity of these organizations is not restricted to certain "weak" populations or to help in times of crises; they are becoming important sources for the satisfaction of certain needs of the entire population. The sociologist wanting to study the welfare state is impeded by the scarcity of specific models and paradigms that aim to explain the dynamics of welfare distribution and the structure of the distributing organizations.

The most interesting analyses of the distributive processes are the work of economists. Many of these are relevant for sociologists, but they have to be translated into sociological terminology in order to expand their impact on the institutional structure of society. There is as yet no single concept covering all the relevant types of distribution, and for convenience I shall label them as "welfare distributions" and characterize them as "the organization equivalent of the unilaterally generous transaction. It incurs costs for the benefit of others, while expecting no payment, or only partial payment in return" (Kuhn 1966).

Welfare distribution appears in three modes:

1. *Public services or public social utility*—"that is providing services as one of the rights of citizenship to all who are eligible, without test of means or contribution conditions, and financed out of general taxation" (Sleeman 1973). Let us add to this that "eligibility is a matter of status (aged, child, resident and so

forth), or the exercise of an option by any potential user (one enters a park or museum or center if one wishes to) . . ." (Kahn and Kamerman 1976). Public services are intended to satisfy a multitude of needs, presumably with a minimum of direct cost to the user. Closer observation reveals that the standard problems of utilization, differential access, and aiming at high priority needs are relevant in this case also. McKinley's distinction (Chapter 8) between a situation of "buyer's market" and "seller's market" is very applicable. Education, vocational training, and cultural events provided as public services are often in the buyer's market situation, and users have to be recruited, wooed, and persuaded.

2. *Social insurance*—"the provision of benefits as of rights to those who qualify by the payment of specific contributions, either by themselves, or their employers, or both" (Sleeman 1973). Social insurance can be regarded as an intermediate form of distribution between the commercial market and the welfare market. It is equally suitable for distributing goods, cash, or services. Nevertheless, it does not have the same appeal to all parts of the population, nor is it equally effective for all types of needs.
3. *Social assistance*—"the provision of benefits financed out of general taxation, central or local, subject to test of the recipient's need and means" (Sleeman 1973). Many of the service organizations are of this type, and it is the most researched. Stigmatization, dependence, conflicting communications, and many of the problems elaborated in chapters in this volume refer mainly to this type of distribution.

These modes of welfare distribution are managed by bureaucracies, small groups of professionals, and voluntary agencies. The most important among these are the big public bureaucracies, which because of their structural constraints redefine needs, create demands, and invent new techniques that can be efficiently managed by bureaucracies.

Two American sociologists present an excellent short description of this process:

> As the size and scope of government philanthropy increase, the services themselves are standardized and rationalized. Standard forms, procedures, programs, machine teaching, standard curricula, larger classes, standardized diagnoses, computerized systems management, and cost-benefit schemes—all work in the direction of the "objectivity" required by large-scale bureaucratized management. In psychiatry, the most individualized

> craftlike service based on a one-to-one relationship gives way to group therapy, lobotomy, chemical treatment, and "mental health" classes. Even the forms of rapport, spontaneity, warmth, and involvement are standardized through the systematic training of professional service workers, custodians, and parent surrogates and models. But even as these new devices are instituted, the objectivity, impersonality, and mass production produce resentment: the client, the individual, is lost in the shuffle. The response to demands for recognition of the individual can be met on a professionalized mass basis by incorporating him into the therapeutic process, sensitivity training, T-Groups, group dynamics, psychodrama, achievement motivation programs—all are designed to produce warmth, spontaneity, individual recognition, and self-motivation within the framework of a large-scale production of services. All of these methods have in common the attempt to reduce the cost per case by large-scale treatment, in other words to expose more and more clients to social service agencies. (Bensman and Vidich 1971).

Service organizations are variants of the bureaucratic organizations, but they are sufficiently different to need new models and new theories. As McKinlay shows (see Chapter 8), a large literature exists that is relevant to the topic. In many of these studies it is shown that variations of the system parameters will affect the conditions that generate inefficiency and the reactions of clients and agencies to conflict and to pressures. Both the modes of the welfare distribution and the content of distribution are in part determining the role of the giver—his or her authority, professional level, and involvement in the process. It would be fruitful to compare on this basis the insurance system and the assistance system. We should be able to delineate the limits of each, their usefulness, and their cost for the client and for society. Usefulness and cost depend on the content of distribution—whether cash, in kind, or services. Gross and Badura (1977) have an interesting analysis comparing income and service provisions and their connection with several organizational and satisfaction dimensions—the production process, rationality of distribution, financing on the one hand; and the measure of the need specificity and utility on the other. A further elaboration of microresearch is needed in defining the situational differences of different types of services such as counseling, socialization, treatment, and care.

CONCLUSIONS: FUTURE TRENDS

Instead of recapitulation of the ideas expressed in the chapter, I shall speculate on some future trends deduced from our present knowledge and suggest the following ideas:

1. In general, a stronger public awareness of the total system of need satisfaction and a tendency to relate to it as an integrated whole can be expected.
2. Collective responsibility for the maintenance and need satisfaction of the members of society is growing.
3. The inventory of needs for which collective responsibility is assumed and the demand for them are both increasing.
4. The level of minimum need satisfaction versus comfort, quality versus quantity, universalism versus selectivity and specificity, will continue to be major points of discussion, both as ideological and as pragmatic issues (Titmuss 1958).
5. "Under continuing industrialization all institutions will be oriented toward and evaluated in terms of social welfare aims. The welfare state will become the welfare society and both will be more reality than epithet" (Wilensky 1975).
6. Industry and administrative bureaucracies develop a tendency of assuming social responsibility for the community in which they function and welfare responsibility for their employees. New concepts, such as the "socially responsible corporation" and the "plant welfare system" are on their way toward crystalization (Anshen 1974; Sethi 1974).
7. Two conflicting trends of the organizational structure are developing. One points toward more bureaucratization and professionalization—proliferation of service bureaucracies, of professional and semiprofessional employees, of bureaucratic trends and procedures that tend to reduce the importance of voluntary agencies, informal help, and self-help. The other trend is partly a backlash to bureaucratization, to the cost of services, and to their impersonality. In some instances a renewal of voluntarism can be observed in practice and as ideology. Informal help arrangements coexist and complement organizational benefits. There is a possibility of integrating these two trends by dividing functions between formal bureaucratic and informal and voluntary help. The professional services are sometimes ready to take into account the existence of the skills and time of private persons and family members whose efficiency can be improved by short training, counseling, and backing. Financial help could ensure the maintenance of the informal need satisfaction system, and it would enable its proper functioning at lower financial and personal costs than the bureaucratic system. There are many projects, such as home care for the aged and the disabled, recuperation and rehabilitation day care hostels, mother's helpers, neighborhood social centers, housing associations, and others.
8. The service society stimulated the emergence of new social

groups, with specific ideologies, interests, social ranking, and power conflict. Three such groupings are visible at present—recipients (users), welfare professionals, and the "distribution elite" (Baier 1977). Although the professionals and the elites are supposed to serve the users, it is not to be expected that the definitions of the needs or the ways toward their satisfaction by each of these groups will be identical. There are strong reasons to expect differences in conception, organizational status, and professional orientation as being bases of conflicting approaches. Users organizations will probably become stronger and more numerous, and their pressure has to be taken into account (Bar-Yosef and Schild 1966; Kramer 1969).

Let me conclude with the words of one of the most important social policy thinkers of our time, Richard Titmuss:

> We have tried to argue. . . that certain instruments and institutions of policy have a potential role to play in sustaining and extending personal freedoms. These have positive and negative aspects; both have to be exercised politically and have to be continually facilitated if they are to survive. . . . Viewed negatively or positively they relate to the freedom of men not to be exploited in situations of ignorance, uncertainty, unpredictability and captivity; not to be excluded by market forces from society and from giving relationships, and not to be forced in all circumstances. . . to choose always their own freedom at the expense of other people's freedom. (Titmuss 1970)

Chapter 3

Social Policy and Social Services: Some Problems of Policy Formation, Program Implementation, and Impact Evaluation

*Franz-Xaver Kaufmann**

A SOCIOLOGICAL CONCEPT OF SOCIAL POLICY

The term social policy has been accepted in the Anglo-Saxon world only since World War II. It had its origin in the middle of the last century in Germany. There, it designated a set of measures aimed at influencing the relationship of state and civil society in a rather broad sense (Panoke 1970). After the enactment of the Social Security laws in the 1880s, the term encompassed all political measures designed to ameliorate the conditions of the industrial workers in order to integrate the working classes into the German Empire. With the progressive extension of labor legislation and Social Security programs to all dependent workers (except civil servants) and the inclusion of social work and other social services in the concept of social policy, the term has been adopted at the international level. Nevertheless, substantial differences in the use of the term in different countries may be detected on closer inspection.

For theoretical purposes it seems reasonable to take a rather broad notion of social policy as our starting point, as was the case at the beginning of the German debate. Social policy in this sense means

*Department of Sociology, University of Bielefeld, Federal Republic of Germany.

action of the state aimed at the amelioration or improvement regarding the living conditions of those members of the Hegelian "civil society" who are considered as disadvantaged (Hegel 1821). This general notion is of course open for criticism from different points of view; I refer only to the Marxian critique of the ideology of "civil society." Nevertheless, it seems that it was the historical process of establishing social policy, with its unanticipated consequences, that transformed not only the civil society, but also the relationship of state and civil society, in a rather differentiated manner (Heimann 1929; Schumpeter 1942). This process is called the emergence of the welfare state (cf. Titmuss 1958; Sleeman 1973; Robson 1976; for empirical evidence Flora, Alber, and Kohl 1977).

During recent years, increasing criticism regarding the concept of the welfare state may be noted. I shall not open this debate here, but I would like to mention two main points of criticism concerning the welfare state. The first objection points out that the welfare state is not able to provide social welfare to those who are especially in need of it. The second objection starts from the assumption that the period of rapid economic growth of Western societies will be followed by a period of moderate growth or even stagnation that may lead to a "Fiscal Crisis of the State" (O'Connor 1973). As a consequence of waning economic growth, the state will be confronted with growing demands from all parts of society. At the same time, the state will no longer be able to support its programs and measures by increasing taxes. Therefore, some writers predict "The Waning of the Welfare State" (Scharpf 1977) as a consequence both of the lack of resources and of the inability of the state to meet the needs of those who are in need. Insofar as the "welfare state" was an ideological concept for gaining the political loyalty of the masses (Offe 1972), based on an almost religious belief in a better world made possible by political action, the "Waning of the Welfare State" means nothing but a new step to the understanding of the toilsome venture of living together without the veil of false hopes, a task suited to social scientists from their beginning.

The presumed waning of the welfare state constitutes then the situation where social scientists are offered for the first time a real chance to gain the interest of practitioners in the field of social policy, a chance similar to that economists had in the period of the Great Depression. But shall we have our John Maynard Keynes?

The case is at least comparable in one respect: Keynes was a theorist who formulated for the first time an economic theory that made political action possible—that is, he explained why a full employment policy was necessary and how it could be carried out.

He and his scholars were able to reformulate the body of neoclassical economics so that explanations for the operating of the economy became linked with devices in the domain of political action to influence economic operations. I argue that sociological theory ought to perform the same function for social policy in the service field (see Gans 1971; Coleman 1972; Herlth, Kaufmann, and Strohmeier 1976).

Social policy is conceived in this study as actions of the state designed to improve the everyday life situation of certain groups of the population considered as disadvantaged in certain respects. The aim of sociology is to explain how these actions take place and to what extent political action is able to lead to the desired improvement.

How can this be done? Our starting point is to consider the difficulties in relating theory and practice in the field of social services. Whereas we have a rather clear conception of the factors influencing the distribution of income and of the measures taken in order to influence the distribution patterns—and thus a theoretical background for the "income strategy" of social policy (see below), we lack comparable conceptions for the "service strategy" (Williams 1971). We have, of course, a lot of reasoning concerning the practical problems in the field—such as budgeting problems, social administration, social work, and so forth—but this reasoning is not being incorporated in a common perspective that embraces the different steps of political, administrative, and social action.

If we want to improve social services—for instance their responsiveness to the needs of their clients—we need, in a certain sense, the practical experience of many people—politicians, board members of welfare agencies, budget controllers, and other members of public administration concerned with financing, regulating, or delivering social services. They all participate in one or another way in the process that determines the kind and the performance of the services. Nevertheless, we do not need much imagination to predict the outcome of a direct confrontation of all this practical experience: it would end either in confusion or in mutual reproaches. The perspective of the practitioners is necessarily restricted to the issues pertaining to their own practice. Nobody can expect from them so much role taking that they forget their own position in the institutional structure with its division of labor. But unfortunately, much theorizing of social scientists remains on a level of abstraction that does not allow them to grasp practical problems at the same time.

If we want to overcome both the insufficiencies of incongruent practical experiences and the deficiencies of theorizing and fact-finding unrelated to practical needs, we need some organizing principle that allows both the consideration of practical experience and an argumentation on a generalized—that is, theoretical—level. What we need is a theory that takes into consideration the different positions of practical experience, in relating them to each other. If we consider the different concrete perspectives as belonging to the same system of practice—that is, the same institutional structure—and if we try to reconstruct this system of practice in terms of its institutional structure, of the processes determined by its functions, and of the states of mind, related to the different positions—that is, the motives, interests, and definitions of the situation of the actors in the institutional structure and its environment—we can arrive at a theory that is related both to academic problems and to practical issues (Kaufmann 1977a). Such a theory would be able to relate the actions and the consequences of the actions of different actors on different levels to each other. And this is what we need if we want to explain social policy in terms of political, administrative, and social action and also in terms of the impact of these actions upon the life situation of the members of our societies.

There are, of course, many restrictions and hindrances to an effective social policy. These restrictions operate at different levels, and we also have to incorporate them into a theory on the operation of social policy. Moreover, what seems to be an obstacle to effective political action may appear in another perspective as conditional for self-regulating processes in the field of the same political action. Social policy is indeed the action of the state on social processes that are not constituted by this action but only influenced by it. The impact of political actions depends to a large degree on the properties of the fields of political or administrative intervention.

We need a theory of the operation of social policies on different levels, including the properties of the intervention field or of the target group. Only if we can explain the difficulties and the possibilities of political action and if we are able to identify devices and limits of political action on the basis of grounded theory both of political and administrative intervention, as well as of the impact on the intervention field, shall we become able to bridge the gap between sociology and social policy.

OBJECT AREAS OF A THEORY OF SOCIAL POLICY: POLICY FORMATION, PROGRAM IMPLEMENTATION, AND IMPACT EVALUATION

This assertion does not mean that we need only one theory with the properties mentioned. In fact, our previous considerations have given some hints concerning the type of theories we need and that have to be formulated with respect to different fields of social policy and different stages of the sociopolitical administrative process. To begin with the latter, we borrow from the theory of political processes the distinction between the processes of policy formation, program implementation, and impact evaluation. These are primarily analytically distinguished perspectives of the political process, but they correspond roughly to the processes of policy input, policy throughput, and policy output, as considered by a systems analysis of political life (cf. Easton 1965; Raskoff and Schaefer 1970; Mayntz 1977).

By policy formation I mean the processes of emerging political issues, of political choice between alternative issues, and of program formulation—in the continental law system, mainly the legislative process. It is the domain of politics and political power seems to be the focal restriction at this stage of the political process. At the same time, patterns of cognitive selectivity and their institutional background also play an important part at this level; insofar as social policy is concerned with the socially most disadvantaged groups, we can even conclude that the chance of their interests and needs being considered depends almost completely on the problem sensitivity of the political system and its parts, given the fact that the political power of these groups tends to be zero.

Whereas it seems rather difficult to modify the everyday theories of administrations in the realm of their own activity, there seems to be a lack of generalized definitions of the situation in the political field. We can observe the way each political actor tries to define a situation in terms of his or her own interests, but it is rather clear that this cannot lead to a common definition of a situation. Here, I see a fair chance for social scientists: they may contribute to the definition of political issues by reinforcing or discarding or even reinterpreting the existing definition attempts made by political actors. This contribution seems particularly promising in three respects:

1. In defining social problems as potential issues of social policy;
2. In identifying the interconnections of different levels of political and administrative action—namely, by a reconstruction of the operation of social policy in terms of implementation as shown before; and
3. In discussing the possible outcomes of alternative strategies in terms of impact and side effects.

By the term program implementation I point to the processes of realization of a certain policy. Once a new law has been enacted or a new program has been set up, it will not operate until a set of identifiable conditions are fulfilled: these conditions depend, as I shall argue later, to a large degree on the type of intervention under consideration. Program implementation consists therefore in the production of the conditions for a policy output (Kaufmann and Schaefer 1977). These conditions can be classified first in terms of structures and resources and encompass norms, organizations, finances, and so forth. The focal restriction at this level may consist in the structure of organizations and their interests that distort the aim of the political action.

If we take social policy seriously, we are right to assume that it is designed to have a certain impact upon the life situation of those who are destined to be the beneficiaries of political action—namely, the target groups. It may be questionable if politicians always really want the effects that they declare to be the aim of any policy to come about; often they may be much more interested in a "symbolic use of politics" (Edelman 1964)—that is, in giving the impression that something has been done concerning a problem, but without provoking a real change in the situation. This seems to be particularly probable in the case of the underprivileged groups.

If we want to overcome a merely symbolic use of politics, we have to question the current dissociation of policy input and policy output in the political debate, and we have to place emphasis on the interrelations of policy input, policy throughput, and policy output. But it is not sufficient to be concerned merely by policy output as measured for instance by the amount of expenditure, the number of social services, or even the number of cases treated by such services. At this level, we still maintain the political or administrative perspective, and we discard the perspective of the official beneficiary—namely, the consequences of the output for the target group. Whereas it would be rather utopian to orient our standards of evaluation only at the so-called needs of the population or of any target group, we have to maintain that social policy standards have to be defined for evaluation purposes in terms of desired outcomes and impacts (see Levy, Meltsner, and Wildavsky 1974) if evaluation is expected to contribute to the greater effectiveness of a policy (Kaufmann et al. 1978).

The aim of a sociological theory of social policy is thus the reconstruction of existing policies in terms of policy formation, program implementation, and impact evaluation. Each of these perspectives needs a different theoretical and methodological approach, and this explains why considerations linking the three levels of analysis are usually lacking. Nevertheless, only the linking of these three perspectives can lead to a type of theory that allows us to understand the whole process of delivering social services and thus to widen the practitioner's perspective of his or her own problems in such a way that he or she becomes able to situate his or her own activity in its relationship to the whole delivering process and the conditions of its effectiveness (Kaufmann 1977a).

Of course, a sociological reconstruction of social policy as a whole would not lead to an elucidation of practical issues. Social policy consists in a more or less encompassing set of programs (laws), administrations, services, and the like whose systemic properties can only be determined by the concrete analysis of a given case. In this chapter we can only point out some general properties of a social policy by examining social services.

FORMS OF POLITICAL INTERVENTION IN THE AREA OF SOCIAL PROBLEMS

To prevent misunderstanding, we now have to deal briefly with the term "social services." It seems to be used in the German context with regard to a more restricted class of institutions than in the French and Anglo-Saxon context. In the United States the term social services designates the five main domains of welfare institutions—namely, education, health, income maintenance (or income security), housing, and employment (or manpower). In the English classifications, the last domain seems to be regularly excluded (cf. Hall 1965; Kameran and Kahn 1976; Madison 1970; Parker 1970; Wickenden 1976; Sainsbury 1977).

If we conceive the term in this broad sense, it covers almost the whole field of social policy. I think that such an approach is not very appropriate for analytic purposes, because the operation of social policy shows considerable variations depending upon the form of political intervention. Let me remind you that in the early 1960s we already had an international discussion about the relationship between social security and social services (see M. Kaufmann 1965, Merriam 1963). It was admitted then that despite some confusion in the institutional mix of the two forms of social intervention, fairly clear functional differences exist between them.

The function of social security is to provide social benefits based upon precisely defined and generalized preconditions. The delivering systems operate in a schematic, anonymous, and egalitarian way, regulated by law. Hence, their benefits consist regularly of money, and the security of income is based here on the previsibility of the benefit for those who are entitled to it (Kaufmann 1970). In view of the fact that the right to these benefits is settled by law and that the characteristics of the individual situation need not be taken into account, a centralized administration seems to be possible and even more effective than a decentralized one (Hentschel 1978).

In contrast to social security, the social services provide benefits with respect to the individual circumstances and needs of the beneficiary; they may be in money or in kind; and their effectiveness depends upon the sensitivity of the providers to the local or even individual situation and upon the motivations and the degrees of freedom that are given to providers to meet individual needs. This function cannot be performed on the basis of specified rules of law and a centralized administration of the services. Therefore a high degree of decentralization both of agencies and of the services themselves seems to suit best the performance of this function.

In the German debate on sociology and social policy that began only a few years ago, we find a similar but not identical distinction: there is a fairly general agreement to distinguish between benefits in money and in kind (Ferber and Kaufmann 1977; Sozialbericht 1976); on the other hand, there is a distinction between two strategies of social policy that we can term following Rainwater (1967) and Romanyshyn (1971) as "income strategy" and "service strategy" (cf. Gross and Badura 1977; Herlth, Kaufmann, and Strohmeier 1976). Following American and English authors, Badura and Gross (1976) have emphasized the particular character of personal services that form the core of the service strategy. Personal services are benefits that are *uno actu* produced and consumed and whose effectiveness relies essentially upon the success of the interaction of the provider and the beneficiary or—in terms of organizational theory—of the basic boundary personnel and the client. The physical presence of the beneficiary and his or her willingness to cooperate represents thus an essential prerequisite for the success of the delivering action.[a]

With respect to my basic problem of how to construct theories that relate the perspective of sociopolitical action and its operation to the perspective of the social field and its target population, I propose a similar but somewhat more encompassing distinction between three forms of political intervention in the social field. As nearly all public actions are grounded on law and need money, I want to emphasize that the following, more selective, distinction is oriented

[a]It seems questionable if the term "person-centred services" (*personenbezogene Dienstleistungen*) of Badura and Gross is comparable to the English term "personal social services" (cf. Sainsbury 1977). For Badura and Gross (and also for myself) the distinction is analytical and not institutional: personal social services are not identical with "social work," but also include services in the domain of health or education, for example.

toward the outcome of the political process or toward the desired impact upon the social field (see Kaufmann et al. 1978).

1. *Intervention by law*, instituting specific rights for the target population in relation to third parties exerting an influence on essential elements of their life situation (e.g., worker versus employer, lessee versus lessor). This form of intervention has its bottleneck at the policy formation level. It needs (in principle) the least administrative structure and extremely few public funds to become effective, because action devolves not on public authorities but on private persons or bodies. Consequently, this form of intervention is particularly susceptible to political pressures intervening already on the legislative level: there is little chance to obtain specific rights for powerless groups. The implementation problem thus consists in bringing about the effectiveness of the instituted rights. This means that those entitled have to claim their rights and those obliged have to respect them. The implementation problem consists in spreading knowledge about these laws, in forming public consciousness of these rights embodied in the law, and in instituting an effective administration of justice and, perhaps, of controlling agencies (e.g., for security measures in factories). The impact of this form of intervention depends upon the ability and willingness of the beneficiaries of law to defend their interests.
2. *Intervention by money* refers to income redistribution by taxes, by social security, or by relief. The aim pursued by this kind of intervention consists of influencing the net income of the beneficiaries in order to enable them to buy goods and services they need in the market. Policy formation is difficult here insofar as the effective distribution pattern depends upon the combination of a set of different measures that are also enacted for other political purposes—for example, fiscal policy and economic policy. The implementation of measures requires general regulations and an efficient administration to lower the costs of the redistribution process. The problems of delivering the benefits are rather simple in comparison with those appearing in the personal service sector. Taking into account the strong interferences of income distribution and economic policy, we consider the effectiveness of this form of intervention as depending essentially upon the ability of the state to control unemployment and inflation. Moreover, the impact depends upon the premises of the market economy—that all which is needed can be bought at market prices, that everybody knows his or her own needs best, and that demand will provoke an appropriate offer of goods and services.
3. *Intervention by social services* concerns the premises (1) that individuals are fully able to defend their own interests and (2) that

all that is needed can (and will) be bought in the markets of goods and services. These premises tend to turn out to be untrue for a growing part of the needs of socially disadvantaged groups. Thus, public intervention takes place to organize the supply of goods and services below market prices, thus influencing the distribution patterns of these goods, and to improve the capacity of self-reliance of socially disadvantaged groups. It is typical of social services that they are concerned both with the substitution of the market economy and with improving capacities of self-reliance. The rationality of the service strategy relies thus on the assumption that people need some services they would not or could not buy on the basis of market prices. As we know, since the time of the beginning of the factory system, there is no evidence that people buy on their own initiative all that they or their children need. The establishment of a system of public instruction constituted then a first grade measure of social policy. Its function was not only to instruct the children but also to deter their parents and the employers from using them for factory work. If we try to discover a perspective that, with respect to social services, allows us to link the perspective of political action and that of the target population, we can find two such perspectives.

Most importantly, an adequate distribution pattern of the services must exist. As social services require the presence of a beneficiary, they lack the mobility of goods as presumed in the theory of market economy. Moreover, services tend to become more and more expensive in relation to other goods, and with respect to publicly funded services there seems to be an agreement that they are needed without regard to the purchasing power and perhaps even to the individual preference for them. Therefore, public intervention has to take place in order to organize the offer of these services below market prices and in the appropriate neighborhood of those in need.

A deeper problem is revealed on closer inspection of the causes that lead to public intervention in the service sector. The economic theory of so-called "merit goods" (Musgrave 1959) presupposes that services are not utilized to an appropriate degree because individual preferences do not correspond to the public preferences, but that an individual need for the services still exists. If the services are offered free of charge and within reach of those in need, they will be used to an appropriate degree. This presupposition has waned under the evidence that the so-called underprivileged groups tend to be underrepresented among the clients of social services, even when the latter are in reach and free of charge. Therefore a noneconomic explanation of the underutilization of social services by lower class people and perhaps also of the overutilization by other social groups is needed (see McKinlay 1970a; Andersen and Newman 1973; Greenley and Kirk 1973; Blum 1975; Skarpelis-Sperk 1978; Wirth 1978).

RESEARCH ON IMPLEMENTATION PROBLEMS IN SOCIAL POLICY AND SOCIAL SERVICES

Most social services have developed out of voluntary social actions and/or out of services on the basis of market prices. The origin of the services lies thus on a local or even neighborhood level, and this proximity seems to be an elementary condition of their effectiveness. Moreover, the use of social services constitutes typically not a unique act, but a sequence of interactions taking place over a certain period of time. Thus, the performance of the service depends not only on the professional skills of its personnel but also on the capacity and willingness of its public to cooperate in the process of service delivery. There is consequently a problem of motivating both staff and public to cooperate in such a way that the aim of the service can be attained (Badura and Gross 1976; Grunow 1978). But this is not the whole problem. As the demand for social services frequently exceeds their supply, a problem exists concerning the selectivity systematically applied by the service staff to the "cases" on the basis of their own definitions of "expected successful treatment" and other standards set up according to the interests of their organization (Greenley and Kirk 1973; Grunow 1977). Finally, we have to admit that the demand for a social service is itself the result of a sometimes complex process of decision making on the side of the potential clients or target group members (Wirth 1978), and the likelihood that the great majority of those who are in need are not demanding the appropriate services seems to be rather high.

We can assume that the output of most social services was originally provided within family households. At the beginning of their separate provision, most of these services, then organized on a voluntary or market basis, did not attain the standards of provision within a functioning household. If there has been any increase in their quality at all, this may be attributed to the professionalization of the services.

In contrast to the interventions by law or by money that are typically original innovations of the state, social services have been, in many cases, pre-existent to political intervention. This is by no means accidental: social services are not suited to the forms of policy formation and program implementation that are characteristic of the modern state with its centralized forms of political decision-making and the complex, multilevel bureaucratic structure of its administration. The typical tools of state action—legal and administrative norms, budgeting and subsidies, administrative and judicial control—are little apt to influence the quality and the selectivity of service delivery and are even less appropriate for motivating the most needy members of target groups. This is, in my opinion, the gist of the problem of a service strategy in social policy. Whereas we find some allusions to it in the literature, the thesis is not yet fully developed. Nevertheless, there seems to be a growing tendency in all industrialized countries to expand the state's intervention in the service sector. This is normally legitimated with the aim of improving the service system in quantity and quality (Dahl and Lindblom 1953; Kaufmann et al. 1971; Offe 1974; Widmaier 1976; Hegner 1978; Kaufmann 1977b).

How does the state operate to achieve a higher standard of social services and to secure their influence? The provisional findings of research groups at Bielefeld (cf. Bohnsack, Schliehe, and Schneider 1977; Grunow, Hegner and Lempert 1979; Domscheit and Kaufmann 1977) show the different strategies pursued in the Federal Republic of Germany. The most far-reaching (and best established) is the professionalization of the services staff personnel. By establishing new professions and by creating new curricula under the auspices of public authorities, the field of social services becomes more formalized and thus more influenced by legal and administrative actions. Another possible strategy would be nationalization, but with exception of the school system, this strategy has been used very reluctantly in Germany—apart from the Third Reich. It is the recollection of that time and also the division of Germany that make any discussion about extensive nationalization impossible.

Nevertheless, social services have not been left in their primary state of mutual help or of a market good: under the auspices of social legislation and with a growing tendency by the state to subsidize the services, there has been a historical trend of forming associations (*Verbandlichung*) in German social policy. This is true for social security (Tennstedt 1976, 1977) as well as for different forms of social services. In this context, a system of ideologically oriented associations has emerged where Catholic (*Caritas*) and Protestant (*Diakonisches Werk*) bodies prevail. These voluntary associations in the field of social service delivery have developed into rather highly organized systems of services with a multilevel hierarchical structure. Thus, the state deals primarily with these associations and tries to influence the services indirectly by sharing its own domains with them. This sharing of areas of competence—that is, the establishment of participation—takes many shapes and operates officially in the implementation process. But our studies also show substantial influences and informal participation in the policy formation process; or perhaps one should say that in the domain of social services, policy formation and program implementation are less separated than in other domains of politics. This means that regulation by law in this field is not very sharply defined and cannot be said to form a program for policy. The decisions—or rather the "agreements"—on the measures to be taken in the field are achieved in partly formalized (e.g., the planning of hospitals), partly informal structures. We should try to find out how effective the regulatory power of these structures is.

But what does effectiveness mean in this context? In contrast to intervention by law or by money, the desired outcome of intervention by services is not easy to define. On the political level, there regularly exist some great words describing the purpose of a program or law—for example, Health, Security, Education, Welfare, or Justice—that often have the function of "precarious values" (see Chapter 11). Sometimes the legislator gives a more precise definition of the subjective rights to social services—for example, the 1975 Code of Social Rights in the FRG. But also in this case the rights have to be specified; they do not become effective until subsequent regulations are set up. Implementation means here not only the realization of the goals fixed by law, but the transformation of the rather general purposes into operative devices. This means that the definition of the population's needs to be met does not take place on the political level, but in the shared implementation process as sketched above. This explains why the responsiveness of social services to clients' needs is a crucial issue of the service strategy.

The aim of the social services is usually not the delivering act itself (its output) but some change in the client's life situation or in his capacities (its impact). This rather obvious fact—that for instance health services ought to be healthy for their clients or that public education has to be measured by the fostering of certain capacities in its pupils—is strangely obscured in the administrative perspective. It is oriented primarily toward efficiency—the relation of costs and outputs—but not toward effectiveness—the relation of desired outcomes and impact (Kaufmann et al. 1978).

THE IMPORTANCE OF IMPACT RESEARCH

It has always been an established matter of political thinking that politics and policies actually affect what they have in view.

This conception of the political process tends to overemphasize the level of politics and to neglect problems of implementation and impact. As we have shown, these are particularly relevant and difficult in the field of social services. None of our established forms of social regulation seems to be suited to improving the responsiveness and effectiveness of social services. Neither the market mechanism nor the established forms of democratic policy formation and bureaucratic policy implementation are sensitive to the needs of persons and of social groups that cannot be generalized in terms of rights and money.

There is also reason to doubt whether the pluralistic or mixed structure of the implementation field—as shown in the example of the FRG—will lead to a better result. In comparison with a nationalized and centralized system it may lead to some opportunities for innovation, but also to a particularly marked predominance of organizational (e.g., domain) considerations on the regulatory level of the delivery system. The only device that may result in an improvement of the service's quality seems to be professionalization, but this mechanism is also open to criticisms insofar as the responsiveness and the effectiveness of the services are concerned (Badura and Gross 1976; Hegner 1979). Or to put it more precisely, I assume that by the combination of professional and bureaucratic patterns of regulation, the tendency for discarding the problems of client's needs is particularly reinforced: professional authority tends to disguise the weaknesses of the bureaucratic structure.

If we want to overcome the dominant administrative perspective at the policy level, it seems necessary to concentrate research on outcomes and impacts of different social services (perhaps in comparison with alternative solutions of the same problem). Evaluation and impact research are promising fields of applied social research, though there are still many problems to solve (Hellstern and Wöllman 1977). The main issues are how the desired outcomes can be determined without a subjective bias and how we can move from observed correlations to causal influences.

From the perspective of the ideas exposed in this chapter we can gain a new approach to impact research: we have to consider the impact of a social policy measure as an element of public intervention in an already established social field. The intervention constitutes a multistep process, and the impact also constitutes a multistep process. To evaluate a certain policy from the aspect of its impact, we have to consider the whole process as a chain of interrelated effects that form in the last instance the impact of some social policy measure (Kaufmann and Schäfer 1977; Kaufmann et al. 1978). Moreover, we have to take into consideration that each step of the process is determined not only by the intervention itself, but by a number of additional factors in the field in which the intervention takes place.

In this context, impact research means controlling the effects of the action of a certain actor upon a "reacting field." Thus, desired outcomes have to be discussed from the aspect of both the actor and the participants in the field, and possible impacts must include not only the desired, but also possibly undesired outcomes. Finally, the potential impact has to be explained not only in terms of the focal action, but also in terms of other features of the reacting field: for instance, if we find a correlation between the participation of parents in the kindergarten and their educational behavior at home, we can conclude that an impact of the kindergarten's parents program on their educational skills exists only insofar as other social factors that may explain differences in parental behavior (e.g. education, profession, social networks) have been controlled (Kaufmann et al. 1978, 1979).

Impact research can take place at different levels of the delivery process: we can study for instance the impact of different legal regulations on administration, the impact of administrative measures on delivery systems, the impact of different organizational patterns on social interaction in the delivering act, and finally, the impact of different treatments on the situation or capacities of people in the target population. Impact research is a necessary tool for testing a theory of the operating of social policy, which in itself may be conceived at different levels of abstraction. However, if such a theory is not to disintegrate in the complexity of a general interdependence, some standards of selectivity have to be held constant. These definitions concern (1) a certain complex of political measures, (2) a target population, and (3) a set of legitimations for the defined political measures. Such legitimations may be only "precarious values," but they nevertheless limit the realm of desired outcomes that have to be taken into account.

Insofar as this admittedly ambitious program could be realized, there would be a fair chance for sociology to develop grounded theories for social policy, especially in the social service sector. This would not, of course, discard the influence of existing power structures, but it would explain their operation and contribute to their control.

Chapter 4

Structural Rationing of Social Service Benefits in a Welfare State

*Else Øyen**

INTRODUCTION

Social policy *(Sozialpolitik)* in Norway is no longer based only on the needs of the weaker underprivileged or low resource groups within our society. Under the label of "preventive measures," social policy is increasingly concerned with the distribution of welfare benefits to all strata of the population. New groups are continually taking advantage of the social services so as to get a share of the benefits. These groups are not recruited from the lower strata of society. The problems presented do not stem from general poverty conditions, and they carry relatively little statistical risk of throwing the affected individuals into permanent need for support.

There are several reasons for this development that will not be discussed in this study. It is sufficient to point to the fact that social benefits during the last few years have to an increasing degree been used as instruments of general economic policy and as part of the wage settlements between public authorities and all categories of wage earners. Rather, we shall be concerned with some of the consequences of this development for low resource groups. Since social service expenditures cannot increase indefinitely, even in periods of

*Institute of Sociology and Political Studies, University of Bergen, Norway

economic growth, acquiescence to new demands from one group necessarily must lead to lessened compliance to the needs of other groups. At the same time it is still more obvious that low resource groups cannot successfully compete in the battle for social benefits. This is apparently an unintentional effect of an imperfect system of distribution and is often interpreted in relation to characteristics of the clients preventing them from effecting their demands and the organizational weakness in a welfare system that is not geared to meet the needs of groups with low resources.

This is doubtless correct, but we should also consider whether this failure is not actually consistent with the more general social principles by which limited goods are distributed. All class societies set certain limits on how much redistribution can be tolerated at any time, and these limits are incorporated in the distributive social service system in the form of "selective rationing mechanisms" directed at certain groups. Some of these mechanisms are explicit, statutory directives concerning who shall receive and who is not entitled to public resources. However, other rationing mechanisms are implicit and informal, based on broad norms and setting limits on the redistribution of resources to marginal and deviant groups.

THE SOCIAL SECURITY SYSTEM

We will take the Norwegian system of social security as our example. There is little research information about this system, its effects, and its clientele, so we must rely on a number of more general observations and on information about bureaucratic organizations and their relations with low resource groups as our point of departure. The literature in this field is by now quite comprehensive (see Sheriff 1976; Nisbet 1975; Leibfried 1977; Schaffer and Huang 1975; Sjoeberg, Brymer, and Farris 1966; Øyen 1974).

The social security system is founded on the National Insurance Act of 1967. Approximately 6000 people are directly employed in the organization, and in 1978 it will administer more than 30 billion kroner. It has functioned in its present form for about a decade, but most of its provisions are older. The organization is built up in the form of a classical bureaucracy with a highly centralized administration, specialization, departmentalization, hierarchical accountability, and a complex set of regulations. The system has a monopoly in administering the benefits granted under the National Insurance Act such as retirement and disability pensions, health and unemployment insurance, family allowances, and so forth. These benefits are not determined by supply and demand in the market, but by politically set rates that will cover predefined needs. The benefits and services that are offered were orginally designed to provide assistance to low resource groups, but have been expanded to include compensation for loss of wages in case of unemployment for all categories of work, social disability in a wider sense, pregnancies, deaths, and the like.

This means that the benefits in principle apply to the entire population, and therefore the clientele is drawn from new groups. The increase in social service expenditures is partly due to the incorporation of these new groups into the system. Instead of being political measures for treating social problems, social service benefits are becoming a more generalized political tool used in wage agreements and the distribution of goods among people who already have work. This can be considered a positive development both on welfare premises and because it builds a bridge between the first and second class citizens in Norwegian society—that is, those whose income comes from their own work and those who receive welfare grants.

However, it is not certain that everyone profits equally from this development. All social systems have a tendency to be influenced by their public, and the social security system is no exception. As a larger proportion of the "normal" public begins to use the services provided by social security, greater emphasis will be placed on administrative responses to normal behavior.

UNDERCONSUMPTION OF BENEFITS

Many people are in need of welfare benefits but cannot receive them because regulations do not recognize their needs. This is an important issue, but not relevant in this context. We pose the question why so many prople who have acknowledged *rights* to welfare benefits do *not* receive the goods and services they are entitled to. Underconsumption of welfare benefits may be a greater social problem than alleged abuse of social services (*Rapport* 1971; *Utredning* 1973).

We know very little about the size of the group that does not get the benefits to which its members are entitled, but several studies indicate that underconsumption must be considerable. A study of the blind and partially sighted, for example, showed that many individuals receive neither the basic pension to which they were entitled, nor the most elementary technical aids whose costs are refunded by the social security system (Odland 1977). A survey in a lower class area in Oslo showed that nearly a quarter of the tenants had not received all the social benefits to which they were entitled (Eskeland and Finne 1973; Kolberg 1976).

A study conducted by the social security system's own administration shows a great general need for information concerning rights to social benefits, and obviously relevant information is necessary before the public can claim its rights (Lyngstad 1974; Linden 1972). Other investigations among different types of handicapped groups, old people, and the poor, both in Norway and elsewhere, give the same picture of a hidden underconsumption.

The studies uncover four types of underconsumption. First, we have individuals who have never been in contact with the social security system and therefore have never received the benefits to which they are entitled. Second, are those who receive only part of the benefits for which they qualify. Third, there are those who discover their rights too late and get help long after they were first entitled to it. As a fourth group, we have those whose applications are incorrectly refused by the system (NOU 1976).

Why is this so? Why are many more people entitled to benefits than actually receive them? This question has been asked many times and is usually answered by reference to characteristics associated with the individual recipients or lack of responsiveness toward the clients from the service organization. Neither of these two explanations seems to provide a sufficient answer. A more detailed analysis shows that the social security system is actually constructed with a number of regulating and rationing mechanisms that are nonstatutory and that necessarily result in a considerable underconsumption.

This is hardly accidental. Some of the rationing mechanisms reflect common attitudes about living off welfare and not being gainfully employed. Other rationing mechanisms are an indirect result of the way the social security system is organized. The management of social problems has been delegated to a traditional bureaucracy without consideration for the specific characteristics of these problems. Social problems have a variety of causes and a highly differentiated clientele, and it is unlikely that an organization that is created to solve certain kinds of problems will be flexible enough to solve others. In the following sections we shall take a closer look at some of the most important rationing mechanisms.

Information Failure as a Rationing Mechanism

The legal provisions governing the social security system are so complicated that there is probably no single individual who completely masters the rules for the distribution of benefits. The social insurance system therefore is organized in a number of departments that administer different aspects of the law and have a specialized staff. Internal memoranda, decisions and interpretations are written in a judicial language that renders them inaccessible to the uninitiated. This precision of expression is important within a bureaucracy to ensure correct application of the regulations, but it can be carried too far.

The law is designed to meet all contingencies, even though some of them may be very hypothetical and apply to only a few potential abusers. This results in excessively comprehensive and complicated regulations which even differ in internal agreement with regard to basic principles. External interests and compromises are reflected in the welfare system as in other administrative organs. Consider, for example, the principles for the benefits offered by disability pensions and occupational disability pensions. These give individuals with the same degree of invalidity very different rights according to whether they were injured in accidents at work or in other places. The needs of the injured do not determine the amount of help that is made available, while the situation of the employment of the injured and the place where the accident occurred do. (Compare also the legislation concerning single heads of households, grants of technical aids to different types of disabled persons, etc.) The regulations are difficult to read and often completely unintelligible to people who can neither understand the judicial language nor find the appropriate paragraphs. The staff in the local social insurance offices master the common regulations, but complicated cases must be submitted to higher authorities.

It is maintained that a social insurance official must have four or five years experience before he or she has sufficient expertise to serve the ordinary public competently.[a] This is the background to the problems facing the official information office when it tries to inform the public about its rights. The information office is supposed to communicate to the public a system of regulations that have become so complicated that neither information experts nor anyone else can manage to describe it in clear and simple terms.

As it is, the information deals mainly with the basic grants and the most elementary rights pertaining to them. It seems as if only the most elementary welfare measures can be presented without reservations. The information leaflets become evasive and vague when they

[a]These figures are not exact, but representatives of the social security system have suggested, in discussion with social workers concerning the optimal length of their education, that four or five years practice is necessary.

present other social benefits available to the public. This is done in order to avoid raising false hopes, which is, of course, a praiseworthy motive. However, it would be more reasonable to admit that it is impossible to explain the complexity of the social security jungle in a simple yet truthful way, because it can only be understood by a small group of specialists.[b]

The authorities are hesistant to ackowledge these side effects of a complicated system. They ascribe the ignorance of the public to its lack of interest in orienting themselves to the system and not reading the leaflets they frequently receive free of charge in their mailboxes. It is also suggested that those who need help the most are those who are slowest to find out about their rights. This is probably true, but it does not change the basic fact that it is necessary to study the regulations intensively before they become sufficiently understandable to make use of them.

The staff of the local offices undoubtedly do their best to help the public, but it is just as difficult for them to simplify the system as it is for the information office. A small group of lawyers now specializes in social legislation and on behalf of their clients track down the relevant information. This is an important development, but there are very few of these specialists in comparison to the approximately 200,000 new social insurance cases initiated every year. Furthermore, the fundamental problem remains, as the public is not able to acquire and process the material that is relevant for their welfare (Kjønstad 1975).

The regulatory complexity that was considered necessary to ensure justice becomes in itself unjust, because it is instrumental in preventing many people from ever getting the welfare benefits to which they are entitled. Moreover, it is also instrumental in stigmatizing certain people as ignorant. It reminds one of the Emperor's new clothes, since neither Parliament nor the local social insurance boards, who are supposed to supervise the system, manage to gain insight into the complex world of the social security system.

Stigmatization as a Rationing Mechanism

Even if everybody knew all about their rights within the social security system, there would still be many people who would never

[b]There is no doubt that the National Insurance System is worried about its failure in the information sector (cf. the most recent volumes of *Sosial Trygd*). Detailed plans have been worked out for improving the public information service. However, all these plans have the present system of regulations as their point of departure and assume that better technical aids, use of mass media, and enough public relations experts in the end will make the public understand the regulations.

claim their rights. This is due to the strong prejudice and stigmatization in our society against people who do not manage to live off their own earnings. There is no corresponding prejudice against employers who do not employ "second rate" workers. The prejudice is not only reflected in the welfare regulations, but also in the organizational arrangements of these regulations. Certain groups are stigmatized more than others, and this stigmatization acts as a rationing mechanism. There are two forms of stigmatization of people who receive welfare grants. The first type is applied by the public in general towards different groups of welfare clients and works independently of the organization of the system. The second type consists of mechanisms within the welfare system that, independent of the intentions of the staff, reinforce the general processes of stigmatization.

Some situations increase the experience of being stigmatized more than others. Selective social services, for example, create more stigmatizing situations than universal social services (Pinker 1971). Situations where people do not understand the decisions concerning themselves, where they do not understand the language used, and where they have to communicate with strangers in order to make their needs known to an out-of-reach decisionmaking body all further the experience of being stigmatized. The experience is closely related to a feeling of powerlessness. Situations where people are required to supply discreditable information about themselves and where they must contribute to the reinforcement of a negative impression of themselves are of the same kind. So are situations that make people at the bottom of a hierarchy beg for help and those that imply unilateral transfers.

If we examine the social security system more closely, it is possible to recognize quite a number of such situations. Most welfare benefits are grants to which the public is entitled, and they are distributed in accordance with established criteria. For some grants, detailed information about the client is decisive in determining whether the requirements laid down in the regulations are fulfilled. This has the characteristics of a means test. The client presents his application without knowing the rules of the game and without knowing what information is pertinent. The transaction becomes asymmetrical as the client stands alone while the staff represent the expertise and the weight of the whole organization. The organization determines the role of the client and has the right to decide what information about the client's life is needed and what informaton shall be defined as irrelevant.

As long as we have a welfare system that is organized as a bureaucracy, many of these stigmatizing processes seem unavoidable. But some reforms have been suggested. There is, for example, no doubt that the universal benefits to which the public has an automatic right and that are granted to everyone regardless of class and position as long as they fulfill some simple requirements are less stigmatizing than grants that are means tested. Old age pensions, family allowances based on the size of the family, and refunding within the heath service are examples of universal benefits that certainly carry no stigma.

However, a move toward more universal services must be viewed against the background of the development described in the beginning of this chapter. Universal services are more costly, and if defined exclusively as social expenditures, they will, in a period of cutbacks in welfare budgets, be established at the expense of more needy groups. If we want to stress the point, we could say that what the poor gain in terms of decreased stigmatization they lose in terms of actual benefits.

Secrecy is one of the foundations of stigmatization. More openness in the social security system might reduce the stigmatization. The complicated and impenetrable regulations and the professional secrecy imposed on welfare officers both contribute to the myths of abuse and immoral clients. The public does not have the insight into the system to reject stereotypes of welfare clients, and cases of alleged abuse of welfare benefits are never contradicted because of professional secrecy. Protection of privacy of the individual is important and might reduce individual stigmatization. When carried too far in order to protect the system from public insight and the profession from public control, secrecy in itself becomes part of the stigmatization process. Clients collectively might be harmed, because stereotypes concerning their behavior are not corrected and because secrecy implies "abnormal" behavior that has to be hidden from "normal" society. Their real problems are not explained to the public, and needed welfare services will not be initiated (Øyen 1978).

Emphasis on the rights of the public to receive welfare benefits will also contribute to reducing stigmatization. Since our society is organized around the idea that all pay is related to work and to having a job, an emphasis on the role of welfare grants in compensating for nonexistent jobs could be helpful. In a tightening job market based on technically trained and younger people, the weak, the old, and the uneducated are bound to lose out. The price to be paid for this type of job market is the size of the social security budget. This price can only be reduced if it is possible to create a job market adjusted to all types of workers.

The size of the grants offered under the social security system is itself an important condition for stigmatization. The grants are small enough to reinforce the impression that the welfare clients come from the lower classes of Norwegian society, and poverty traditionally is an invitation to stigmatization. An increase in the minimum pension would be a good, helpful protection against stigmatization (cf. Hogan 1977). It is also important to realize that unilateral exchange will always be stigmatizing, no matter how it is made. There is no way of repaying the social security system. The client will always have to assume the humble and grateful role that the benefactor expects of the beneficiary.

Built-in Queues as a Rationing Mechanism

There are no price mechanisms in the welfare system that regulate demand and supply. In principle all consumers are equal, and ideally it is the need that should determine the form and size of the grants. Need, however, is an extremely variable phenomenon that grows parallel to services offered and a rising standard of living. As was said at the outset, new interest groups continually present their needs, and new needs are recognized and incorporated into the system. However, the welfare system does not develop as quickly as needs are recognized, and therefore queues form at many points within the system.

Formation of queues acts as a rationing process, because queues contribute to restricting demand (Bramness and Christiansen 1976). Position in the queue is not decided purely by chance; neither are dropouts in the queue random. Those who are active, know the rules of the game, are able to organize interest groups, and arouse public opinion will, in all probability, move forward in the queue, while those who are passive and not able to mobilize either themselves or others will remain in the queue longest. Individuals or groups who can procure the same benefits through other channels will obviously do so and leave the queue. As always, those who have many resources will have the most choices, while those with few resources stay longest in the queue and are repeatedly pushed back. Moreover, many individuals will never make any demands because they know about the length of the queues and therefore give up beforehand.

There are at least two types of queue within the social security system—those created within the system and those created in social service agencies lovated outside the system but hooked up with the social security system through funding and organizational arrangements. The first type of queue is usually considered to be a result of inadequate staffing in the offices that handle applications. Statistics of this kind of delay are carefully kept and used as an argument for expanding the staff. However, the most important cause for delay is ignored—namely, the complicated regulations that make detailed investigation necessary before a decision can be made. It is likely that the number of experts within the system could be increased considerably without appreciably shortening the queues.

The social security system has less control over the queues formed in social service agencies outside the system. Many of the delays and queues are caused by the organization of refunding, however. Underconsumption is probably large, but is hidden because no systematic information is provided about how slowly the queues move, how long they are, and how many clients are referred to other institutions. Clinics and rehabilitation institutions have long queues that are not regulated by antecedents. These institutions have inadequate capacity, and their choice of clients is influenced by their goals of showing successful treatment. Within the rehabilitation sector, for example, services are more or less reserved for the most adaptable clients and those having the best prognoses for getting back to work. Other services, such as physiotherapy, treatment by specialists, and psychiatric counseling, are also examples of scarce commodities that people queue up for. Economic compensation for time spent in the queue is no substitute for treatment, since problems increase as the months roll by. And the longer the clients have to wait in line, the further their resources become reduced.

The Passive Bureaucracy as a Rationing Mechanism

The bureaucracy is in many ways an effective form of organization. It assumes, however, certain qualities in its clients that make it less suited for handling certain problems in the social service sector. The public is heterogeneous, without common interests and mostly unaware of its rights. The traditional clientele also is recruited from the lower class and often stigmatized before entering the system. Their demands are socially not fully legitimized and cannot be enforced as they have no services or production of importance to society to withhold. As a result, the individual client as well as the group is in a weak position when dealing with the bureaucracy. It is hardly an exaggeration to say that the social security bureaucracy has little need to pay much attention to its clients because they cannot retaliate. Only through intensive pressure group activity or when surveys and research throw light on the way the system works can the bureaucracy be forced to change its course.

The rationing mechanisms described above prevent a large number of individuals from receiving welfare benefits to which they are entitled. We can only guess how many people are involved and who they are. It is not considered the duty of the social security bureaucracy to ask these questions or to initiate research into the problem. Its duty is only to inform the public when asked. It has no obligation to go out and try to find potential clients.

The social security system pays no attention to research showing underconsumption; it does not publicize the results, nor does it use them in the education of future bureaucrats or try to estimate the size of the underconsumption.

The philosophy of much of the social security system is based on the premise that active individuals, who know their rights, should present a clearly formulated application, preferably in writing. When the client does not come to the social security office, this is interpreted as a defect in the client and not in the system. Automatic registration of new clients who are summoned for information exists only for old age pensions and some family allowances. The underconsumption for these benefits is minimal.

Each client is dealt with individually, and at no time are clients with similar problems brought together. While this is advantageous for the system, since it needs only to bargain with one individual at a time, it is disadvantageous for the clients, who do not have a chance to learn from each other, act jointly, and back each other up against the bureaucracy. Welfare clients are mostly unorganized, and in the well-organized Norwegian society, unorganized groups are politically weak and without influence. It seems important to construct an organizational structure that furthers the formation of interest groups among clients with similar problems. At present, it is primarily clients with greater resources and nonstigmatized problems who manage to form interest groups and achieve advantageous reforms. However, since the welfare public is heterogeneous, interest groups would have to be organized in such a way that different groups do not damage each other's interests while competing for limited resources.

In cases of disagreement between the client and the social security system the client is more or less left on his or her own. The staff are assigned the dual role of helping the client appeal the decision and being loyal to the system whose decision is being appealed. An independent board of helpers within the social security system would be a better support for the client in appeal cases. At present, it seems likely that many rejections are not appealed because the staff do not believe that an appeal will be successful. Therefore dissatisfaction is not registered, and we have no statistics on how many cases are involved. In this connection it is interesting to note that nearly a quarter of the appeals made to the court of appeal were decided in favor of the clients while they were being processed and before coming to court (NOU 1976). This means that when given a chance the system corrects its own mistakes. Elsewhere the social security system is responsible for providing free legal help for some of the clients who appeal a decision. (This is a new statute in Israeli Social Security Law, which was enacted in the fall of 1977.)

IS RATIONING NECESSARY?

It seems to be important to ask what the functions are of these rationing mechanisms. Are they unintentional or intentional, and what would happen, in our society and in our welfare system, if they were removed?

Norway is a welfare state whose social security system is considered worthy of imitation by other countries. The National Insurance Act is a banner of considerable pride, because it contributes to increasing the standard of living and quality of life of many Norwegians. Our pride has, however, prevented us from admitting the existence of flaws in the system and has encouraged us to conceal a tendency to favor high resource groups and to discriminate against low resource groups. This is perhaps not surprising. The social security system operates within the society that created it; and Norwegian society being a class system, goods are unequally distributed and mechanisms are at work to preserve and even increase the inequalities (Øyen 1976).

The hierarchical pecking order is closely connected with the distribution of power within the society, and the social security system does not try to challenge the power hierarchy as it might if it strengthened the position of the poor, organized them, and ensured that they received all the benefits to which they were entitled. It remains "neutral," though its neutrality is tinged with middle class sympathies and flawed because it has greater loyalty to other bureaucracies than to its lower status clients. The rationing mechanisms become another tool to reinforce the existent inequalities in our society, although the National Insurance Act is designed as a tool to promote our beliefs in equality and just distribution of common goods.

The rationing mechanisms also have economic consequences that should not be ignored. If these mechanisms were to be eliminated, and everyone received benefits due under the law, it would have drastic consequences for the social security budget. Expenditures would rise so sharply that an extraordinary parliamentary grant would be necessary. Opposition to the increased social security expenses would surely grow among the general public and demands would be set forward that no further increases should occur and that transfer of benefits to new groups should imply deductions in benefits for other recipients within the system. It is difficult to guess what principles would be used to decide priorities if the welfare budget should be reduced, but an explicit priority system, which we do not now have, would undoubtedly be introduced. A reevaluation of the social security system would be painful and disruptive, because it would involve defining our views on the future position of the poor in our society and would stress the concept of class in the social policy discussion. On the whole, there has been political agreement about our present social policy, and it is unlikely that the reform we can realistically expect will primarily deal with the rationing mechanisms that have been discussed above. It is more likely that resources available to the system will be spread thinly and that the social security bureaucracy, with its 6000 employees, has so much momentum that it will continue in its present path with very few changes.

Since this was written, a government-appointed committee concerned with welfare benefits has delivered its report. It suggests that the minimum pension should be raised by 40 percent in the course of five years. It will be interesting to see whether or not this interest group, mobilized to represent a low resource group, will be successful and even more interesting to see which demands from high resource groups will be presented to compete with this increase.

PART II

Organizational Dimensions and Problems of Social Service Delivery Systems

The contributions to Part I emphasized the societal level of analysis and a more or less historical perspective on the development of social needs and the growing societal responsibility to react collectively to these needs. It is a very important feature of the "welfare state" that the politicoadministrative system as well as society at large acknowledge the fact that a great number of individually felt needs are caused by society and can only be solved collectively. If the fact is accepted that our modern industrial and postindustrial societies witness a still increasing demand for social services—in order to solve social problems and to satisfy the needs and demands of a large number of groups in society (not just some marginal ones)—one consequence seems to be quite evident: we will have to observe and evaluate quite different modes of dealing with these needs and problems at the same time. If one looks at the increasing public expenditure in the social service sector, one tends to forget or overlook the fact that most of the social services are still "produced" in the primary social environment of those people in need of support. Thus we will have in the future as we have today a great diversity of service delivery processes and respective institutional infrastructures.

In fact, this can be described as a dialectical relationship between need development and service provisions: we produce within the same societal framework the problems on needs and the solutions for problems. From an "optimistic" point of view, we can declare that the appropriate solutions are found; from a "pessimistic" outlook, we can expect that our so-called "solutions" generate new problems while solving the old ones.

Whatever perspective we choose to select, we will have to work on a thorough analysis of social service processes and their contribution to the solution to social problems. One of the fairly new features (historically speaking) of service delivery is its allocation in large organizations (or bureaucracies) that are ever more connected with each other in order to cope with the increasing number of societal groups or classes served and the differentiations and complex combinations of needs and problems to be dealt with.

In this part we will point out some of the organizational aspects and difficulties of service delivery systems: Chapter 5 deals with the increasing necessity of cooperation and coordination of action between a large number of service organizations; Chapter 6 with the selectivity of organizations in the relation to possible client groups and clients' needs and its organizational causes; and Chapter 7 with the complicated and varying relations between the dynamics of organizational development, interests of the personnel, and the clients' interests and need fulfillment. These contributions show quite clearly that the lack of responsiveness of service organizations is not just a matter of "selective perception" or ignorance, but that the "natural" dynamics of inter- and intraorganizational processes gives much more reward to nonresponsive reactions to clients' needs and problems.

In his study of interorganizational service networks, Dieter Grunow formulates some structural principles of the enduring self-interests of networks—in contrast to the demand of a responsive service delivery system. Drawing from the empirical results of two large-scale research projects he illustrates such deficiencies as lack of goal formation, lack of transparence of implementation and decision processes, lack of positive coordination, and predominance of only symbolic goal fulfillment of social service networks.

In Chapter 6 James R. Greenley discusses some of the features of organizational processes of service delivery in a more systematic way. Giving a review of the relevant literature he focuses on "systematic selection patterns of organizations, not the more random-appearing selection errors resulting from the inabilities of agency staff to deal precisely and consistently with complex and ambiguous client problems." Among a great number of topics, he draws attention to the hidden and overt organizational rewards for selective behavior—

including the "cooling out" of clients and the reinforcement of negative attitudes of clients toward welfare organizations.

This diagnosis should not obscure the fact that these selection patterns only operate fully if each organization and its personnel is interested in making use of them. In Chapter 7, Antoinette Catrice-Lorey takes up some aspects of the organizational and personal infrastructures of service delivery systems (i.e., the Sécurité Sociale) by considering problems and possibilities of integrating service orientations into a bureaucratic organization and its personnel. She indicates the importance of personnel management in each organization on deciding in favor of a more technical administrative or a more client-oriented perspective and activity of the boundary personnel.

Chapter 5

Constraints on Organizational and Personal Responsiveness Toward Clients' Needs as a Consequence of Interorganizational Service Networks

*Dieter Grunow**

INTRODUCTION

The contributions to this volume indicate quite clearly and almost without exception the difficulties practitioners and scientists have to face in the field of social service delivery. The evidence of the interrelatedness of many difficulties is as solid as the lack of suggestions about how to deal with them theoretically and practically. The fact that social programs "did not work" (i.e., did not reach their declared and/or intended goals), that instead social institutions produce individual and social situations and dispositions that they were supposed to abolish, that a gigantic redistribution of resources takes place in the social sector, but does not reduce inequality among the client groups—all this has become a truism that everybody knows but increasingly does not care about (Scott 1961; Sykes 1958; Fisher 1969). This development leads us to question whether "innovations in the service sector" are still possible and can be at all effective (OECD 1976).

In the FRG we have also experienced reactions to the failure of

*Research Group, Social Planning and Social Administration, and Project Group, Administration and the Public, University of Bielefeld, Federal Republic of Germany.

many reform activities in the early 1970s. There has not only been a general disappointment but also an explicit conservative reaction to this in terms of a rejection of the so-called *Reform-politik* of the SPD/FDP coalition in Bonn (Grottian and Murswieck 1974; Murswieck 1976). But fortunately this has not been the only type of reaction and result: quite a few practitioners and scientists tried to learn from these experiences. This has led first to an intensified analysis of policy restrictions and second to the conceptualization of implementation processes (Mayntz 1977). Although rather new as a central focus of discussion and research, implementation "theory" has advanced as a major attempt and means to close the theoretical and practical gap between the formulation (and codification) of social programs, their administration, and their effectiveness. It has become quite clear from the results of evaluation and of implementation studies that it is ever more important to include aspects of the implementation structure and possible implementation processes in the phase of program formulation (Bunker 1972; Gilbert 1977; Dye 1972).

Although this fact seems to be trivial—at least for those who know something about the concept of "innovation in organizations"—it is very often neglected in the policy formation process. If anything, new programs try to keep up with the rules that so far are supposed to govern the activities in the field of concern. But not even the legal implications and consequences of new programs are sufficiently known. The most recent experience of this in Germany was the so-called "finance reform" of 1975-1976, which has reinforced interest in founding a political party of discontented taxpayers. Even less can be anticipated in regard to the factual structures and processes of the action field in which the innovations are planned. Social programs often enough deal with the action fields as if they were a *tabula rasa* ("empty blackboard") whereas in reality they are already fields of interests and actions. The constellation of an action field is by no means sufficiently described through lobbying—which is closely connected with policy formulation—because the lobbyists are quite often as remote from the action field as the politicians.

One main type of reaction of officials to this situation—if it is recognized at all—is just to ignore it (unless there is a strong public reaction); another reaction is to go on making new programs of the same ineffectual kind. A third type of reaction is the attempt to reorganize the field of social policies and programs in general. In Germany, for example, an attempt has been made to integrate and adjust the whole social welfare and social security legislation and to create the *Sozialgesetzbuch* (General Code of Social Rights). The first, general part of this code of social rights (SGB/AT) is already in effect: for the first time it formulates the rights and obligations of the citizen (in terms of social welfare and security) in a general fashion and thereby includes explicitly the relationships between citizens and the responsible public institutions. Although the most difficult parts of this project—the mutual adjustment and the simplification of existing laws—are not yet realized, it seems to be a very important step toward a more visible field of social service production and delivery.

To be successful in the reorganization of the delivery systems or the implementation of new programs in a structured action field, the horizontal and vertical interorganizational networks are of ever-increasing importance. (This was the major topic of the European Consortium of Policy Research workshop in Grenoble in April 1978). In Germany the interorganizational networks have to be seen in the light of federalism—that is, the division of responsibility between the national, state, and local level—and with regard to the division of labor between private groups and organizations, voluntary associations (*Wohlfahrtsverbande*), and the state-communal institutions according to the *Subsidiaritatsprinzip* (a principle by which the state is confined to activities that are not or cannot be executed by private actors or local government). These two types of interorganizational networks are relevant for the implementation process and for the ongoing process of services delivery.

The following remarks try to indicate some features of the inter-organization network that constitutes the service delivery system. Although there is—as far as I can see—neither a data-based theory of implementation processes nor of interorganizational networks, it seems necessary to me to stress the importance of this point of discussion (Majone and Wildavsky 1978). It should at least be seen as a major demand for future research activities. This demand not only includes the problem of theory building and of practical innovations but also the development of appropriate research methods. A review of the latest implementation studies shows very primitive and ad hoc research designs and research strategies. Thus we have to acknowledge that many of the deficiencies mentioned above are a consequence of the lack of appropriate methods.

ORGANIZATIONAL AND PERSONAL CONSTRAINTS TO THE RESPONSIVENESS OF SERVICE DELIVERY SYSTEMS

If we choose the responsiveness of delivery organizations (or networks) to the clients' needs as a point of evaluation, we can relate our arguments to many research results. These results—as this volume demonstrates—give evidence of many deficiencies in terms of the responsiveness of welfare agencies (in almost all countries). It cannot be of interest to repeat these findings in detail; it might be helpful, though, to try to accentuate some areas of special importance.

Within our own empirical research projects (Grunow and Hegner 1977a, 1978b; Grunow 1977), we have identified four main areas as the most important indicators of responsiveness (cf. the overview of variables in Table 5-1):

Standards of problem identification and problem definition (i.e., in which mode and intensity information about clients and client groups are collected and used for decisionmaking in regard to the services to be offered: the negative extreme would be a stereotyping and stigmatizing usage of this information);

Standards of client selection (i.e., how selective the services offered are in terms of client characteristics or client groups; in addition, the question of the degree of awareness the organization has in regard to its selectivity);

Standards of service production and preparation (i.e., how services are prepared and produced and which characteristics the production process and the product have—in relation to the clients' needs); and

Standards of service delivery (i.e., how services are delivered to the clients and what intended and actual impact they have on the clients' situation).

Although there are overlapping areas between these standards of responsiveness, it is important to indicate the special features of each of them. Therefore we cannot judge the responsiveness of welfare institutions just from the perspective of one measure—as has been done too often already.

In addition, it is necessary to consider these standards in relation to the organizational and personal characteristics of the institutions under study. Often this fact is ignored within practical discussions of the responsiveness of welfare institutions: in this context either the personnel or the bureaucratic structure is blamed—with the intention of finding a scapegoat for the problems and difficulties in contact with the clients. It is necessary, however, to see both factors (personnel and organizational structure) as conflicting or intensifying in their mutual relationships. This leads us to demand a very careful empirical analysis of all standards in terms of individual and organizational structural aspects (Grunow and Hegner 1978b, 1979).

By following this demand we should exclude other forms of

Table 5-1. Responsiveness of Delivery Systems and Social Policy (an Overview)

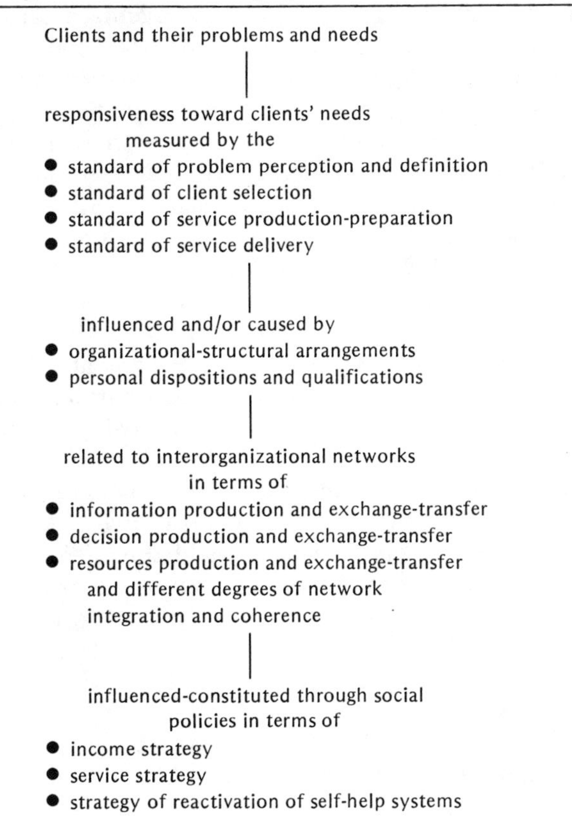

argumentation and conceptualization that seem to be very up to date, such as the equalization of responsiveness (of welfare organizations) with a general (probably ideal!) type of organization (Muller 1973; Rosengren and Lefton 1970; Pankoke 1971)—for example, the "participative" organization, the "situational" organization, the "professional" organization, and the "nonbureaucratic" organization. It should not be obscured that first of all these terms stand for a descriptive differentiation of types of organizations according to some dominant features. For each type it has to be shown that it actually implies or causes a more responsive relationship to the clients and their needs. Neither other studies nor our own research results convince us that an increase of professional orientation, for example, leads to a more responsive reaction to the clients in terms of the four "standards" described above (Blum and Rosenberg 1968; Innes 1977).

It can be concluded that it is mainly an empirical question as to which type of welfare agency has been organized most adequately according to the needs and problems of the clients. Whereas this empirical approach might be plausible and acceptable to the scientist, the practitioners very often try to escape this kind of "evaluation." They prefer to blame definitively someone else (although not only the victim-client): in Germany very often some bureaucrats at higher administrative levels or the legislative boards are blamed by the responsible officials. These arguments are only partly true, but they nevertheless indicate one important aspect of the service delivery processes correctly—the ever-increasing interrelatedness of the many relevant actors in each field of service. Although this fact is broadly acknowledged in journals, in books, and at conferences (e.g., under the headings of service integration, coordination necessities, merger of service agencies), our empirical knowledge is rather meager (Gans and Horton 1975; Brown 1974; Rowbottom et al. 1974; Groell 1972). Little is known about the actual consequences of interorganizational networks on intraorganizational processes and the relationships between service agencies and the clients. In the following section I describe some features of interorganizational networks and the possible effect they might have on the formation of the four standards described above in a focal (social service) organization.

INTERORGANIZATIONAL DIMENSIONS OF SERVICE DELIVERY SYSTEMS

At first glance it seems to be quite easy to deal with the concepts of interorganizational relationships; there are, at least, many conceptual propositions (Tuite et al, 1972; Neghandi 1971). This does not allow the omission of some critical remarks. In our developed industrial societies we have observed the process of functional and structural differentiation of private and public activities in the production sphere as well as in the reproduction sphere. This has led to the reintegration problem in terms of joint decisionmaking, cooperation, coordinated action, and so forth. Problems of this type have been a central topic of many different organizational analyses. Along with vertical, horizontal, or even diagonal concentration processes in private economic and public administration organization, theorists have become more interested in the relationships between organizations and their environment(s) than in intraorganizational processes. As long as "environment" was conceived as a residual category, it was easy to separate organization and environment quite clearly. With the discussion of interorganizational relationships (as a concept of structured environment), the concept of organization tended to become a residual category—which implies many difficulties with defining the boundary of an organization. This fact can be proved in almost all contributions to interorganizational theory (Warren 1976-78; Metcalfe 1976; Marret 1971): the term "organization" is used in a vague and empty sense. This brings us to the conclusion that it remains completely open to question what the differences between interorganizational relations and interdepartmental relations (within one organization) are.

If we look at the many listings of so-called "interorganizational dimensions" (Fritschler and Segal 1971; Hall et al. 1977; Rogers 1974), we find hardly any term that is not used for intraorganizational analysis. This leads us to the suspicion that interorganizational analysis is nothing more nor less than organizational analysis at a higher level. Therefore, the crucial question of the conceptual arrangement seems to me to be whether the theorists apply a "closed system approach" or an "open system approach" to interorganizational analysis. From the above arguments we can conclude that interorganizational analysis deals mainly with intranetwork problems and thus uses a closed system approach (at a higher level). Typically, the network as such becomes the main focus of attention, which implies a separation from or neglect of the problem (or function) the network is supposed to deal with. In these terms, interorganizational analysis does not contribute any new idea to the general problem of the division of labor in our society and its consequences of integration problems.

Thus we have to ask again, What are the network specifics? I am convinced that it is not sufficient to point to the number (n 1) of organizations under study when answering this question. The immediate reaction would be to ask for the *qualitative differences* of the implementation process *within one* organization (which in itself is functionally differentiated) in contrast to the implementation process *within the network* of two or more organizations. This question can be answered only with regard to a problem to be solved (as a starting point). The lack of relevance of most of the interorganization-network discussion has to be seen in the lack of a focal or reference-point (outside the network) for analysis. These conceptual deficiencies correspond with the pre-occupation of 'implementation theorists' with policy realization and output measures—while *excluding* the problems of the impact of the administrative output. Both trends (interorganizational relations as closed systems and implementation as a process of internal enforcement of norm-conformity)

Table 5-2. Deficiencies of the Delivery Systems in Terms of Lack of Responsiveness to Clients' Needs

	Dimensions of Delivery Systems		
Standard	*Personnel*	*Organizational Structure*	*Interorganizational Network*
Problem perception definition	perceptual distortion	goal displacement	lack of goal formation; goal conflict
Client selection	"creaming" processes	stigmatizing client groups	lack of clarity; no control of resulting total selectivity
Service production-preparation	deficiencies in personal qualifications	dominance of organization technology and/or professional standards	only negative coordination; seller's market situation; bureaucratization of the whole network; time losses
Service delivery	lack of interaction competence; problems of motivation	low prestige and incentive for boundary personnel	impact evaluation hardly possible; no accountability for failures; increasing relevance of symbolic goal fulfillment

can be described as a *technocratic perspective* to public policy-making. To avoid this perspective as the focus of our dicussion we'll have to relate the interorganizational analysis closely to the exploration of the organizational responsiveness (in terms of the four above formulated standards) to clients' needs: *what (if any) are the specific interorganizational problems of responsiveness of personnel or organizations or even the delivery system in toto?*

In Table 5-2 some of the well-known problems or deficiencies on the personnel and organizational level are repeated—they need not be described and discussed again. We focus on the interorganizational specifics of the responsiveness of service delivery systems (networks). Arguing about these specifics requires at least a determination of major components of the network. For our purposes it should be enough to talk of the interorganizational network in terms of production and exchange or transfer of information, decisions, and resources aiming at the satisfaction of clients' needs. In addition, the mode and the intensity of the relationships between the organizations in the network have to be described for every single arrangement. In their study of 156 social service organization networks Konglan et al. (1976) propose the following scale of relationships:

Interpersonal awareness of officials,
Interpersonal acquaintance of officials,
Systematic information exchange,
Exchange of interorganizational resources (personnel, rooms, technical instruments),
Overlapping boards or council cooption,
Joint programs (coalition), and
Written agreements.

This scale can be used as an indicator of the integration of the social service delivery system and the coherence of the interorganization network. Within our line of argument it can be said that the stronger the existing integrative characteristics, the greater are the similarities to organizational problems of service delivery that have to be expected (compare Table 5-2). In the following we want to look at the less integrated networks and try to indicate some of their deficencies with regard to the fulfillment of the clients' needs.

Problem Definition

On the level of each single organization, a high degree of perceptual distortion and goal displacement has been described in many empirical studies (Merton 1940; Estes 1974). This evidence shows that there is a lack of ability or willingness to perceive and define the problems and needs of the clients without prejudice. But it still implies the possibility of standardizing the problem definitions at the organizational level: the definition of common (even if inappropriate) goals in dealing with clients' needs.

For the interorganizational network this does not hold true; here we can expect a lack of goal formulation processes and thus a great number of goal conflicts that are deduced from very different problem definitions. In Germany especially, this is a consequence of contrasting philosophies of service provisions between public agencies, voluntary associations (mainly tied to the churches), and private initiatives (which often operate with profit interests) (Campenhausen 1976). For the client this has a qualitatively different impact: it is not just the fact that his or her needs are not met adequately by the network—it is also the fact that these needs might be defined in contradictory terms if he or she moves (or is referred) to another organization in the network. Thus clients lose the possibility of identifying their own position and relationship with the delivery system as a total network. To illustrate my argument I want to refer to research results from an empirical investigation of the implementation of new forms of domiciliary social and health care services (*Sozialstationen*) in the FRG (Grunow, Hegner, and Lempert 1979). The original problem that led to the discussion of the *Sozialstationen* concept was a minor one—a lack of personnel in the former, church-related agencies of domiciliary health care (*Gemeindepflegestationen*) in contrast to the growing demand for these services in the population. As these agencies could not solve this problem by themselves it became a political issue, first to the voluntary welfare associations (*Wohlfahrtsverbande*, especially CARITAS), and later—to secure the financial support of the state—to the political and the administrative system as well.

In the following public debate (from the early 1970s), which included almost all potential members of the implementation network (for the development of *Sozialstationen*), the dominant problem definition changed quite often and rapidly. In general, the original problem was largely replaced by cost increases of institutionalized health care. *Sozialstationen* were now defined as a major contribution to the cost reduction of hospital services. With this shift in the problem definition, the conflicting interests of the relevant actors in the field became much more articulate. Those actors were (1) the state administration, which wanted to establish a large-scale domiciliary service network; (2) the voluntary welfare associations, which wanted to gain more power (in terms of monopoly) in the delivery system of a specific region and at the same time tried to avoid regulatory state influence in the implementation of *Sozialstationen*; (3) the physicians, who were afraid of losing parts of their clientele to *Sozialstationen*; and (4) the systems of health insurance, which were afraid that they would have to pay for most of the services delivered and that there would be a rapid increase of demand for these services.

Very little (or almost nothing) was said in relation to the people who should be the beneficiaries of the services offered. Neither the physical, psychological, nor social problems they had were described and discussed, nor was the question raised whether the services to be offered would be adequate to deal with these problems. At the local level, not only did the individual interests and problem definitions of single actors prevail but also the existing network as such. Very often the relevant local actors would not decide who should apply for state funds, who should be the first to implement a *Sozialstation* in their community. They rather sent many applications to the state agencies, to let them decide who should get the funds. This procedure was chosen although they all knew that the state agencies would not give any money to this community under these conditions. But, as the actors said, they did not want to damage the good relationships in the network just for the implementation of a *Sozialstation*.

Client Selection

This situation also describes the problem of client selection through personal and organizational arrangements very well (Cloward and Epstein 1965; Leibfried 1976). The number of clients who do not get adequate service is increasing in a network where all organizations not only select certain groups of clients but realize this selection on the basis of different of even antagonistic measures. If the delivery of services is possible through the participation of all network organizations only, the probability of failure is higher the greater the number of organizations. The network is very often not able to perceive and control its overall selectivity in regard to client groups and clients' needs. Each organization tends to believe that its own selectivity is compensated for by another organization in the network. Thus the task of integration of many single service elements is left to the client—although it is quite clear that he or she usually does not have the necessary information and skills to deal successfully with this task (Bujard and Lange 1978; Gordon 1975).

To add some empirical evidence from our study of the administration of the local social services at this point, I want to refer to some results from our survey of the local social administration officials ($N = 412$) (Grunow and Hegner 1978b):

99 percent of them are convinced that not all persons receive social welfare who are entitled to do so;

90 percent of them are convinced that a large proportion of those people receiving social welfare do not receive all the benefits they are entitled to;

Two-thirds of them know that this "selectivity" takes place mainly with regard to old people and to mentally and physically handicapped persons, but at the same time one-third of them could not indicate any agency in the community that offers help to the elderly (one-third gave just one correct answer, one-third gave two or more correct answers), although there are on an average more than a dozen of those agencies in each community;

94 percent of them declare that they are willing to give clients all kinds of information about additional sources and agencies of help, but in only 19 percent of the observed contacts with their clients ($N = 2312$) did they really give this information.

Thus it is of great importance that, for example, the previously mentioned Code of Social Rights (SGB/AT) relates to this problem when it defines the obligation of each organization in the network to advise the clients in all aspects of the social services that are included in the whole code. We can omit speculations about the chances of realizing these obligations. To describe the factual situation, it is much more plausible to expect each organization to "excuse" its own selectivity by referring to the responsibilities of other organizations in the network. This can lead to the extreme situation where clients (within the most complex problem situations) are referred from one organization to another in a constant circular process.

Service Production

Although the four "standards are discussed separately, they are very much interconnected. The problem definitions and client selections are of great importance to the mode and adequacy of service production. If one accepts the notion that different types of social services require different organizational settings (for example in terms of more or less formalization and standardization of procedures), an important question deals with the effects of bureaucratic organizations on other less bureaucratic or nonbureaucratic organizations in the network. From research findings that are already available we can conclude that there is a strong tendency to bureaucratize the whole network if there are only a few bureaucratic organizations engaged in this network (Schluchter 1972; Touraine 1969; Grunow and Hegner 1977b). To refer to our research about *Sozialstationen* again, this is a very good example of the bureaucratization of the network (of domiciliary health care services). As soon as parts of the services offered or the necessary investments are financed by the state and controlled by local and regional authorities, the preparation or production of services becomes much more "organized" and "bureaucratized," and through this the service system loses flexibility and responsiveness:

Sozialstationen are forced to strictly and efficiently "organize" the activities of the staff (mainly nurses);

When making the first contact with a patient, *Sozialstationen* have to find out, first of all, who will pay for which kind of service;

To apply for state support, *Sozialstationen* have to carry out even more administrative work;

By financing only specific care services (for instance no social services), the state "motivates" *Sozialstationen* to restrict their services in a selective and artificial sense.

Another important aspect is the production time. Under the

condition of different intraorganizational structures of the relevant organizations we can expect frictions as well as loss of time if production procedures have to cross organizational boundaries. These frictions and losses of time increase in situations where differently trained and differently oriented personnel have to participate in the process of service production. The preoccupation of the network with its own structural and procedural problems leads to a situation that McKinlay (Chapter 8) calls a "seller market." The production process is separated from the financing process and from the evaluation and impact of the services produced.

Service Delivery

This last point is a consequence as well of deficiencies in the standards of service delivery. If the single organization delivers only marginal services (in relation to the clients' problems and needs), it cannot be forced (or is not able) to evaluate the impact and relevance of its own activities. Thus the means become ends: everybody does his duty; nobody is responsible for the failures observed. The accountability can be as easily referred to other organizations as to the clients (Ryan 1971; Piven and Cloward 1971; Goffman 1952; Weirich et al. 1977). The network as such is not an entity that can be called to account. It thus becomes a typical procedure to blame someone else (if not the client herself or himself) for the deficiencies in the contents and procedures of service delivery. Last but not least, the computer might become the scapegoat. Again I want to give an example from the research done in the social services administration. When we asked the officials ($N = 412$) how they would operationalize the main goals of the relevant law (*Bundessozialhilfegesetz*), 14 percent could not formulate any specification; 51 percent referred to existing operational rules; and the rest mentioned the necessity of responsive behavior by the officials.

Thus almost everybody declared existing work procedures as being functional in reaching the legally defined goals of social welfare—although, on the other hand, 80 percent of them acknowledged that only a small proportion of the welfare recipients are able to become independent of the welfare system again, which is one main goal of the welfare provisions. These empirical results show quite clearly that the officials do not relate the failures of the social programs to their own praxis. When asked, they would rather "blame the client":

70 percent of them believe that the anxiety of clients about contacting the social services is the main reason for the existing barriers;

50 percent think that the negative image of welfare recipients keeps people from asking for help;

Only very few refer to the lack of responsiveness of the delivery system—for example, long waiting time, complicated application forms, officials' lack of time, unkind behavior of the officials, and so forth.

The more each organization within the network can free itself from direct accountability for its output, the more it can concentrate its energy and resources on public relations and propaganda instead of adequate service production and delivery. It becomes ever more important to produce the image of goal adherence and goal fulfillment (in a purely symbolic sense) (Meyer and Rowan 1977; Krause 1968). Many of the activities of organizations in the service network are already devoted to this symbolic representation of organizational responsiveness (instead of adequate delivery procedures)—namely, lots of written materials, a "telephone hour" with high officials or politicians, the so called *Meckerbander* (tape recording of clients' grievances), and so forth. Although the points mentioned above are by no means a complete list of special effects of interorganizational networks on the service delivery procedures, they clearly indicate their relevance for any innovative conception and action in this field.

CONCLUSION: INTERORGANIZATIONAL NETWORKS AND SOCIAL POLICY

Our short analysis should have made clear the importance that interorganizational networks have for the theoretical and practical attempts to reach new solutions in the field of social service delivery. This factor is at least as important as the often described personal and intraorganizational aspects. If we relate this conclusion to the question of innovative social policies again, we have to stress the necessity of looking at this factor of interorganizational relations much more than has been done until now. If we see the major options for future social policies as

Income strategy,
Service strategy, and
Activation or reactivation of self-help systems (see Badura and Gross 1976),

We have to explore the limits and possibilities of these strategies not only in the light of single service delivery organizations and their personnel. The decision about adequate policy strategy will have to be established more and more on the basis of an analysis of delivery networks. Without this analysis a calculation of the costs and effects of social programs would not be at all possible. It will not be possible either to improve service delivery just by changing one organization in a direction that implies more responsiveness to clients' needs. For the future, any improvement has to presuppose the innovation of whole networks of service delivery.

It is my impression that we—as social scientists—still lack many prerequisties (in terms of theory, research methods, and empirical data) for the formulation of relevant contributions to the practical problems we are confronted with in the field of social service delivery.

Chapter 6

Organizational Processes and Client Selectivity in Social Welfare Services

*James R. Greenley**

INTRODUCTION: THE CONTEXT OF STAFF-CLIENT INTERACTION

Social selection processes necessarily operate throughout all societies because all societies need mechanisms to distribute goods and statuses. This chapter concerns social selection processes that result in the distribution of goods and statuses by social welfare organizations. Following Blau and Scott (1962), social welfare organizations are defined as those organizations in society having clients as their prime beneficiaries, even though there may be indirect benefits for society at large. These would encompass all traditional welfare organizations, including those designed to provide financial, health, employment, rehabilitation, personal, or psychiatric counseling, and other such services.

The services provided by social welfare organizations are distributed selectively. This is both necessary and desirable. Certain people need these services and others do not. Since the amount of service any social service agency can supply is limited and usually must be rationed, difficult selection decisions must be made.

High rates of referrals and rejections give us cause to examine

*University of Wisconsin-Madison, Madison, Wisconsin, U.S.A.

social selection processes. Approximately two-thirds of all applicants to U.S. social welfare agencies are either referred or rejected (Kirk and Greenley 1974). The distribution of services often appears systematically biased or productive of morally undesirable outcomes. For example, we are distressed to learn that the blind person most in need of agency aid is least likely to receive it (Scott 1969). This study focuses on such systematic selection patterns, not the more random-appearing selection errors resulting from the inabilities of agency staff to deal precisely and consistently with complex and ambiguous client problems.

The overall results of these social selection processes are most often thought to be aggregates of individual decisions made in the interaction of basic boundary personnel and clients of social welfare organizations. By basic boundary personnel, we mean those professional or nonprofessional staff who directly interact with clients concerning eligibility and the provision of services. By social welfare organization or agency, we mean a formal organization (Blau and Scott 1962) located in a particular community and providing services directly to people of that community.

Individual decisions concerning the provisions of services are the outcome of negotiations between client and staff (Thompson 1962). While selection processes occurring at the micro level of staff-client interaction are crucial, much social selection (or the pressure toward it) occurs outside of this staff-client contact. Potential clients select themselves out of service by deciding not to seek certain organizational services. Client selectivity is influenced in part by professional ideologies and the publicity of and about social welfare organizations. In addition, many of the forces which mold selection processes at the staff-client interaction level, such as eligibility rules and organizational staff reward structures, are the result of decisions made by the organization's administration and influenced by the organization's environment (Grunow and Hegner 1977a). Thus, even though individual selection decisions are made in the interaction between client and staff, the causes of considerable selectivity lie in the context of this interaction.

This chapter will focus on questions related to the context of staff-client interactions. What are the organizational processes that give rise to staff discretion? How do organizational processes and environmental conditions influence the types of clients who receive or do not receive services? How do governmental bodies and other institutions that establish and fund local social welfare agencies influence client selection? How do both professional and nonprofessional basic boundary personnel cope with the pressures of having to be selective of clients? How do answers to these broad questions relate to the particular client selection practices of basic boundary personnel? How do the social selection practices of social welfare agencies affect client attitudes and help-seeking behavior?

DOMAIN ADJUSTMENT

A major source of autonomy and resources for welfare organizations is their claimed domains (Greenley and Kirk 1973; Meyer 1975). An organization's claimed domain consists of its written and verbal pronouncements regarding the problem it deals with, the population it serves, and the services it offers (Greenley and Kirk 1973). Rather than constituting a fixed territory, a claimed domain may be relatively flexible, representing the outcome of the organization's continual negotiation with its relevant environment (see Strauss et al. 1963). Typically, the claimed domain would be negotiated annually with funding or governing groups (e.g., charitable organizations, government bureaus or legislatures, or agency boards) and would be negotiated by top administrative staff for the purpose of obtaining funds or raising prestige. Often claimed domains are expanded in search of additional organizational resources, such as when a welfare organization publicly announces new programs or auxiliary services. As Meyer (1975) has noted, claimed domains rarely contract in scope.

An organization's claimed domain may not be congruent with its de facto domain (Greenley and Kirk 1973). The de facto domain consists of the problems presently or actually dealt with, the population served, and the services rendered. Often the two domains are not congruent in that they do not cover the same problems, populations, and services (Stanton 1970; Scott 1969; Perrow 1961). This can result in a difference between claimed and de facto domains that will be called domain discrepancy.

Domain discrepancy commonly occurs when de facto domains become smaller than claimed domains. From its inception, a welfare organization may be unable to provide all promised or mandated services due to insufficient resources or unavailable technologies. Certain organizations are established with unrealistically wide claimed domains for essentially political reasons, such as to shield themselves from criticism. These organizations never fully intended to provide all services in their claimed domain. Public employment agencies were mandated and funded to establish outreach programs to serve persons with exceptionally poor employment records (Randall 1973).

Despite this expansion of their claimed domains, certain agencies did not serve this population for fear of losing needed support from large local employers who might have been angered by receiving referrals of these poor employment risks. Also, de facto domains may shrink due to contracting organizational resources that force reduction of services. Professionalization of agency services may cause claimed domains to contract. Other conditions being equal, there is a tendency for agency de facto domains to contract over time (Hasenfeld 1972; see also Rosengren 1970), leaving claimed domains larger than de facto domains. In such a situation, potential clients drawn by an organization's claimed domain will apply for services that the organization is not providing.

Less commonly, de facto domains may become larger than claimed domains. This may occur when serving a particular population is valuable to the organization, but including this population in the claimed domain is not. For example, a public mental health clinic funded to provide acute psychiatric care for the poor was observed by the author to allow certain staff to provide long-term psychoanalytic psychotherapy to some high income people. This was allowed to improve recruitment possibilities and morale of staff, even though recognition of this service in its claimed domain would undermine the organization's ability to get public funds. Provision of services to clients defined as outside an organization's claimed domain reduces the services that can be supplied to those defined as within the claimed domain. The discrepancies between claimed and de facto domains that are attendant on goal displacement do create a need for staff members to be selective in services provided.

Organizations tend to choose to serve those clients whose cases result in maximization of resources and autonomy (Greenley and Kirk 1976). There are substantial data to support the proposition that the more an organization values a client as a resource or sees a client as a source of organizational autonomy the greater the likelihood that that applicant will be accepted as a client. Clients are a necessary resource in and of themselves for welfare institutions. Without them a service agency cannot survive (Gore and Dyson 1964). However, clients vary to the extent that they are a resource or a liability to a welfare institution. Certain clients can overburden an agency by demanding special attention; by requiring staff overtime; by consuming scarce resources such as staff, equipment, or space for long durations; or by failing to exhibit the proper improvement desired by the agency. Thus it is understandable in terms of goal displacement processes (which are often the consequences of an agency's search for resources and autonomy) that de facto domains will reflect an organization's preference for clients who are more of a resource (Greenley and Kirk 1973).

Faced with an ability to be selective, agencies will tend to serve higher status clients and those with a greater potential for improvement or rehabilitation (Greenley and Kirk 1973; Levine, White, and Paul 1963; Bredermeier 1964). Welfare institutions are therefore often in the position of attracting a broader range of clients than they are equipped to serve and accepting from a diverse pool of applicants those who are generally higher status and less severely impaired or impoverished.

Our unpublished data show that highly selective agencies, as indicated by their high referral and rejection rates, have greater autonomy and more stable resources (Greenley and Schoenherr 1978). Agencies with more autonomy and resources are better able to absorb the costs of selectivity—for example, client dissatisfaction from rejections or staff time that must be devoted to client selection. Autonomy and resources may not only result from domain discrepancy and client selectivity but also may reinforce an agency's ability to maintain domain discrepancy and selective practices.

ORGANIZATIONAL REWARDS AND CLIENT SELECTIVITY

The reward structure of a welfare agency may promote certain types of client selectivity as staff try to meet established performance standards in order to obtain organizational rewards. Staff are often rewarded more if they adopt certain patterns of client selectivity. For instance, agencies providing rehabilitation for physically handicapped people sometimes evaluate staff according to the number of clients that they "rehabilitate," place in jobs, or assist to achieve some particular level of functioning (Levine, White, and Paul 1963). This may encourage staff to select as clients those individuals whose disabilities are less intransient and to avoid those clients whose problems are difficult.

Performance standards are usually adopted to increase organizational autonomy and resources or to protect the position of the agency's administration. Under certain circumstances, welfare organizations may seek autonomy and resources through establishing performance standards by which they can document the value of their service. Standards may be imposed on the organization by funding bodies and higher governmental units or be negotiated with them, in which case the importance of meeting these performance standards is usually clear. Also, establishment of performance standards by which to evaluate staff is a means of asserting control over staff by the organization's administration.

Through goal displacement processes, performance standards become the operative staff goals, often regardless of whether client interests are served. These performance standards are usually an attempt to operationalize official goals (Perrow 1961) in a quantifiable manner, as when agency staff are evaluated according to the number of clients "rehabilitated." Organizational members have a tendency to deflect their energies toward the achievement of the more quantified activities (Etzioni 1964; Warner and Havens 1968). This may be more common in welfare organizations delivering complex human services where precise goals and desired outcomes are difficult to formalize.

Staff members will favor accepting clients who will more likely lead to their positive evaluation by the organization (Sjoberg, Brymer, and Farris 1966; Nagi 1974; Greenley and Kirk 1976). In making selection decisions, staff often experience a conflict between what they see as good service or good professional practice and activities that will result in their obtaining a good organizational evaluation (cf. Grunow and Hegner 1977a). Over time, staff not performing according to organizational standards will tend to leave because they will be unrewarded or discouraged. The remaining staff will be overrepresented by those more likely to be selective of clients in ways that may promote their own careers through fulfilling organizational needs. In sum, improving agency autonomy, resources, and internal integration are the intents of these standards; organizational reward structures are the means of enforcing these standards; and social selectivity of clients is one result.

ORGANIZATIONAL STRUCTURE AS A REFLECTION OF SOCIETAL BELIEFS

Meyer and Rowan (1977) indicate that ideology and beliefs lead organizations to incorporate into their structure and activities those items expected of it. So persuasive is a belief in the medical profession, they write, that "A sick worker must be treated by a doctor using acceptable medical procedures; whether the worker is treated effectively is less important." Similarly, welfare institutions dispensing funds often expend considerable effort in eligibility checks, not because this may be cost effective, but because the public and legislators expect them to engage in this precautionary activity.

Meyer and Rowan (1977) argue in general that organizations that incorporate accepted legitimized "elements in their formal structures maximize their legitimacy and increase their resources and survival capabilities." It is clear that organizations do employ particular professions and engage in particular activities because they are expected to by their sponsors or the general public. Meeting these beliefs and expectations is necessary for their autonomy and claim to resources.

To the extent that an organization secures its autonomy and resources through conformity to social beliefs or expectations, the organization is less dependent on providing itself through outcome performance. Thus, welfare agencies may survive and prosper with structures and activities that are not rationally built around solving problems or delivering services. Social welfare organizations often do not need to be tightly and rationally organized around producing a certain outcome for clients. Many are not evaluated on the basis of client outcomes. They achieve necessary organizational autonomy and resources by being isomorphic with societal beliefs. To the extent that producing specified client outcomes is not necessary for survival, monitoring of service activities will tend to have less value to the welfare agency, and the discretion supplied to staff will consequently be greater (cf. Nagi 1974). This discretion increases the possibility of client selectivity in the interaction between basic boundary personnel and clients.

COPING WITH SELECTIVITY: ACTIVE AND PASSIVE SELECTIVITY

Basic boundary personnel are faced with many choices concerning the selection of clients and the strategies to manage the selection process. Selectivity is created, as argued above, in large part by the organizational structure and processes that necessitate selectivity and provide discretion to basic boundary personnel. Also, the variety and ambiguous nature of client problems generate uncertainty concerning the proper provision of services. In order to manage their work lives, basic boundary personnel may adopt active strategies, not unconscious or psychological mechanisms, to cope with pressures created by the necessity of selectivity. The type of coping strategies that are adopted are influenced by the degree of boundary control possessed by a particular welfare organization.

"Boundary control is an organization's ability to influence the outcome of its exchange with its environment" (Greenley and Kirk 1973).

Applicants for service are one aspect of an organization's environment. Welfare organizations will try to minimize the adverse impact of applicant demands on the organization's core technologies in order to maximize resources and autonomy (cf. Thompson 1967). Managing client demands, especially in circumstances of surplus applicants, requires client selectivity.

Certain organizations are severely limited in their ability to manage their relationships with their potential clients through refusal of service or simple referral at time of initial application. Funding agency requirements, regulations imposed by higher levels of government, and laws are examples of environmental constraints that limit an organization's ability to control the impact of applicant demands at the point of initial applicant contact. For example, public mental hospitals are often required by law to accept and treat persons committed to them by courts. Other organizations have considerably more freedom to reject clients or refer them to other organizations when they initially apply.

Basic boundary personnel in organizations that have sufficient boundary control to reject or refer clients at the point of initial contact will generally choose to do so at this point. Discarding unwanted clients at the earliest possible opportunity limits immediate costs to the basic boundary personnel, such as time, emotional involvement, and diversion from other activities. Given sufficient boundary control, basic boundary personnel will tend to utilize active selection strategies in which staff make eligibility decisions and communicate these directly to applicants. In active selection, the staff controls the provision of service through supplying the client with reasons for limiting or continuing service.

In situations of low boundary control where applicants must often be accepted for service, staff tend to employ passive selection. In passive selection, the staff does not directly make eligibility decisions but rather provides a context shaping client desires for service. The decision to continue or terminate service, however, is left to the applicant or client.

Both passive and active selection may occur temporally at any stage of a client's career. For organizational reasons, passive selection will be more common at later stages in a client's career than will active selection.

Active Selection

Active selection usually involves the construction of different reasons used to explain eligibility to a client. Professionals often employ rationales and explanations to clients that are developed out of professional ideologies. Clients commonly accept these explanations as legitimate due to the professional's status and implied expertise. When professional grounds for rejecting clients are not available, as in organizations staffed largely by nonprofessionals, use of bureaucratic explanations centering on organizational rules and regulations are more common. Nonprofessional social welfare workers have been observed to retreat into ritualistic "compulsive defending behavior" in order to manage the pressures necessitated by obligatory selectivity (Wasserman 1971). Ritualistic behavior refers here not only to a narrowly conceived deviant adapation (Merton 1958) but also to a more broadly defined tendency to focus legalistically on rules and regulations. While Blau (1955) notes that ritualistic behavior is often a defense against the complexity of bureaucratic rules, ritualism is also a useful strategy in client selection.

The necessary gate-keeping functions of staff cause them considerable role strain, as they must often reject persons whom they see as needy. Most staff do not like to have to reject applicants. Ritualistic behaviors may supply rationales to basic boundary personnel that allow them to manage the emotional costs of selectivity. In particular, the "eligibility" rules often used in client selection are worded in a way that deflects the onus onto the client and away from the staff or the organization. These rules proclaim the client "inappropriate," not the organization or its staff as "insufficient" to supply the needed services. Thus the emotional costs of selectivity are reduced through placing the responsibility or blame for necessary selection on the client rather than on the staff member. Professional ideologies often serve the same purposes.

Ritualistic behavior in itself may create additional emotional costs to staff when it heightens pressure from clients who are, for instance, angry or disappointed. Ritualism may intensify the pressures that originally inspired the ritualistic behaviors, creating a vicious cycle in which the results of ritualism promote further ritualistic behaviors. When a client population does not accept bureaucratic authority and when a professional's appeals to a client are not effective or possible, basic boundary personnel may employ still other active selection coping strategies, such as appeals to nonorganizational values or enlistment of their colleagues for support (Bar-Yosef and Schild 1966).

Passive Selection

Welfare organizations unable to reject or refer applicants at the point of initial contact tend to use passive selection methods designed to get clients to drop out or withdraw their demands for services (Hasenfeld 1972; Carlson 1964). For instance, Mechanic (1976) observes that prepaid group medical practices may insulate themselves from excessive patient demands by bureaucratic barriers to service such as long waiting times and difficulties in patients securing prompt appointments (see also Vinter 1963). Levine and Levine 1970) describe how child guidance clinics in their early years reacted to a surplus of demand for their services by establishing waiting lists and other bureaucratic barriers to restrict the number of clients. Staff may express negative attitudes towards clients, such as unconcern for, dislike of, or boredom with clients, that serve to encourage clients to drop out of treatment (Baekeland and Lundwall 1975). Creation of primarily custodial "back wards" in public mental hospitals may be seen as an organizational response to low boundary control. The public mental hospital reduces the impact of unwanted clients by giving them only the most minimal service. Long waiting times, extensive forms to fill out, and certain negative staff attitudes can discourage clients in their help seeking to the point where only the most persistent eventually secure service. The magnitude of the passive selection should not be underestimated. Depending on the type of service offered, studies show anywhere from 20 to 75 percent of all beginning clients drop out without receiving full service (Baekeland and Lundwall 1975).

Passive selection practices are usually not seen by organizational personnel as methods of selecting clients or restricting access. The results usually are interpreted as reflecting lack of client motivation, insufficient client "bureaucratic competence," and other client deficiencies. These interpretations, of course, permit the organization and its staff to make sense out of these activities in terms of its overall mission. An interpretation of these activities as client selectivity is suggested by the fact that most clients who drop out of service or cease requesting service eventually go elsewhere to seek such service (Baekeland and Lundwall 1975). This implies that clients are reacting to organizational barriers and not to a spontaneous remission of their problem or diminution of their need.

If passive selection systems function to support organizational autonomy and resources, clients withdrawing from service would be expected to be the least desirable from the organization's point of view. Clients dropping out of various treatment programs tend to have worse prognoses and be of lower socioeconomic status than ones who remain (Baekeland and Lundwall 1975). This type of client is usually seen as less desirable by social welfare organizations (Greenley and Kirk 1973; Levine, White and Paul 1963; Scott 1969; Bredemeier 1964).

Carlson (1964) suggests that when organizations have less control over their intakes—that is less boundary control at the point of initial contact with applicants—they will more likely "cool out" clients. "Cooling out" implies that clients would withdraw their demands for services but not leave with active hostility or negative feelings toward the welfare agency (cf. Clark 1960). In our study of eleven social service agencies, 27 percent of all applicants were seen as rejected by agency staff, yet only 3 percent of applicants to these agencies reported being rejected (Greenley and Schoenherr 1975a). This suggests that many clients seen as rejected by staff of social service agencies do not experience their contact with the agencies in the same way.

Effective tempering of potentially negative client reactions is more likely to the extent that an agency obtains its legitimacy from conformity to societal beliefs. One way agencies conform to societal beliefs is through professionalization. Clients who believe service from a professional is legitimate and appropriate are less likely to feel adequate to criticize the service. Nonprofessionals are less buffered from client criticism by these beliefs, and therefore their selection practices are more likely to be viewed negatively. Nonprofessionals are more likely than professionals to ritualistically use eligibility rules or passive selection by bureaucratic barriers in client selection. Because nonprofessionals are less buffered by client beliefs from criticism than are professionals, selective practices of nonprofessionals and the "bureaucracy," symbolized by agency rules and procedures, will generally be viewed more negatively than similar selection practices of professionals. Incorporation of professionals, and possibly other ways agencies obtain legitimacy from conformity to societal beliefs, make "cooling out" clients easier and reduce the costs associated with selectivity.

In sum, we suggest that basic boundary personnel will cope with pressures of client selectivity in various ways and that these coping strategies will vary by the degree of boundary control the organization has at the point of initial client application for services. Active selection at the point of initial contact will occur to the extent possible, and the staff behaviors most likely to be observed may be described as highly professional or ritualistic in form. In other circumstances, where welfare institutions have less control over client selectivity, passive selection will more often be employed.

CLIENT DISSATISFACTION AND HIDDEN SELECTIVITY

The interaction of client selection practices and client help-seeking processes produces a hidden form of selectivity. Client and applicant attitudes toward welfare organizations affect the decision to seek help or not. Individuals who express dissatisfaction with agency services, skepticism of the value of these services, fear concerning the consequence of seeking help, and other attitudes reflecting negative reactions to welfare organizations are less likely to seek help from them (Ware, Snyder, and Wright 1976). By giving less satisfactory experiences to certain groups, such as lower class groups, basic boundary personnel may produce negative attitudes and thus reduce demand for their services in this population (cf. Elliot 1972). Other population subgroups with more positive attitudes may have increased service utilization (Kadushin 1969). In effect, this process is a hidden selection system operating entirely outside the walls of the welfare organization and even beyond the knowledge of agency staff.

Negative client attitudes toward welfare agencies become aggregated and reinforced within societal subgroups. For example, social class or ethnically defined subgroups tend to have similar agency experiences and similar positive or negative attitudes toward agency services, relative to members of other subgroups (Greenley and Schoenherr 1978). Social interaction within the subgroup will provide the context in which these attitudes are reinforced or solidified. Individuals tend to have attitudes toward specific welfare organizations that are similar to those of their friends and relatives (Greenley and Schoenherr 1978). These beliefs and attitudes become part of the general subcultural understandings within these groups.

As these groups are the basis for one's "lay referral" system, they influence decisions to seek agency services. Lay referral systems, or those individuals with whom one consults and whose advice one often heeds in making a decision concerning seeking help, are operative in major ways in medical (Freidson 1961), legal (Ladinsky 1976), psychiatric or counseling (Gruin, Veroll, and Feld 1960), and other areas. When subgroup attitudes are predominantly negative toward an agency, use of its services would be discouraged by a person's lay referral network. Through a subgroup's lay referral network, negative attitudes toward an agency will reduce service use even among those subgroup members who have never had any personal contact with the agency.

Negative attitudes toward welfare organizations are self-reinforcing. In our study of eleven social welfare organizations, client dissatisfaction with agency services was greater among those applicants who came to the agency with preformed negative expectations and attitudes (Greenley and Schoenherr 1975b). Applicants who came to an agency expecting low quality, ineffective service tended to leave the agency with their expectations confirmed. Negative attitudes toward welfare institution services may undermine the trust on which staff-client interactions are often based. In such an instance clients may tend to focus on "specific service activities of a direct instrumental value to the client-member. . . . in this case one may find not only client-member disorder and confrontations with the staff, centered on the regulations immediately at issue, but more pervasive client-member disaffection" (Bidwell 1970). Applicants with negative attitudes toward agencies are likely to be rejected or referred elsewhere (Greenley and Schoenherr 1978) and are more likely to drop out of service (Baekeland and Lundwall 1975). These negative selection experiences are associated with client dissatisfaction. In sum, clients with negative expectations and attitudes toward agencies will tend to perceive actual experiences more negatively and to interact with staff in ways that create undesirable experiences for themselves.

This hidden selectivity reduces the number of potential selection problems faced by basic boundary personnel. Subgroups composed of generally less desirable clients (from the organization's point of view) would "underutilize" services. Many of these less desirable people never apply for service. Staff are thus spared the difficult and presumably unpleasant task of rejecting, referring, or cooling out many of these applicants. Clients will be more dissatisfied with agencies facing the largest or more difficult social selection problems, because these agencies will be rejecting, referring, and underserving a larger share of their applicants. Thus the hidden selectivity due to the accumulation of negative attitudes in subgroups will tend to be greatest for those agencies in which the problem of client selectivity is the greatest.

Hidden social selection is initiated by agency activities, but is usually attributed to client attitudes. These client attitudes are usually attributed to some general subcultural orientation toward bureaucracy or lack of modernization (Danet and Hartman 1972; Suchman 1965). This is another example of the imputation of selective effects to client attributes and serves to isolate welfare organizations from the negative implications of these selective processes.

CONCLUSION

Organizational processes based on the difference between claimed and de facto domains result in various forms of client selectivity. At the same time service organizations succeed in shifting the responsibility for the dropping out of clients to the rejected clients themselves. Doing this, the agencies can conceal the discrepancy between claimed and de facto domains from the public at large. To break this vicious circle, it is necessary to point out and to change the organizational processes that produce client selectivity.

Chapter 7

The Acquisition of Service Values in a Predominantly Administrative Social Organization and the Structuring of the Staff Function

*Antoinette Catrice-Lorey**

THE BASIC FACTS: THE ORGANIZATIONAL CONTEXT AND ITS ACTORS

The implementation of social security policies and the carrying out of welfare rights programs provided by legislation—in short, the distribution of social security to individual claimants—involves a special sort of welfare organization that is predominantly administrative. Relations with clients in this sort of service are achieved through an administrative screen that acts as both a means and an obstacle.

The structure of the French system for distributing social security was originally and deliberately planned to be decentralized in order to be closer to clients' needs. Thus, some 250 organizations pay out sickness benefits, family allowances, or old age pensions—122 sickness benefit funds, 118 family allowances funds, and 16 regional old age pension funds. However, thirty years of operation have considerably added to the administrative screen: on the one hand, rises in social security coverage and in the number of claimants have led to a continuous, and accelerating, increase in the size of the organizations and a dulling in the communication system; on the other hand, the

*Centre de Recherches in Sciences Sociales du Travail (CRESST), University of Paris-Sud

development of modern management techniques such as computer science has introduced new factors that make for rigidity. In short, the developing distribution system has tended to introduce an increasing distance between organization and claimant and at the various levels in the hierarchy has acted to diminish the perception of the client held as much by the leaders of the welfare organization as by its basic grade staff.

In such a context, one might well ask how the organization's initial aims can be maintained and service values acquired. The problem arises at each level of responsibility held by the two sorts of actors in the organization—for management, when defining their objectives and choosing management methods; and for basic grade workers, when handing out benefits at the client relationship level, a relationship established in increasingly technical conditions and involving less and less direct contact. The problem however, also arises when these two sorts of actors interact within the organization itself—an interaction to be observed in the operation of the staff function.

As it is a case of management and of the reconciliation of the aims being pursued with the organization's overall social aim, one must first note that those responsible feel very little pressure from the consumer of the service.[a] This is partly because, given the nature of the service provided, the claimant is located outside the organization in his own environment and partly because social security is in a monopoly situation and the absence of competition removes certain sanctions otherwise available to consumers. Thus it has been shown that a monopoly encourages evasion of tasks and closure of an administrative system in relation to those under its jurisdiction (Crozier et al. 1974). It is true, however, that a democratic system of representation for those insured has been built into the French social security system through trade union organizations. But analysis has shown how and why the relationship between unions and consumers has become strained as the presence of trade unions in the institution has tended to become increasingly independent of its original legitimating principles and as the power granted to claimants' representatives has become a permanent source of tension because of its societal and political significance (Catrice-Lorey 1978). The consumer thus has little control over the operation of the system and little influence with which to work toward improving his or her lot.

All these elements mean that the welfare organization risks being in operation while remaining relatively indifferent to its own public: and so the question arises of establishing, as regards the aims being

[a]On the subject of consumer control in different types of organizations, see Etzioni (1964).

pursued, how far those responsible for social security organizations go beyond their simple executive tasks—that is, the implementation of legislation—in order to extend the service provided and reduce the difficulties encountered by a varied public when seeking its rights. There is also a question of how the staff function is perceived and guided for the management of resources—for example, is this function not more often a juxtaposition of responses to various economic situations that have occurred, rather than the result of real policies? Does it focus on the attainment of caring objectives in all its various aspects, and in the search for a reconciliation of staff interests and the organization's requirements?

The question of the acquisition of caring values by front line staff takes on a particular significance in a predominantly administrative organization. Through the technical tasks of handing out benefits, basic grade staff have a degree of decisionmaking power that can lead to a more or less rigid or well-disposed interpretation of claimants' rights, and they are also largely responsible for the quality and efficiency of relationships between the administration and its consumers. The application of the formal rules of social legislation to individual situations is by no means a mechanical operation. Such work often involves a search for some adaptation in order to reach a favorable conclusion. In fact, in the name of the rules, the employee may well be tempted to exercise a measure of discipline over the client; or, being too inclined toward procedures and ritualism, the employee may tend to adopt overrigid attitudes (see also Merton 1958). In the same way, the official can come to limit his or her intervention simply to a technical role, treating a "file" of a "case" rather than a living person. Yet he or she is the best-placed person to discover the need for much more information or, in cases felt to be difficult, to involve other administrative or social services. In short, whether he or she is in direct contact with the client at the point of entry or in writing, he or she has the responsibility for "debureaucratizing" the encounter by transcribing and decoding the legal language generally used. The technical work carried out by the employee can involve an important social dimension, provided that he or she has a degree of personal commitment and some motivation to broaden his or her role beyond that of fixed tasks.

On the other hand, while it is possible to control the technical task of establishing rights in a particular case, it is not as easy to control the quality of the relationship and the amount of help given. In practice, research has shown that here the application of rules by front line workers displays a certain independence of operation within the welfare organization. The adoption of a caring attitude is largely left to the personal initiative of the employee, who is in any case conditioned by the support received from his or her work group in so far as the latter is the informal meeting place where colleagues consult each other (see Blau 1955). Naturally, the adoption of such an attitude at the front line also partly depends on the behavior of the supervisor, through whom initiatives in favor of the client can either be praised and rewarded—at least as regards financial rewards—or conversely, implicitly discouraged. In the administrative systems studied, at the front line one most often deals with staff who, unlike social workers, for example, have no professional interest in the "social" sense. But this has not always been the case: in the early years of social security in France, for example, the decision of basic grade staff to join the service certainly included a caring motive. This arose largely from the fact that at that time social security was run and inspired by trade union organizations in a spirit of mutual aid, and recruitment was guaranteed by co-option from militant elements. However, the administration's rate of increase led to a rapid broadening of the recruitment base, and the institution became no different from any other administration as far as employees at social security are concerned. From that time on the caring motive could only be acquired—but on what conditions?

It is our intention here to emphasize the importance of organizational conditions and the contribution of management to the emergence of caring values in nonprofessional staff. In this context, the involvement of staff in the specific aims of the organization seems conditioned largely by what the latter has to offer its wage earners in exchange for their work, by what it offers as much as by what it requires—in a word, by the way in which the staff function has been structured. Whether it is a question of recruitment and promotion methods, of training conditions, of overall wages, of guaranteed social benefits granted to them, or of working conditions, all these factors carry positive significance for the functions performed and potential to encourage the worker to feel committed to the organization. For the workers, they constitute a starting point from which the individual absorbs and interprets his or her own experience, as much regarding the balance reached between contribution and reward as the degree of participation and of withdrawal. Thus on the one hand, one can say that the enterprise controls the overall shape of the work force it attracts to enter, and then stay in, the organization and, on the other hand, that it creates a collective infrastructure that either encourages or discourages the acquisition of caring values by the individual.

MANAGEMENT AND THE DIRECTION TAKEN BY MANAGEMENT POLICIES

Being in charge of the direction of policies, management is

responsible for maintaining the original values legitimating its social organization—a responsibility it discharges through the development taken by the organization and its relations with its surroundings. It is up to the management to give form to these values in objectives, which constantly need redefining and adapting. In addition, as regards the choice of methods and decisions on internal organization, management must ensure that these values spread among members of the organization and get the widest possible consensus on aims to be achieved, beyond the involvement just of executive grades.[b] How far the caring organization is open to the needs of those under its jurisdiction will depend on this double mission.

Research carried out in branch social security offices enabled the study first of the structuring of the aims actually pursued by management. A wide variation in policy was observed as regards on the one hand the extent of the definition given to the service to be provided to the public and on the other hand the adapting of management methods to the aims of the organization. It must be said also that, concurrently, the study showed up the almost complete absence of any system controlling results with which to sanction either positively or negatively the action of managers in local branches as regards the quality of the service provided.

The Range of Objectives

It has been noted that certain organizations tended to limit their action toward the public to the technical tasks of applying the system of welfare rights, whereas other organizations gave themselves the additional aim of acting as mediators on behalf of claimants, of trying to help them get best value from the social insurance programs provided by the law. The enormous increase in and unwieldiness of communication channels in social administration, the impersonal relations, and the complexities of the law in fact often result in a limitation on consumers' access to their rights. Some managers therefore seek to remedy the situation either by evolving a policy for communicating with the public, by multiplying and decentralizing contracts, by managing to provide the chance for individual exchange not just of mass treatment for consumers, or by setting up a permanent information policy that in spite of the complexity and dispersal of the relevant texts, is intent on informing consumers in due time of their rights as well as of their obligations—that is, as their needs emerge.

[b]On the leadership function, and particularly its role in the symbolic representation of the organization and the latter's response to social needs created by the exigencies of the environment, see Selznick (1957).

The range of aims covered by social security organizations at branch level is thus revealed as more or less broad or narrow, and great flexibility is found in management's idea of the service to be provided.

However, the quality of a service organization's responsiveness to the needs of the public also depends on the choice of internal management methods—notably on the direction given to the staff function. In this respect, it appeared that in the French social security system, the staff function was not actually very well integrated into the efficient running of the service. Likewise, its development showed few attempts to assess and control results and little capacity to adapt to change. As will be shown below, an analysis of the reasons for this state of affairs points to the particular nature of the employer; to the fact that in view of the system of power to give rights and to fix duties, the employer is actually a multiple employer; and to the impact of the staff as pressure group. In certain respects, especially in relation to the control of results, analysis also points to divergent processes arising from a preconceived idea of how a decentralized organizational whole should operate—a point that will not be pursued further here. In short, as a result of a combination of these factors, the staff function, rather than acting as mediator for the specific aims of the institution by reconciling them with the interests of its workers, tends to develop as a relatively independent subsystem within the operation of the social security system.

The Structuring of the Staff Function and Its Variety of Significations

The following method was adopted in our study: After having assembled and united the elements of the staff function in the particular social situation under consideration, we tried to interpret them within the framework of a problematic that saw the staff function as resulting from a dialectical confrontation between two forces—the needs and interests of the organization on one hand, and the needs and interests of the workers on the other. Finally, as the subject was social security, we attempted to discover the outcome of the different elements in this staff function, in terms of how they are experienced by the workers themselves and their impact on attitudes toward participation in the organization's aims. The management of human resources in a fixed organizational whole implies a degree of tension between the needs of the organization for its aims to be met and the safeguarding of workers' interests. The question that arises in any organization, as regards the management responsible for the staff function, is that of knowing the extent to which decisions actually made have considered and attempted to reconcile the two sides of the problem. If labor history too often illustrates how totally dependent workers are on their enterprise, some independence of human need is now being recognized in organizations. However, unlike a production organization, which aims to produce a concrete object as well as profit, the welfare organization operates in a disinterested way to serve a given population. Consequently, possible compromises at the staff function level occur between two sorts of people. According to the sort of service organization in question, greater or lesser pressure can arise in favor of consumer interests, but this runs the risk of emphasizing employees' dependence. This would be the case in a hospital, for example, but as we have seen, would not be the case in the framework of a welfare administration.

The staff function, as it emerges through a number of more or less institutionalized decisions or regulations, amounts to the expression of the employer's power and attitudes; however, it also expresses the balance of power in employer–employee relations and the impact of the staff and of its representatives as a source of pressure and negotiation. As concerns employer attitudes, the staff function not only points to the employer's fundamental attitude on the safeguarding of worker interests, to the quality of agreements reached when the interests of staff and organization diverge, but also to the way in which the employer perceives technical procedures for managing the labor force and to how much they contribute to the achievement of organizational ends.

We shall also attempt to systematize the two essential directions taken by the staff function in an organization. On the one hand, it organizes a professional system that foresees the means whereby the work will be carried out and rewarded; under this heading, in addition to the definition of tasks and scales of remuneration, one can list recruitment conditions, promotion prospects and criteria, and the role of training, as well as the degree of control wage earners are given over the administration of their work. Within the framework of the dialectical relation described above, decisions on the professional system should also consider the requirement for quality work to be achieved at every staff level, from the organization's point of view, and, from the employees' point of view, the means of obtaining the necessary skills from a human work force that also makes an implicit demand for work enhancement both internally and externally. In addition, the staff function tends to determine a certain guarantee of workers' individual rights and also defines the degree of independence

THE ELMER E. RASMUSON LIBRARY
UNIVERSITY OF ALASKA

granted to them in the face of the network of constraints developed by the enterprise.

That is also where one finds decisions regulating hours of work and how they are organized, the degree of job security and job protection in case of dismissal, the question of the exercise of trade union rights and the right to strike, the various extra holidays given beyond the legal minimum, and the extra sickness benefit for loss of working power. The system of guarantees and of protection for rights should, in principle, result from a reconciliation between the need to ensure a satisfactory performance by the organization and the need to reduce the dependence of those who contribute to that performance.

Returning to the case of social security in France, it should be noted that for a long time the staff was actually employed by trade unions, as the boards responsible for administering the funds were mainly composed of union administrators representing those insured.[c] In their capacity as employer, the trade union organizations reached a collective agreement with the staff right from the beginning of the institution, which, as regards the organization of the profession and the protection of workers' rights, is wide open to claims by the workers. This is because one of their concerns was to make this contract, if not a model contract, at least a starting point for use in other sectors.

However, judging by the operation of the institution over a long period, it would appear that because of their traditional function as defender of the workers, the trade union employers have underestimated—and in the staff's favor—the essential operating requirements of welfare organizations such as the Funds, both as regards the system's performance and as regards the skill requirements of the professional tasks to be performed. Also, as far as internal administration was concerned, they did not pay sufficient attention to establishing the necessary conditions for the provision of a quality service for those insured.

THE IMPLEMENTATIONAL LEVEL AND THE OVERALL EXPERIENCE OF WORKING CONDITIONS

The approach followed led to a new look at the organization's offer to its staff, then to the adoption of the point of view of

[c]On the administrative boards of the Social Security Funds, trade union organizations held three-quarters of the seats and employers one-quarter between 1946 and 1967; the former lost their majority in 1967, when parity was achieved on the boards and the employers' side increased in power. The analysis of the

the front line staff: in the social security context studied, an attempt has been made to understand the manner in which the employees collectively perceived and absorbed into their plans and into their behavior the various elements in the conditions offered to them. As the negotiated system of guarantees carries the obvious, well-meaning stamp of a trade union employer, the social security front line staff enjoy a set of provisions amounting to considerable social insurance. Take for example the assurance of complete job security after six months' work, compensation of wages in case of sickness, a gradual reduction in hours worked, the granting of various holidays beyond the legal holiday period, an extension to maternity leave, the right to days off when children are sick and for trade union activity, a favorable retirement scheme, and so forth.

However, when considering the question from a financial point of view, one must admit that the wages offered to front line staff are hardly to be envied. In fact, discussion about wages lies largely outside the scope of contract negotiation, and another actor-employer comes on the scene—the state, in the form of an interdepartmental commission that regulates wages in the nationalized public sector. In a wider context the multiple character of the employer and the tensions that can arise between the two parties certainly tend to introduce factors that are incompatible with the aims to be achieved in the organization's offer to its staff. Be that as it may, the wages offered to basic grade staff are low—and in this system recruitment only occurs at the basic grades. Such wages are admittedly also a response to a fairly unselective recruitment method, written into the career structure by the trade union employer under strong pressure from staff. The tendency to limit selection procedures to existing staff is indeed a characteristic of this career structure. As we shall see, it is illustrated by the rewards given to length of service.

In this respect, one could also quote another important provision in the statute book, which commits itself to ensuring as far as possible that promotion to executive posts is done internally within each local branch. In any case, one might ask whether the various factors of low wages, limited requirements at the hiring stage, and closure of the profession except to an internal market indicate that employment as a social security officer is not highly regarded by public opinion. The fact remains that when faced with a scale that shows

---

staff function made here refers in essence to trends right at the start, insofar as they are fundamentally conditioned by the current situation; since 1967, the scope for flexibility by the employer (half trade unionist and half employers) has in fact been reduced because of a great resistance to change.

the prestige attached to various activities in the tertiary sector, the general public finds that it is better for a young man or woman to start work in a bank or at the post office than at social security. (Note that whereas the wages earned by front line staff at social security are lower than bank wages, they are rather higher than those of post office employees.)

On the other hand, there is a limited number of grades to be passed through by the officer who calculates and determines claimants' benefits, and the attested technical qualification stage is reached quite quickly. In fact, stagnation at this level and the wages received are both the subject of claims by interested parties who deplore the inadequate recognition given to the complexity and multifaceted nature of their work. As for the training provided to reach this level, this is essentially based on an apprenticeship spent learning how to handle legislation and is hardly concerned with the client relationship.

Promotion prospects bring the following extra dimension: through the cumulative interplay of selection and length of service criteria, and by dint of remaining in a given post, the satisfactory employee can see his wages increase by 40 percent over ten years or so. However, this provision is almost automatically applied; for employees with a less satisfactory work record, it is spread over a larger number of years, and length of service takes precedence over selection criteria. It is therefore not considered to represent a stake in the system and does not in fact act as a stimulus. There remains the possibility of becoming an executive officer through internal promotion; but first, the proportion of such jobs is relatively low,[d] and second, despite a largely female basic work force, the executive grade is mainly male.

The overall effect of these factors is to show objectively and definitely the low prestige accorded to that sort of work and how its social responsibility dimension is underestimated, as well as a degree of inflexibility in the system of organizational rewards that leads to a lack of stimulus toward a greater commitment to the work. In parallel, social security employees subjectively feel their social status to be inferior and inadequate. In practice, the gap between the level of guaranteed social benefits separate from the work itself and the material and moral rewards for the actual professional tasks is quite considerable and acts for those involved as a sort of compensation:

[d] Changes actually under way seek to broaden the future prospects for basic grade staff somewhat by creating supervisory grades. In addition, in the question of access to executive posts by internal promotion, they aim to make the training conditions and the passing of examinations more stringent requirements.

right from the start, the working situation is accepted for what it is—low wages, few future prospects, a function that attracts little recognition either inside or outside the workplace—in exchange, one gets a certain degree of security and freedom. And as a motive for entering the service, this sort of calculation leads the employee to withdraw from the organization and its specific aims. Finally, overall the workers at the basic grades tend increasingly to be female, young, with little general education, and no career plans. The fact that this work force has, typically, very little capacity to mobilize around a collective, caring aim is somehow the result of the enterprise's own policy and of a particular way of structuring the staff function.

The organization of work in the Social Security Funds and the structure of individual jobs as they have developed have not been conducive to the acquisition of a caring motive. A Taylorian division of tasks, which has also reached administrative organizations, tends to cut the employee off from the result of his or her work. The intervention of computers and the consequent centralizing technical processes generally mean that files are considered and payments made at different stages. Information science thus tends to reduce both contact at the point of entry and the direct impression the employee used to get of the insured person. In addition, the codes it introduces into work processes are so many extra abstract factors, which ultimately contribute to less representation for the client. In short, the question of restructuring such work is posed in acute form in social administration organizations and should be high on the list of problems posed by the staff function.

SUMMARY

The situation outlined here shows how a certain disaffection has been noted in front line staff in social security organizations. As regards internal management, there are complex signs of this phenomenon—high levels of absenteeism and of staff turnover and the consequent impact on the quality of the organization's performance. As regards responding to the needs of the public, the phenomenon is to be seen in the low perception of the role played by such staff. The improved operation of social security to the claimants' advantage and the disposition of basic grade staff to lay claim to caring values require management to apply innovative policies to the staff function. Not that the organizational conditions here questioned are sufficient to lead to participation and commitment; however, at the social infrastructure level of the organization, they undeniably mold the collective potential for participation (see Dachler and Wilpert 1978).

From top management to basic grade staff, each of the hierarchical grades within the administrative systems that distribute social insurance and security is thus called upon to ensure the best possible outcome to the welfare rights programs provided by law. It nevertheless remains the case that the absence of a caring ideology at the various specific skill levels in the organization will, in the first instance, affect its least-favored clients; in fact, as a consequence, it emphasizes and multiplies the layers of bureaucracy acting as obstacles to access to their rights by people ill-equipped to overcome them (Catrice-Lorey 1976). Being more likely, first to be particularly discouraged by the need to find their way through an abstract and anonymous administrative world, and second, managing only with great difficulty to understand complicated social legislation, these least-favored categories of claimants require from management policies for information and communication that have been especially designed for them. However, in addition such claimants are, typically, often very complicated cases and are frequently in marginal situations. Thus they are the ones that require the most special consideration and initiative on the part of front line staff in their task of applying the rules. Lacking all these attributes, social administration organizations may well hide behind their own bureaucratic complexities and actually operate certain restrictive practices on the distribution of benefits, and social insurance programs may well not reach all those who have most need of them.

PART III

Professional Work and Interaction with Clients as Constituents of the Process of Delivering and Denying Services

In Part I the general limitations of the adaptation of social services to the needs and problems of the target population were outlined (limited resources; biases in the process of social policy formation and implementation; rationing mechanisms resulting from the social order, from vested interests, and from cultural patterns). It has been shown how these general limitations are incorporated in, and reflected by, the structures and functions of service delivery systems. The articles in Part II focused on specific limitations resulting from the proper dynamics of delivery organizations and interorganization networks. A fundamental ambiguity of the welfare state has been elaborated:

On the one hand, formal organization and bureaucracy are widely used "tools" for maintaining or improving conditions for those who enjoy a good lifestyle and for raising the standard of living of those who fall below accepted social standards of well-being;
On the other side, these "tools" are by no means instruments in the hands of those who are in need of social services; rather, they incorporate specific interests and dynamics, originating within their organizational structure and personnel.

The question arises whether there are any social mechanisms to overcome or mitigate this ambiguity. Here, three mechanisms are discussed regarding social service delivery: (1) training the clients to become capable of handling contacts with delivery organizations more successfully; (2) substituting professionalized staff members for administrators or bureaucrats and overcoming bureaucratic organization by professionally and more flexibly structured delivery systems; and (3) substituting centralized organization by decentralized and more participative (participatory) service delivery organizations with the aim of expanding and intensifying interpersonal contacts between staff members and clients. Some of the implications of these types of reforms or innovations are discussed in Part III.

In Chapter 8, John B. McKinlay summarizes findings that question the assumption that professionals (i.e., "any possible group to which the term by being publicly believed has been successfully applied and sustained") are more apt than bureaucrats to fit clients' needs. He even argues that most of the research done on "client satisfaction" mystifies the work of professionals instead of analyzing the deficiencies and faults of service delivery processes. Trying to elaborate the reasons for the causes of these deficiencies, McKinlay analyzes the dynamics of professional "standards of client selection" as well as the characteristics of professional work within formal organizations. Finally, he presents some explanations of the misfit between services and clients' needs with a view to different types of relationships between service organizations and their target populations (differentiating between "buyer and seller market services").

The inherent limitations of professional work with regard to responsiveness to clients' needs are empirically diagnosed in Mathilda Goldberg's chapter on the consequences of organizational reforms in English social work services. It is shown that these limitations result as much from the characteristics of specific clients' problems and needs as from characteristics of work organization and the corresponding perceptions of the personnel. The findings of one of the few systematic empirical studies, comparing "social worker and client perspectives," demonstrate the necessity to plan and implement innovations from both points of view.

Any serious reforms or innovations in a field of social services should start with a comparison between the objective structures and subjective perceptions of clientele, staff, and delivery organization. Considering only one of the two sides—that is, confining examination to either target population or service delivery—necessarily leads to prejudices concerning the room for innovations with a view to more responsiveness to clients' needs. Friedhart Hegner, in his study of "the gap between service organizations and the public served," tries to develop a frame of reference that relates the two sides. He asks whether "microinteraction" is an appropriate social mechanism to bridge the gap between the structure and inner dynamic of clientele and delivery system. Some of his theoretical observations are illustrated with empirical data from investigations in German public welfare agencies.

In spite of their skeptic orientations, the different authors point out that there is still some room with regard to innovations that could augment the responsiveness of social service delivery to clients' needs.

Chapter 8

Professionalism and the Imbalance Between Clients' Needs and the Organization's Interests

*John B. McKinlay**

INTRODUCTION

Until quite recently, discussions of the ways people utilize or underutilize social or human services have focused on various characteristics of the recipients. Some have identified economic variables (e.g., prepayment mechanisms, extent of insurance coverage, etc.); others turn to socioeconomic characteristics (e.g., age, sex, socioeconomic status) or social psychological considerations (e.g., fear, stigma, alienation, perception of need) or cultural associations (e.g., race or ethnicity) and geographical distance. While such research has provided some useful data for administrative and managerial purposes, it is currently frowned upon as lying in the "blaming the victim" tradition (Ryan 1971). I am aware that some of my own earlier work lies within this broad tradition and appreciate and accept some of the ideological and methodological criticisms that are made of it (McKinlay 1970, 1972a, 1975).

There is now no disputing the fact that organizational phenomena and the behavior of "professionals" may be as related to the ways

*Department of Sociology, Boston University, and Consultant Sociologist, Massachusetts General Hospital, Boston, Massachusetts

social services are used as to the personal characteristics of recipients of services. This study rests on such an assumption.

WHO ARE SERVED?—SOME NOTES ON "CREAMING"

Many studies have uncovered a tendency for client-centered bureaucracies to dissociate themselves from groups that the organization was established to assist. The use of referral to other agencies as a mechanism for closing out contact with the poor has been noted by Maas, who observed that disproportionately more lower occupational status families terminate in consultation or referral (Maas, 1955). A further study showed that

> except for the top class, closings at client initiative dropped as social class declined. In the upper middle class, nearly six cases in ten took the initiative in terminating in contrast to only one in three of the lowest groups. Termination of the relationship at the initiative of the employee, while unusual at any level, was more than twice as frequent at the lowest level than at any other. (Beck 1962).

Coleman and his colleagues (1957) have compared the selection of applicants for psychiatric treatment in a clinic and in a family agency. They found no significant differences in the distribution and severity of psychiatric diagnoses in the two agencies. Class V (lowest patients), regardless of diagnosis, tended to receive less favorable consideration for continued treatment in the clinic and also in family service—although to a smaller extent. The study by Beck (1962) notes that the average number of interviews decreases as social class status declines—the drop is from an average of nearly eleven interviews per case in the higher social classes to less than six for the lowest social class—and shows that the tendency to preselect high income people is not limited to private agencies. It has also been noted that in public agencies, the decision to treat or continue in treatment is often discretionary with treatment personnel (Cloward and Epstein 1965).

Although it can be argued that high income groups will always be favored in a fee-for-service situation, one study of a tax-supported child guidance clinic, available at no cost to the residents of Illinois, found (consistent with many other studies) that while a representative cross-section of the total population applied for service with this agency, the characteristics of those who actually received treatment are far from representative (Stevens 1954). For example, while 37 percent of the applicants for service came from low income groups, only 25 percent were accepted for treatment. In contrast, while 29 percent of the applicants were from high income groups, 47 percent of them were accepted for treatment. The report concludes that although high income level does not affect intake, it does influence the probability of entering treatment.

Hollingshead and Redlich (1958) reported relationships between social class, diagnosis, and treatment of persons with mental disorders in a community survey in New Haven, Connecticut. In particular, the manner in which patients were treated was linked to class position. The lower the social class, the greater the tendency to administer an organic therapy—shock treatment, lobotomy, or drug therapy—even when the agency administering the treatment was held constant. The number of times patients saw their therapists per month, as well as the length of the visits, were significantly different from one class to another—higher status clients receiving more frequent and longer treatments than those from the lower classes. It is often held that the cooling out of certain clients occurs as a consequence of the differential availability of certain forms of treatment. However, studies of similar agencies treating different social categories have shown that this simply is not so. One study investigated the relationships between social class, psychiatric diagnosis, and treatment in three hospitals that had comparable treatment facilities available to patients from different socioeconomic levels (Siegal et al. 1962). Differences in diagnosis, treatment selection, and duration of hospitalization were found in all three hospitals. The hospitals that treated higher ratios of patients from the lower socioeconomic groups had larger proportions of patients diagnosed as psychotic and employed organic therapies more often (a finding consistent with those of Hollingshead and Redlich). Social class position was also positively related to the length of time a patient spent in these hospitals—the lower the status, the shorter the stay.

PROFESSIONALISM AND STANDARDS OF CLIENT SELECTION

Given that some selection process exists, why do agencies disengage from certain clients (usually those of lower socioeconomic status)? One explanation may be associated with the tendency for clients to be served by "professionals" in organizations. It is not intended to enter the endless argument over what makes an occupation a profession or what makes one profession "more professional" than another. There is little agreement on the precise definition of a professional, and this is not the place for consideration of the many attempts to clarify the meaning of the term through the use of lists of characteristics (Greenwood 1957; Cogan 1953; Goode 1961; Wilensky 1964; Freidson 1970a, 1970c).

While such listings may be useful criteria for describing the training and everyday activity of professionals and for comparing one profession with another, each of them is inadequate as an explanation of either the emergence and perpetuation of professions or various aspects of professional behavior. It may be, as Becker (1962) suggests, that the label "professional" is no more than an everyday usage, lending some prestige and general approbation to certain occupations that have more or less "arrived." If an occupational group defines itself as a profession and manages to receive public acceptance of the term, then to all intents and purposes it can be regarded as a profession. In other words, the notion of a self-fulfilling prophecy may more adequately explain the nature and emergence of professions and aspects of professional behavior than a searching of the numerous descriptive inventories. Once an occupational group makes a claim to the definition professional, they may as a consequence of their own and public reaction to this claim appear to become professional in practice. By way of summary, therefore, we may say that the term "profession" can be employed to denote any possible group to which the term by being publicly believed has been successfully applied and sustained.

The status of any profession may be a function of the status of its clientele, whether that clientele is defined in terms of age, sex, socioeconomic status, ethnicity, or other factors. Indeed, because the designation professional may be more dependent on societal reaction than on the intrinsic character of tasks or training, we find certain groups sensitive to association with people or tasks that would question the applicability of the label. One dilemma confronting socialworkers (perhaps also criminal lawyers or welfare physicians) is that there is little prestige to be derived from serving groups that in our society are defined as lacking in moral virtue, ambition, self-dependence, and so forth. Hughes suggests that one means of identifying "highly professional" occupational groups is through the clients they serve (Hughes 1966; Beck 1967). Becker (1956) supports this with the suggestion that the typical process of professionalization involves the shedding of "dirty work" in an attempt to devote one's time—and be seen as devoting one's time—to "more professional" activities.

A professional is supposed to serve equally all those in need of his or her skills. In reality, however, this is not the case. In the competition for increased prestige, it may be that one way to advance one's claims is to seek a "higher" class clientele rather than being identified as a lower status servant of the poor. Whether or not an occupational group's claims to professionalism are successful may also be dependent on the relative positions of related occupational groups. Goode (1961) has described this process as a kind of zero sum game—one in which there is only a limited supply of professional kudos—as one group rises, another must decline. Given a limit to the number of groups that can claim whatever advantages professionalism offers and the reliance on societal reaction, certain professions may have a vested interest in the process that Cloward and Epstein (1965) call "disengagement from the poor."

As certain human service workers and agencies equate "dirty work" with handling undesirable problems and clients, officials tend to avoid these as obstacles to professionalization or gaining higher professional status. Goffman (1963) has described the bearers of "courtesy stigma" as those having a spoiled identity because they are affiliated in some way with the stigmatized. Since this type of stigma is affiliational and not actually physical, it is relatively easily managed by certain distancing tactics or by deviance disavowal. A study by Walsh and Elling (1968) centered on the orientations and behaviors of three occupational groupings within public health—physicians, nurses, and sanitarians. They found that within formal organizations members of highly striving occupational groups were significantly more negative in their orientation toward the poor and lower class clients than non-striving groups.

A second reason for both professional and agency disengagement from certain clients may lie in the threat such people pose to service organizations. Sjoberg argues that in order to maintain itself, client-centered bureaucracy tends to neglect those in greatest need of its services—those, in fact, whom the organization was primarily established to assist (Sjoberg, Brymer and Farris 1966). Certain clients tend to challenge organizational effectiveness by presenting a range of problems that are perceived as less easily resolved. A disproportionately large amount of time and effort must be devoted to such clients and problems, even though success cannot be predicted with confidence or, in fact, ever be realized. An organizational achievement ethic prompts bureaucracy to select for processing those who are perceived as most amenable to the fulfillment of defined objectives and to exclude those whose needs pose a threat to organizational effectiveness.

Similarly, it has been found that lower class clients in child guidance clinics are generally neglected in favor of middle class clients who appear to respond better to therapy (Hunt, Gurrslin, and Roach 1958). In the same way, the Job Corps in the United States is said to bypass men with criminal records, even though they may be in the greatest need of assistance. Against the advice of a Social Workers Association, the prime minister of New Zealand (Mr. Muldoon) recently denied a state-supported youth worker position to a professionally qualified person who had several years earlier been a gang leader and served a period in prison. The process by which local authorities in Great Britain allocate council houses certainly reflects this bias in favor of people who are not necessarily in the greatest need of public housing. Scott (1961), in a study of agencies serving the blind, reports that their programs concentrate on clients who "enjoy the highest probability of success." Even though the elderly blind account for 56 percent of the blind population, the great majority of these services (67 percent) have programs that are geared to serve the needs of children and employable adults.

A feature of all these studies, is the evidence concerning the process of "creaming"—the elimination of those cases that are perceived as likely to jeopardize the realization of certain professional or organizational goals. It is suggested that this creaming, which may take the form of initial, biased selection, removes those very cases that would constitute a real test of organizational effectiveness.

The role of officials in service organizations as mandated labelers is, of course, of primary importance in the creaming process. If an official "accepts" a client, he or she is publicly declaring that the client is in some need and publicly exposing both her or himself, and the agency, to the likelihood of being unable to assist. Having made such a declaration, the official exposes the organization to the liability that a whole range of related problems, which the client may have not yet declared, may eventually emerge. Such possibilities may be rendered invisible and avoided if bureaucratic regulations can be discretionarily invoked by the official to disqualify the client. There are at least four main techniques of invisibility by which certain clients and problems can be effectively concealed, and it is likely that their usage varies both between different social agencies, and between different types of people presenting problems.

First, the eligibility requirements for the agency's service can be constructed in such a way that the official can exclude the client on first encounter. This exposes the agency to challenges of callousness or inefficiency. Second, after accepting a client, an official can prematurely terminate contact while at the same time giving token recognition to some problem. Exposure to criticism from outsiders may be reduced by the use of this technique. Third, an official may only recognize a highly segmentalized area of the client's social life as relevant to his agency and disregard other spheres of activity or problems that are in fact causally related, but probably threatening to the organization. Fourth, and probably the most effective and frequently employed technique of invisibility, is to recognize related problems, yet abdicate responsibility by referring the client to another agency. In such a situation the client is likely to believe that he or she is receiving some service rather than simply being disengaged, and potential hostility is averted. As a result of this fourth technique, however, certain services (usually publicly assisted) become repositories for the disengaged and fail through unmanageable burdens.

PROFESSIONALS IN ORGANIZATIONS

Skepticism is increasingly voiced concerning the professed activity of certain formal organizations. There is a body of evidence accumulating that suggests that organizations seldom accomplish what their formal charter and the claims of administrators or representatives suggest (Goss 1970). Organizations are thought to have both manifest and latent functions, but it is often difficult to determine what precise latent function its members subscribe to. Some organizations—with a variety of resources, manpower, access to mass media and so on—are able to persuade the public that their manifest functions are, in fact, the real and only functions of the organization. So we see in the United States, for example, that EXXON oil is primarily interested in dissolving oil slicks and purifying water, Ford Motors is "concerned" to reduce exhaust emission and minimize air pollution, and Chevrolet is anxious to ensure that every American has a "better way in which to see the U.S.A." If one was to take such claims seriously, it would be seen that the generation of hollow consumer needs and the desire for profit are the very last interests of multinational financial and industrial institutions.

The closer one looks, however, the more one finds that, despite claims to the contrary, hospitals are really not patient-oriented, prisons seldom rehabilitate inmates, universities and schools are prey to market rather than educational demands, industrial concerns are really only interested in maximizing profits, and even voluntary organizations serve to dissolve employee conscience pangs as much as they improve the lot of those they are supposedly assisting.

These rather superficial and somewhat ephemeral organizational "concerns" for certain groups and issues illustrate the way in which organizations use ideologies with the explicit intention of energizing certain groups toward acting in the organization's interests and perhaps those of groups who are in a position to benefit from such action. With this phenomenon in mind, Krause investigated the ways in which the concept "citizen participation" is being used by certain bureaucracies (urban renewal and community action programs) in the United States in an ideological manner (Krause 1968; Stanton 1970). He suggests that certain target groups (usually the poor) may be placed in an invidious position when bureaucracies offer them the "citizen participation" ideology. They may lose if they participate, and they sometimes lose if they do not participate. Krause concludes that either participation in the manifest activities espoused by the bureaucracy is directly detrimental to the welfare of those asked to participate (urban renewal) or the bureaucracy whose activity is unacceptable to the wider population becomes involved on behalf of a powerless or unliked target group (Office of Economic Opportunity). Rather then dying away in Western societies, as Bell (1960) has suggested, Krause claims that ideologies are becoming primary tools used by large and powerful bureaucracies. If his conclusions are correct, and present trends continue, then the use of ideologies by large-scale formal organizations constitute a threat to the individual's capacity to exercise some control over development in society.

Faced with manifestly deceptive or exaggerated claims by organizations, clients may decide to reject the publicly presented ideology. In such a situation, according to Fisher (1969), the organization or helping group may move in four different ways: (1) it may try to alter its ideology and the nature of the helping claim; (2) it may try to alter its structure in order to effect its claims; (3) it may seek to change the response of its clients; (4) or it may attempt to change the makeup of its clientele. It is suggested that changes in any one or more of these directions are ultimately far-reaching, for they all involve some change in the organization or helping group itself.

Fisher divides the ways in which organizations may alter their ideologies or claims into six main categories: (1) scale—how much the organization claims it will do for its clients; (2) scope—how wide a group or how many sorts of clients the organization promises to service; (3) time schedule—when or over what periods of time the organization claims it has serviced or will service its clients; (4) location—the place at which service is claimed to be best given; (5) technique—what technological or organizational measures the organization claims will result in the most effective means of service; and (6) the end—for which the organization claims it is undertaking its service work. Given the apparent disparity between the claims and performance of certain organizations, there appears to be a general public tendency to turn to and place reliance on the role of professionals as a counterbalance to this emphasis (Haug and Sussman 1969). This public conception of professionals and the general credibility given to the altruistic claims of professionals underlies a central theoretical question that is presently claiming the attention of many sociologists. Simply put it is: How autonomous are professionals in formal organizations? Various aspects of this question are, of course, addressed by Daniels (1975).

The traditional model of the professional has always been one of the free agent contracting to perform a service for a client (Carr-Saunders and Wilson 1933; Scott 1966). It is thought that the client can choose his or her own professional and that the first loyalty of the professional is always to his or her client. This conception has recently been challenged, however, on the grounds that it gives little attention to the numbers of professionals who have always been employed in organizations and the changes that such employment brings about in the professional relationship over time (Ben-David 1958; Engel 1969). Unfortunately, the notion of the "free professional" ignores the ways in which conflicting values exert pressures upon the professional, particularly where third parties intervene in a relationship with a client. Professionals with a basic mandate to provide a personal service to some individual may find this mandate directly or indirectly challenged by organizational priorities that require either the practitioner or his client to give primacy to other considerations. Recent sociological studies of professionals in organizations seriously question how "free" professionals really are (McKinlay 1977).

Where the rewards are high enough, professionals may adapt their professional ideas of competence, rewards, and status to the value system of the organization they serve (Mills 1951). Kornhauser (1962) shows, for example, that scientists in industry are pressured to subordinate their basic research interests to applied commercial problems of concern to their employers. Goldner and Ritti (1967) show how readily professionals abandon their own work for administrative duties so as to rise within the status hierarchy of their employing organization.

Merton (1958) has suggested that intellectuals who enter government service face similar predicaments. In the area of psychiatry, Szasz has argued that once the professional moves into a bureaucratic setting he becomes unrecognizable (Szasz 1967; Daniels 1969; Garfinkel 1956). The focus of the psychiatrist's concern can no longer be on helping the patient, since his or her professional rights and duties have been redefined by the organizational context. Indeed, Burchard (1954) observed that conflicts in basic differences between the professional and organization values are sometimes so readily resolved in favor of the organization that often no conflict is seen. When military chaplains were asked how they resolved the discrepancy between biblical commandments against killing and their loyalty to the military organization, most reported that they did not see any conflict. Barber and his colleagues (1973) show that the social structure of competition and reward in science for priority of discovery and the recognition and prestige that go with it leads to the devaluation of therapy and to more permissive behavior in the use of human subjects for experimentation. Is there any reason to believe that human service workers in formal organizations should behave any different from what has been found for most other categories of workers?

BUYING AND SELLING SOCIAL SERVICES

There are two ways in which the estrangement of the poor from formal organizations can be explained. The first, which can be termed "client culpability" or "blaming the victim" (Ryan 1971), lays emphasis on the knowledge, skills, and lifestyles that clients lack, which, if present, would prevent or minimize any breakdown. A second explanation of the estrangement locates the source in both the structure of organizations and aspects of professional behavior. These approaches have already been considered in relation to the creaming activities of officials or professionals in organizations. Attention will be directed here toward organizational factors that make it difficult for the poor to use certain types of service, so that they do not receive the benefits to which they are entitled.

Given the relative neglect and even disregard of the needs, wishes, and demands of potential consumers by health and welfare professionals and organizations, one is tempted to draw an economic parallel with a buyers' and a sellers' market. In a sellers' market, demand exceeds supply, and it is the seller who is in a position to determine price, conditions, and the extent of services. This is contrasted with a buyers' market in which supply exceeds demand, and sellers have to be consumer oriented in order to sell to consumers who may perceive no immediate need for a service or who are able to choose between many similar groups of services being offered. Since health and welfare services appear to operate predominantly in a sellers' market, they tend to be oriented toward the fulfillment of some perceived need (medical or social) often irrespective of the consumer's demand.

Most of the health and social welfare "needs" of the poor can be established by reasonably objective criteria, but if this "need" is not translated into "demand" for service, the "sale" has not very much chance of being made. Perhaps planners and service administrators could borrow a page from marketing textbooks and seek to determine the extent to which a sellers' or a buyers' market obtains in the area of health and social welfare. Attention could be given to the increasing number of "preventive" services, which appear to operate in a buyers' market. In a buyers' market, attention must be paid to techniques for encouraging people to purchase an item and/or to retain loyalty to it.

Buyer market services are usually person oriented, and efforts are made by officials to encourage them to come and to retain them in service. Clients are often rewarded in various ways for "buying" the service. In such person-oriented situations, the treatment received is frequently designed to encourage the clients to continued use of that service.

In contrast, seller market services are usually object oriented, with officials remaining rather formal or impersonal and less interested in the unique characteristics of the client. Efforts may even be made to turn people away or to deter them from returning in order to regulate a threatening workload. These two general orientations (whether person oriented or object oriented) may form extremes on a continuum that in effect describes the form in which the service is presented to potential clients.

A second dimension that may also shape the type of service delivered concerns who takes the initiative in establishing some relationship with an agency or official. At one extreme a potential client may take the initative in deciding that he or she has a certain need, identifying it as amenable to ameliorative action, selecting a possibly suitable agency, and utilizing it. One may term this type of behavior self-initiated action. At the other extreme, some official or agency may take the initiative and decide that some person or group has, or may be in danger of having, some need that could be removed or assisted in some way and acts to help them (Gans 1962). One may term this other-initiated action.

The types of services that would result from the combination of these two dimensions—the form of service (whether person oriented or object oriented) and the initiation of contact (whether from the client or the service)—can perhaps be summarized in the simple diagram presented in Figure 8-1. Given the absence of a high priority need, it can be postulated that the rate of utilization for the poor will increase from type A to type D services, in alphabetical order, as presented in the figure.

A study of the use of a wide range of health and social welfare services by the lower working class in Aberdeen, Scotland, suggested that a person-oriented service is preferred by this group, however the contact is initiated (McKinlay 1970). Through the use of various research instruments—attitude profiles, intensive tape-recorded interviews, and observational work—it was found that A and B type situations were particularly distasteful for the lower working class sample studied, while C and particularly D type situations were tolerable and perhaps occasionally even enjoyed. However, although clearly preferring D and C type situations, it appears the people of low socioeconomic status are being increasingly directed to A and B type encounters.

Not only are there differences in the nature of the agencies encountered by the poor and the treatment orientations experienced, there are related differences in the levels of staff encountered, with important consequences for the treatment received. Encounters by the poor are usually restricted to "the man at the desk"—often the lowest incumbent who is the most bound by formal bureaucratic constraints. For higher socioeconomic categories, contact with higher ups is more readily available and even fostered in many formally organized agencies. Note the connotations of such terms as "my

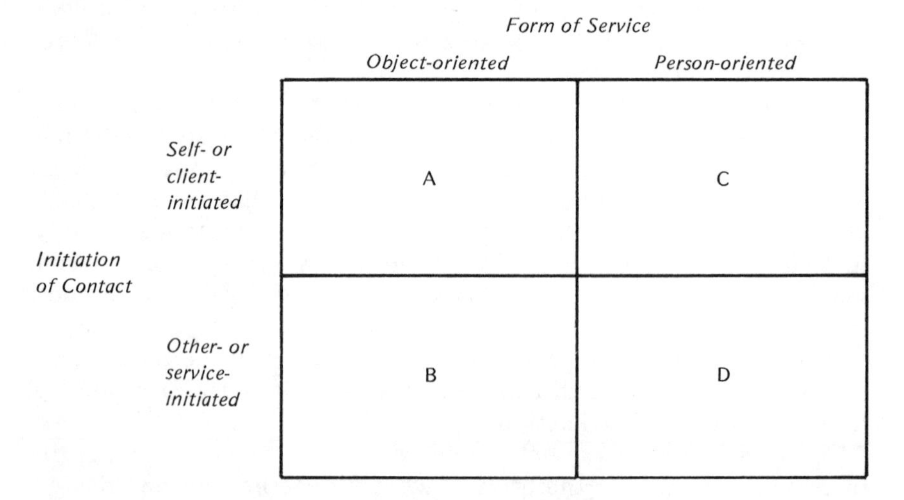

Figure 8-1. Different orientations and types of service.

broker," "my doctor," "my accountant" and the intention behind the television advertisement depicting a bank manager secreted in one's cupboard at home for instantaneous consultation.

A consequence of such differential contact may be that the poor have fewer chances of increasing their understanding of organizations. Employing Mannheim's distinction between "substantive" and "functional" knowledge, Janowitz and Delaney (1957-58), for example, show that those employed at the lower levels of large-scale organizations generally possess a range of social understanding, knowledge, and attitudes (their informational perspective) that is limited to matters experienced directly in performing their specialized jobs—"functional" knowledge. Only at the higher levels of large-scale organizations are there occupational possibilities that permit broader knowledge, attitudes, and understanding—"substantive" knowledge—that involves a more generalized understanding of how the goals of social life may be linked, and how these goals can be achieved.

Overriding all these considerations, however, is the immediacy of need. The presence or absence of such a need will largely determine utilization behavior. While the majority of those in poverty never apply for or receive taxation rebates, one cannot automatically maintain that such a group is underutilizing taxation or internal revenue departments. As is well known, most in this social category are either chronically unemployed or underemployed and therefore seldom qualify for taxation rebates. In contrast, the same chronically unemployed groups will, of economic necessity, utilize such services as the Labour Exchange or the Supplementary Benefits Commission (Great Britain) or the welfare departments in the United States. Using a similar argument, if someone breaks a leg or experiences a severe heart attack, this person would most probably utilize an emergency (survival) service, given such an immediate and obvious need to do so. The same individual, however, may or may not perceive the need for either a regular medical checkup or immunization.

Some needs, however, are not so universally obvious and immediate. Many are differentially perceived, and may be given varying priority depending on situational and cultural factors. For example, some may perceive a chronic cough as needing attention, while others may consider it a "hazard of living" and not worthy of any medical attention at all. Differential patterns of utilization by the poor may be partially explained in terms of this differential perception of the importance of need and of taking some ameliorative action.

Associated with this phenomenon is the appropriateness or goodness of fit between services and the values, norms, beliefs, and lifestyles of the subgroups of society for which they cater. Some needs, perceived or actual, may be recognized as important enough for attention from, say, a social welfare service, and yet the form in which the service is presented may be perceived as so abhorrent or debilitating that it is underutilized. Or, where there exists a choice of services catering for the same need, one service may be preferred above others because of the form in which this particular service is delivered.

It is likely that service preference is largely a function of the types of agencies and officials one has routine contact with. Generally speaking, the poor have regular contact with A type agencies out of necessity, and these typically operate on seller market principles (welfare agencies, emergency rooms). The middle and upper classes, in contrast, also experience A type services, but for them such contact is relatively infrequent, and when it does occur is by choice—banks, insurance and trust companies, building societies, and the like are some examples.

The implications of these different experiences with different agencies and levels of staff cannot be overemphasized. While all social categories probably have encounters with A and B type services, they may do so for entirely different reasons and experience quite different treatment from officials. The use of these types of services by the upper and middle classes is largely a matter or choice with the consequence that they can withdraw if dissatisfied—which is unlikely, since these services usually have a buyer market orientation. In contrast, the poor are forced to utilize services out of need and consequently do not have the freedom to withdraw if dissatisfied—which may be most of the time, since the services they routinely encounter operate on seller market principles.

Certainly, the inability to distinguish between the activities and orientations of what appear to be quite different agencies seems to have two deleterious consequences for subsequent utilization behavior. During the course of field work for the study referred to, the author was struck by the way in which many of the respondents had quite detailed knowledge about and negative attitudes toward particular agencies, even though they had never been in contact with these agencies or the personnel from them (McKinlay 1970).

Many typifications of certain services were not necessarily emergent responses to current situational experiences on the part of the respondent, but were communicated by others who had direct experiences with the service in question. Moreover, many of these negative typifications, while perhaps true for certain services, were apparently transferred and applied to other quite different services.

This process was probably assisted by the inability of the respondents to discriminate the predominant functions of different services. These "transferred typifications" came to constitute grounds for underutilizing other services. If a respondent did utilize a service, these transferred negative perceptions appeared to act almost as self-fulfilling typifications: after having been defined as negative and debilitating, agencies and officials almost certainly appeared to become so in their consequent behavior. The other deleterious consequence concerns the effect this may have in constricting one's repertoire of persuasive appeals, as well as in determining the appropriateness of any one appeal for presentation in a particular situation. Logically it would seem that services that are regarded by clients as indistinguishable would be likely to call forth the same general appeal strategy, despite possibly different situations. The behavior deemed appropriate and effective in, say, a welfare or employment office most probably will be quite ineffectual in a neighborhood health clinic or outpatient department. By perceiving services as indistinguishable, the poor may employ the "wrong" persuasive appeals in the "wrong" context, with the consequence that service to them and the reactions of officials are measureably affected. This lack of congruence between service and appeal may consequently affect the degree of client satisfaction. Most respondents in the Aberdeen study who underutilized services spent a considerable period of time in and around public assistance agencies, consequently developing techniques to present themselves in a particular way and to withhold information. During observational field work in a maternity clinic, it seemed that these tactics were inappropriately transferred to this organization, calling forth certain unfavorable definitions and responses from the clinic staff.

Certainly it would seem that in many instances, the ability of a client to extract some service from a formal organization or professional has little to do with public entitlement. Rather, it is dependent to a large extent on his or her repertoire of persuasive appeals and the ability to discriminate service type so as to correctly present oneself. For many reasons, some of which have been outlined above, such a facility with organizations does not appear readily present for many of the poor.

SOME DOUBTS ABOUT CLIENT SATISFACTION

In recent years attention has been devoted to the influence of patient satisfaction on utilization behavior. It is assumed the people expressing satisfaction with some type or aspect of social service will be more likely to utilize facilities, follow regimens, comply with advice, and so forth. Such an assumption appears unwarranted, since researchers have pointed out that few studies have been able to establish any sort of correlation between attitudes and subsequent behavior (Festinger 1964; Kegeles 1967). Despite this and other known limitations, such studies, for a variety of questionable reasons, continue to engage the attention of researchers.

There is, of course, a range of different techniques for measuring attitudes and satisfaction. Some researchers make vigorous efforts to measure satisfaction in an "objective" and structured fashion (Hulka et al. 1971). Others, adopting less structured approaches, have listed several major factors associated with patient satisfaction (waiting time, spent with the physician, ease of communication, exactness of diagnosis, etc.) and have requested responses regarding satisfaction or dissatisfaction with each of them. Another approach is simply to ask respondents what they like or dislike most about utilizing a particular social service; a more recent, imaginative technique is to offer subjects several hypothetical situations or short vignettes and require them to state feelings and attitudes.

Many researchers employ some combination of structured and unstructured techniques. Subjects may, for example, be interviewed about their expectations before utilizing a service; then, by content analysis of the recorded happenings, an effort is made to determine the influence of expectations on satisfaction (Francis, Korsch, and Morris 1969; Reader, Pratt, and Mudd 1967; Deisher et al. 1965).

When reviewing the plethora of studies of client satisfaction and allowing for the wide variation in methods employed, one is struck by the surprising consistency in findings. Expressed satisfaction with services is phenomenally high for all social categories. Where there is variation, it is presented as varying levels of positive attitudes, rather than as really negative sentiment. One of the very lowest levels of satisfaction appears to be the 76 percent reported in a study of doctor-patient communication (Francis, Korsch, and Morris 1969), but the usual figure is around the 98 percent found in a study of mothers' opinions of their pediatric care (Deisher et al. 1965).

The high expressions of satisfaction found may be a function of who sponsors the research, the subject content of the inquiry (nearly always associated with pediatrics), and where the interviews were conducted. It has been reported that respondents tend to reply in a stereotyped, socially acceptable manner and that hesitations are often noted. One group of researchers concedes that those conducting the survey had some feeling that the respondents were generally reluctant to express any dissatisfactions they might have had because of the nature of the doctor-patient relationship (Deisher et al. 1965).

With such constraints, it is surprising that researchers continue to elicit responses through interviews and/or written questionnaires at the very place that respondents are expected to provide comments on and continue to utilize. Respondents in several earlier investigations of patient attitudes and satisfaction reported positively (and therefore produced the phenomenally high rates of satisfaction) for fear of possible recriminations. A comparable situation in criminology would be a study by prison guards of the satisfaction of long-term prisoners with the treatment received from the guards.

Information concerning satisfaction with services that is elicited from respondents when they are not actually utilizing a facility may also show a higher degree of satisfaction. When not actually receiving a service, respondents may overlook matters that trouble them when they are using it; satisfaction is expressed rather with its availability. The person only occasionally utilizing a service may tolerate irritation or inefficiencies that accompany such infrequent visits without becoming dissatisfied with the system. Or the costs of potentially dissatisfying aspects of care may, for the client, be outweighted by the long-term benefits of the intervention. Kosa and his colleagues (1967) noted that the "errors of recall are not simple functions of forgetfulness but tend to follow a complex, psychologically motivated selectivity." They report that a person "when furnishing information, feels impelled to apply a selective censorship, separating the reportable events and suppressing the others."

Kegeles (1967) is openly skeptical of earlier work on attitudes and beliefs and writes:

> as to attitude surveys as means of gathering information, people will generally answer questions posed them by interviewers in surveys. This will happen whether they have ever thought of the question or not. There seems to be a growing body of data which indicates that such expressed attitudes have no functional significance unless they fit into the cognitive organization of the person.

Converse (1963) has labeled such statements "nonattitudes"—those that seemingly bear no relationship to the behavior of the informants or to anything else—and argues that "without demonstration that such attitudes have relevance for behavior, they provide merely interesting and perhaps useful hypotheses for further testing." Kegeles also suggests that there are few indications of the persistence of the beliefs and attitudes studies and that the best prediction of subsequent behavior is previous behavior.

These criticisms of attitude and satisfaction studies are clearly not exhaustive but relate principally to utilization behavior. Many other researchers have considered a number of the more technical methodological problems with attitude studies per se. Certain questionable ideological factors appear to perpetuate those studies, despite their dubious status on other methodological grounds.

Studies of patient satisfaction often appear to be value-laden and biased in their allocation of responsibility for dissatisfaction. When almost everyone is considered satisfied with some seemingly negligible minority, the danger arises to play down the deficiencies of service delivery. Responsibility for dissatisfaction and underutilization is allocated to the clients—especially since it has been "shown" that dissatisfaction is more often present among the aged, the less educated, and lower socioeconomic groups. Hulka and her colleagues (1971) in a recent paper claim that the "use of the medical care system and knowledge of how to use it, as evidenced by having a regular doctor and hospital insurance, are associated with increased total satisfaction." What appears to be implied in such a statement is that those people unfortunate enough not to have a regular doctor or health insurance do not know how to use the system correctly and have brought upon themselves any dissatisfaction they might experience. The same implication is present in some of the earlier work of Suchman, who suggests that if an individual maintains an informed, objective, professional, and independent approach to illness and health care, then he or she will be likely to express satisfaction with it (Suchman 1964). Such research appears to justify the status quo and provides a rationale for either inactivity or lack of progress. According to this view, it is not that the service is inequitable or inefficient, but that the nature and characteristics of the recipients obstruct delivery and undermine purposeful social policy. It follows that such a perspective and the findings of the studies that it employs tend to support the existence of demonstrably ineffective programs. Accompanying federal and private funding in the United States has been the formal (or informal) requirement that service agencies that receive funds must occasionally justify their continuance. Evaluation studies, with patient satisfaction as a principal component, have been conducted as one of their primary aims.

For some time behavioral scientists (especially sociologists and psychologists) interested in utilization behavior have ascribed culpability for underutilization (or overutilization) to particular individuals or groups—usually the poor—employing such labels as distrustful, disreputable, irresponsible, alienated, parochial, dissatisfied, and the like. By adopting such a perspective, we have attempted to deemphasize social structure or organizational determinants of utilization and have highlighted the features of clients. Social scientists, among others, guided in part by the availability of funds, have acted as midwives during the birth of much of present-day punitive welfare legislation. While most of them have not actually designed and administered the legislation, they have, through certain findings and concepts, facilitated its delivery. Coser (1969) has noted that researchers tend to espouse a status quo ideology and fail to consider the unanticipated consequences of their liberal theorizing. It surely must be time for researchers to reappraise the effects of their involvement and their perennial invention of new words and concepts. Becker (1967), for example, has described how officials develop ways both of denying the institution's failure to perform as it should and of explaining those failures that cannot be hidden. He also reminds us that researchers who favor officialdom are almost always spared the accusation of bias. Perhaps we should, along with Becker, consider whose side we are on, the various consequences of our research involvements, and the extent to which we are prepared to participate in the coverup of the real sources of client dissatisfaction.

Chapter 9

Social Worker and Client Perspectives: The Delivery of Area-based Social Work Services in an English Town

*E. Matilda Goldberg, O. B. E.**

BACKGROUND: CHANGES IN LOCAL GOVERNMENT AND SOCIAL SERVICE DELIVERY

Within a relatively short time major changes have taken place in the British local authority social services in which over 90 percent of socialworkers are employed. These services have been transformed from three separate specialist departments with fairly well-defined functions in the field of welfare for the disabled and elderly, the care of deprived children, and social services for the mentally ill and handicapped into one integrated social services department that serves all comers. Recent legislation concerned with the welfare of childern and the care of the chronically sick and disabled has added new statutory duties to the steadly increasing volume of referrals to the integrated social services department. These developments coincide with a steady growth of the population aged seventy-five and over, with the continuing increase in juvenile delinquency, and with the apparent spread of violence within the family. Requests for help range from simple information and advice to the most intractable problems our society is capable of producing. The activities of these social services departments include extensive domiciliary services,

*Senior Fellow, Policy Studies Institute, Great Britain

such as home helps (accounting for about a quarter of all staff employed and 14 percent of the net expenditure), meals services, and various forms of day and residential care—the latter accounting for about half of all the social services expenditure. Socialworkers, though central to decisionmaking and to the delivery of services, comprise only 10 percent of all staff in the personal social services. Income maintenance is not included in these services but is administered by the central government, although the social services department has small cash resources at its disposal. The social services personnel, headed by a director of social services, are accountable to the Social Services Committee, comprised of elected councillors, so that decisions about the allocation and deployment of resources are in the last resort political ones.

The convergence of many influences, among them some memorable passages in the Seebohm Report (1968) "to make the social service more accessible and acceptable," the injunction of the 1970 Chronically Sick and Disabled Act to ascertain the number of chronically sick and disabled in need, the media's increasing preoccupation with social problems, the growth in self-help and pressure groups, the welfare rights movement, and last but not least, scandals arising from nonaccidental injuries to small children—all these influences contribute to more publicity, debate, and criticism about the social services and social workers in Britain.

It is taking us a very long time to recognize the changed nature of the personal social services and the requests coming to it and to adjust social work methods accordingly and, most important, to examine and adapt the training of socialworkers to meet the changing service demands on them. Many young socialworkers come out of their training courses unprepared for the multiplicity of undefined problems and situations bombarding them. A large proportion are hoping to do casework—coming to grips and working through their client's problems in a sustained relationship. But faced with requests for bath rails, home helps, holidays; surrounded by unpaid electricity bills; harrassed by problems of homelessness or vagrant alcoholics, they take fright and take up a defensive position. They feel impelled to limit their functions to those of a kind of welfare sifter, instead of opening out and exploring the social repercussions of the presenting problem and the resources both within themselves and within the community that may be brought to bear on these problems. On the other hand, statutory obligations, pressure of public opinion, fashions in social work, and lack of time for thought and planning may lead to cases consuming precious skilled socialworker time to no specific purpose. A rational and systematic look—needs to be undertaken into the problems and requests coming to the social services departments. We need to explore afresh, and with as few preconceived notions as we can possibly manage, what skills and resources seem to be required to meet the wide range of requests, what mix of social work teams and organizational structures appear to be most effective, and so on.

Many social services departments are already evolving new ways of working, but mainly on a trial and error basis, and these new methods may come to be adopted without sufficient empirical enquiry and testing. Take for example the concept of the "intake team" in which a group of socialworkers deals solely with referrals and short-term work, only passing on to other colleagues those cases that appear to need long-term involvement. This is an excellent idea in many ways—referrals can be dealt with promptly; clients do not have to be passed on from duty officer to another socialworker; and socialworkers can develop expertise in assessment, resource finding, and short-term social work. But this kind of solution raises other problems. What about the so-called long-term teams? Will it make their work less varied? Will it reinforce the open-endedness of drifting, goal-less social work? Will it encourage a kind of sausage machine mentality in the intake team to get rid of as many people as quickly as possible?

It is becoming clear that the integration of hitherto fragmented services, while sweeping away some of the old notions of water tight specialties, does not carry with it the implication that one type of worker can help all types of clients with all types of problems arising in all conceivable situations. But how can we differentiate functions and tasks requiring different skills? One way is to study systematically types of problems presented and types of help given by people with varying degrees and types of training, as for example we tried to do in our field experiment with the aged (Goldberg, Mortimer, and Williams 1970).

THE RESEARCH TASKS

So far we have discussed some of the issues raised by the reorganization of the social services and the tasks that confront socialworkers. Where should a practice-oriented social work researcher put his or her emphasis when so many questions clamor for answers? At least six areas suggest themselves:

1. The *tasks* to be performed by those who man the social services will have to be systematically studied.

2. The *skills* needed to perform these tasks will have to be defined and tested.
3. Thought and research need to be devoted to the professional's *accountability* for individual clients and to the community.
4. *Systematic record* and review systems need to be developed to provide basic information about socialworker activities and their effects on different client groups and in order to provide monitoring and educational and planing tools.
5. Studies about the relative *costs* of various forms of social services will have to be undertaken.
6. Last, carefully controlled experimental studies will have to be mounted to test the client's and the care giver's *evaluation of the outcome* of social work, using criteria that are meaningful to both client and socialworker. Such studies need to be concerned with effectiveness—is the client better off?—as well as efficiency—at what cost?

It will be noted that experimental studies are put last. This is deliberate: until we know what it is we are evaluating and can formulate relevant and descriptive categories for types of client's problems and social work or social service inputs and finally for the desired objectives, there is very little point in mounting such experimental studies. Hence, the studies with which I was concerned concentrated first on the clients' and socialworkers' perspectives on the newly organized social services and their effects and second on the creation of a systematic record and review system, which enables socialworkers to plan more and to become more evaluative in their work with individual clients. In aggregated form it enables management to ascertain how social work resources are being deployed (Goldberg and Fruin 1976).

These studies were carried out in a medium-sized town on the south coast of England, which we have called Seatown. The attitudes of a random sample of 300 consumers of the social services in this town and of all the area-based socialworkers were studied at two times—in 1972, soon after the integration of the services and the establishment of area offices, and again in 1975, to see what changes, if any, had occurred during this vital period of reshaping the personal social services (Neill et al. 1973; Neill, Warburton, and McGuinness 1976; McKay, Goldberg, and Fruin 1973; Glampson and Goldberg 1976).

THE SOCIALWORKERS

The aims of the socialworker studies were to discover what their perceptions were of the size and type of their caseloads, the time pressures they experienced, the areas of new knowledge they felt they needed, and the aspects of integration they found difficult or rewarding. We also wanted to learn how they perceived their clients' expectations, likes, and dislikes about the service.

The early 1970s were generally a period of great restlessness and mobility among socialworkers. Many senior jobs had become available for the professionally trained as a result of the reorganization, and opportunities for promotion seemed almost limitless in the fast expanding services. Thus in 1972 staff turnover in the social services department of Seatown was very high: half of the seventy area-based socialworkers intended to leave their jobs within two years.

Over half the workers felt under considerable or severe time pressure, which was only partly related to the current workload. Unsorted caseloads, unclear goals for social work intervention, and lack of criteria for assessment, allocation, and closure were mentioned as reasons for the workers' feelings of pressure as much as the amount of work to be done. The merging of three separate services had made socialworkers aware of persistent gaps in services that they had previously assumed were filled by other departments. Now there was no escape from them, and again this was felt as a stress factor. In these early days the caseloads of the socialworkers were still highly specialized, and most thought that specialization by client group would continue indefinitely and considered this to be desirable. One of the most striking findings in the study, which has been confirmed by subsequent studies (Stevenson et al. 1978), was the socialworkers' very great preference for work with family problems and children. Yet the highest proportion of the department's clientele at that time consisted of the physically disabled and the elderly, for whom the least preference was expressed. Work with the elderly was perceived as requiring practical services and surveillance. This was mirrored by the consumer study in which the old people interviewed stated that they had mainly received practical services while the younger clients also described receiving what might be termed casework.

Nearly two-thirds of the staff thought that integration of the personal social services had in general been a good thing, but the majority considered that most other aspects of the service had deteriorated or remained the same. One telling quote, from a person interviewed, sums up these feelings: "There has been a decline in services that we have spent years in struggling to improve. The major frustrations are the feelings that senior management staff appear to know very little about managing—this is a national feeling, not just a local one. The clamouring for higher salaries and top positions has been very disillusioning. The better deal for the clients is rarely spoken of these days."

When asked what they thought about their clients' satisfaction with the department, most of the socialworkers were unsure, while the clients' feelings were distinctly positive: two-thirds of the clients in the consumer study expressed satisfaction, and 80 percent considered that their socialworkers were understanding, sympathetic, and easy to talk to. Another discrepancy between socialworkers' perceptions and clients' perceptions was revealed when the socialworkers were asked what types of help they felt clients expected from the department. Most socialworkers thought that clients expected, above all, sympathy, information, and freedom to discuss personal problems. Most clients on the other hand said that they wanted practical help, and few expected help in the form of sympathy or listening, although they appreciated the socialworkers' understanding and capacity to listen. When asked what they thought clients most liked and disliked about the department, the socialworkers took a gloomier view than their clients. They listed far more client complaints than client likes, possibly mirroring their own current difficulties. The majority thought that clients would complain about administrative delays, unclear definitions of the department's functions, and the problems of contacting socialworkers. In fact nearly two-thirds of the clients had no overt complaints about the services.

The social workers imagined that their clients were finding it difficult to get socialworkers on the phone and would complain about the long delays in the reception area and of infrequent visits. However, the clients who had called at the office did not find access to their socialworker difficult. Most socialworkers thought that clients valued a feeling of security from knowing that support was available from a beneficent department. This view was in part accurate. A third of the clients mentioned a feeling of security and relief of emotional distress, and a quarter said that they had received helpful advice. About a third, however, also mentioned benefits derived from the provision of aids to daily living, practical services, and material goods—such as clothes or bedding—while the socialworkers seldom mentioned these sources of satisfaction for their clients.

By 1975 the atmosphere seemed more settled. While in 1972 four-fifths of the socialworkers under thirty intended to move within two years, less than two-fifths expressed a similar plan in 1975. More socialworkers said they enjoyed their jobs despite continuing problems over the increased size and hierarchical structure of the large social services department. Although the socialworkers' caseloads were considerably smaller than in 1972 (the average size had decreased from ninety-two to fifty-seven, they felt similar degrees of pressure. Again this was only partly related to the amount of work, but also to their perceptions of whether their work was worthwhile and appropriate. Over half the socialworkers described a range of clerical and administrative tasks that they considered to be a waste of time. Some described a feeling of pressure and conflict over deciding priorities, and many commented on the need for more precise definitions of social work roles and tasks. Anxiety was evident among many about the potentially infinite demands that might come through the "one door" of an area office. The preferences for work with children and families had persisted. Although caseloads were more mixed in 1975 than in 1972, a considerable number of socialworkers expressed reservations about the general practitioner type of socialworker. A typical opinion was: "I have reservations about every good socialworker being generic. Although there is some enjoyment in variety, lack of knowledge and experience inevitably leads to a feeling of impotence and less efficient service."

The perceptions of clients and socialworkers still diverged on many topics. While the majority of the socialworkers thought that at least half the clients expected to discuss their personal problems, only 8 percent of the clients expected to do this. While half the socialworkers thought that the personal relationship with the socialworker would be one of the positive things the client would point to, this was only mentioned by 16 percent of the clients. Here we may have the nub of the difference in perception between socialworkers and clients. The clients appear to take a sympathetic, receptive attitude by socialworkers for granted: she or he understands your problems (81 percent), is able to see things from your point of view (71 percent), is sympathetic (77 percent), is easy to talk to (84 percent), and is a good listener (81 percent). But the majority of clients do not single out the relationship per se as an important ingredient in the help received. This is not surprising when one considers that the majority of clients have infrequent and fleeting contacts with the socialworkers and receive in the main practical help and advice, as we shall document later on.

As in 1972, socialworkers felt more pessimistic about their clients' satisfaction and attitudes toward the department than the clients did themselves. Thus, practically all the socialworkers thought that almost all clients would have a complaint, while this actually applied to only 37 percent. As we shall see presently, it seems as though clients have more realistic expectations about what is possible under present staffing conditions and with the skills available, although they were by no means uncritically accepting of the services offered.

THE CLIENTS

The aims of the consumer studies in 1972 and 1975 were to explore the clients' expectations, feelings of satisfaction, and views on the services they had received and to test their general knowledge of the functions of the social services and their perceptions of social-workers. Some 300 randomly selected clients were interviewed in Seatown along the lines of a structured questionnaire by a team of specially trained interviewers.

The majority of the consumers in both surveys said that they had received some help, and almost two-thirds felt that they had got what they hoped for. The two groups who received mainly practical help were the elderly and the physically handicapped and those who came with housing and financial difficulties. Casework type of help was most often mentioned by those whose reason for contact was mental disorder and those with child care and family problems. This accords well with the socialworkers' descriptions. Two-thirds of the physically handicapped—young and old—in both surveys said that the help they had received had made a difference either to them personally or to their lives generally. The handicapped, whatever their age, valued a feeling of security and support in the background on which they could rely: "I think it's the very fact that they're there and you get in touch when there are difficulties. The word security comes to mind" (widow aged sixty-three living alone). About three-quarters of the people replied positively to the question about how satisfied they had been with the services, but while in 1972 the degree of satisfaction was fairly evenly distributed throughout the client groups, in 1975 satisfaction varied in different client groups. The elderly and the physically handicapped and those who approached the department with housing and financial problems were the most satisfied. These were the two groups who received predominantly practical help.

Similarly, while in 1972 equal proportions in all client groups had complaints, in 1975 interesting differences emerged between client groups. The elderly and physically handicapped over sixty-five made fewer complaints than the rest, and when they did it was mostly about infrequency of visiting or about delays in receiving services. In contrast, half of those with child care and family problems made complaints, which most frequently referred to the socialworkers or the service given. Comments often referred to the youth and inexperience of socialworkers dealing with children or complex family problems. These clients did not refer so much to lack of empathy on the part of younger socialworkers as to the immaturity and resulting lack of understanding. Interestingly, some uneasiness about lack of specialization had permeated to the consumers; a small proportion (6 percent) voiced this problem, feeling that workers could not hope to deal adequately with every type of problem.

The consumers' perceptions of socialworkers also had changed between 1972 and 1975. In 1972 more than a third of the consumers stressed the need for practical knowledge and skills, and one-quarter mentioned the importance of a good basic education. In 1975 only a quarter of the consumers thought that socialworkers should have practical skills such as first aid or domestic work, and even fewer stressed a good basic education. Instead, twice as many consumers emphasized the need for training and specialized knowledge.

The famous Seebohm Report (1968), which formed the basis for the reorganization of the social services, emphasized the importance of the local community's participation in the running of the social services, and we explored the views of consumers on this issue in 1972 and 1975. In 1972, 28 percent of the consumers felt that they would like to have some say in the running and planning of services. In 1975 considerably more—38 percent—said that they would like to participate. The main reasons for wanting to participate were that the experience of users was thought to be important for planning and organization. Some consumers made concrete suggestions about the ways in which they would like to be involved, such as offering advice through liaison groups. Others wished to participate by the interchange of information through meetings and lectures. Some consumers felt that they could most usefully contribute their views through surveys, and others expressed ideas of self-help.

Appropriate use of the social services is very much dependent on adequate knowledge about services available; hence, in both surveys we tested how much knowledge clients had of the social services. We presented respondents with six fairly common problem situations and asked them what sort of help they would suggest. We were also interested to find out which problems consumers thought needed professional rather than informal help from the community and how far they themselves would be prepared to get involved. Several important points emerged:

1. On the whole clients appeared to be well-informed about the functions of the social service and made many useful and appropriate suggestions.
2. The social services department was increasingly seen as an information and advice center that can direct clients to more specialized forms of help. Thus the boundaries between the social services department and the citizen's advice bureau tended to become blurred.
3. Users of the social services department made more suggestions to each problem situation in 1975, possibly indicating an

increase in knowledge and sophistication about sources of help, which in turn may reflect the increase in publicity and information about the social services.

Finally, a most interesting development was the greater importance that consumers in 1975 placed on informal rather than professional help. Particularly striking were the growing number of consumers—both young and old—who would be prepared to have a go themselves. If this means that more people are ready to help their neighbors, it may carry important implications for the future use of resources by the social services. Further studies will have to show whether what people say coincides with what they will actually do.

Perhaps one can see the dim outline emerging of a social service agency being there in the background in time of need, much as the general practitioner service is available when one's health breaks down. Many consumers now expect socialworkers to be trained professionals rather than practical "universal aunts" with little specialized knowledge or training. These perceptions of a professional social service do not apparently lead to greater passivity and dependence but coexist with a blossoming of interest in mutual support and in involvement in the social services. An intriguing result of the explorations into the subjective perceptions of socialworkers and clients is that the work that the socialworkers preferred most, that with children and families, evoked most complaints, while the practical service support to the elderly and disabled, representing the least favored client group, resulted in most satisfaction.

CREATING A MONITORING TOOL

So far we have considered the subjective perceptions of clients and socialworkers in the reorganized social services, but what did actually happen? While these two surveys were carried out, some of us engaged in an action project in one area office. We began by reviewing with each of the twenty socialworkers some half-dozen cases that were chosen more or less at random. We hoped to gain an idea of how the socialworkers saw their jobs, what skills they were using, and what aims they were pursuing in different case situations. Four features stood out among these preliminary 113 case reviews:

1. The indeterminate nature of the aims the socialworkers were pursuing;
2. The difficulties the socialworkers experienced in formulating a plan for the future rather than a description of the present situation;

3. The very long-term nature of the majority of cases discussed, which had been known to the department for a long time and which were expected to remain open more or less indefinitely; and
4. The reluctance of the socialworkers to involve others—possibly less trained colleagues, volunteers, or other community resources—in situations that appeared to be stable and not to require the special skills of a trained socialworker.

Further, the consumer and socialworker studies had highlighted certain discontinuities and difficulties in service delivery: for example, as we have seen, differences emerged in what clients expected from socialworkers and what socialworkers thought their clients wanted from them. Ambiguities about closure of cases became apparent. A number of clients thought they were still in contact with the services when officially their cases were closed; conversely, others believed that their contact with the department had ceased while the socialworkers considered them current. All these factors pointed at the operational level toward the need for more clearly defined aims of social work, a more explicit understanding of these by client and worker, a regular system for reviewing progress and readjusting aims, and a broader perspective and more use of outside resources that might provide relief for the socialworkers and a better service for the client. At this stage we defined our action research aims as follows.

1. To develop a model information and review system that would enable field workers and management to monitor their social work and social services activity in order to discover how professional skills and other social service resources are used in relation to different problems presented and to different aims pursued; and
2. To encourage socialworkers to become more explicit about both means and ends of their activities.

The climate was ripe for the practitioners to work closely with the research team in creating a basic tool they lacked—a case review scheme that would eventually become part of an ongoing computerized system. This system was developed through the course of some two years in a "bottom-up" way. A working party consisting of five field workers and a senior socialworker met regularly once a fortnight with two of us. Categories for problems, services, socialworker activities, and so forth were developed, and gradually the case review instrument emerged after many trial runs, tests, and criticisms. The form consists of three sections: (1) past activities, (2) the present situation, and (3) the intended future activities and aims. The socialworkers filling it in ask themselves four kinds of questions: (1) What is the problem I wish to tackle? (2) What have I achieved so far? (3) What am I aiming for within the next period? (4) How do I intend to achieve these aims? Finally, the scheme was launched at an area meeting when all the socialworkers undertook to review their current allocated cases and to review their caseloads thereafter at intervals to be determined by them, according to the needs of the particular case.

It is likely that much of the resistance of socialworkers to providing codified information on their cases is due to the fact that they hardly ever receive any interesting feedback that makes sense of the data they are supplying. We therefore decided early on to make the review system as relevant as possible to their needs and interests and to encourage a constant dialogue of questions and answers based on the data we were accumulating with them.

What did this monitoring tool reveal about the clients' problems and the socialworkers' responses to them? We analyzed one year's intake to this area office, largely dealt with by the intake team on a short-term basis, and we similarly scrutinized the ongoing cases handled by the two long-term teams during the same period, using the case review data. (Goldberg et al 1977; Goldberg and Warburton 1978).

THE SOCIALWORKERS' TASKS AND QUESTIONS ARISING: A REDEPLOYMENT OF SOCIAL WORK SKILLS?

Let us now summarize the socialworkers' tasks as they emerged from this monitoring exercise and from other less detailed studies (Stevenson et al. 1978):

1. Screening incoming demands, many of them for straightforward practical services;
2. Providing practical help and services of many kinds for the disabled and elderly;
3. Acting as a kind of citizen's advice bureau for a great variety of material and interpersonal problems;
4. Acting as a gobetween or advocate vis-à-vis the Department of Health and Social Security, housing departments, and other statutory and voluntary bodies;
5. Conducting long-term surveillance of the elderly and disabled (directly or through others) and of children in care;
6. Conducting crisis work among the frail elderly on the borderline of requiring residential care and among families in a chronic state of disequilibrium; and

7. Conducting casework. Although this is usually taken to be the main activity of socialworkers, in the sense of helping people to engage in a clarifying and problem-solving process in a calm atmosphere, it only constituted 20 percent of socialworker activities in the area studied. A caseload study in an eastern county of England (Booth 1977) reported that only 5 percent of clients received any form of individual casework.

The findings of the consumer and the socialworker studies and from this monitoring exercise raise a number of questions, particularly in relation to the deployment of social work skills. Are socialworkers being used to the greatest benefit of the clients and to the optimal work satisfaction of socialworkers? Take for example the elderly, who though satisfied with the practical services, sometimes complained about infrequency of visiting, and who received hardly any help with their nonmaterial problems. One might consider channeling requests for specific domiciliary services as a matter of routine to social service officers without using socialworkers as screening agents; but some resources would be devoted to training these social service officers to spot those clients who appear to need help beyond the specific service requested. Only at that point would the trained socialworker enter the case.

Second, frail elderly and disabled clients might benefit by the curtailing of the endless round of ineffective occasional surveillance visits. Instead some social service input might go into the creation of neighborhood support networks using both statutory personnel (home helps, meals on wheels) and volunteers. Those socialworkers who wish to develop such skills would then take on a quasi-community worker role as initiators and advisers.

How appropriate is it for a social services department to become an information and advice center on such a large scale? Do socialworkers have the requisite skills for the roles that they are currently taking on as information givers and advisers on such a broad front, or are they landing themselves between several stools, being neither information experts nor advocates nor caseworkers? Would it be more helpful to clients to create a special information and advice section manned by information officers with additional specialized training, either within the social services department or outside it, by transferring some resources to citizen's advice bureaus?

Third, the intractable problems of the chronically disorganized and disturbed families presented the greatest challenge to social work skills. On the other hand, over a quarter of the family problems were closed during the intake phase as "low priority" when problems were not as yet very severe. It may prove more effective in the long run to reverse this policy and to limit the resources that are at present poured into work with chronically disorganized families and to spend more casework resources on work with families who have not as yet become severely disrupted. It is also worth noting that we observed relatively favorable outcomes of work with families where material problems were tackled as the most outstanding ones.

Would casework aimed at more specific and concrete targets also repay in emotionally disturbed families, which are often beset by many pratical and environmental problems? Consumer research, as well as experimental studies on social work outcome, testify how much clients appreciate practical help given in an understanding way (Mayer and Timms 1970; Goldberg, Mortimer, and Williams 1970; McKay, Goldberg, and Fruin 1973). Furthermore, findings on task-centered casework indicate that clients gain a considerable sense of achievement and learn from the experience of tackling their problems one at a time in the pursuit of small achievable aims (Reid and Epstein 1972; Goldberg et al 1977). These considerations may also apply to some of the long-term cases of emotional disorders where ongoing "ventilation" of problems and "support" seem to result in few if any changes.

The redeployment of skills sketched out above would give rise to a certain amount of specialization (information, practical service delivery, neighborhood work, group work) within the framework of an integrated social services department. Inherent in these suggestions is the concept of delineating clearer tasks in response to specific needs within the context of a social services team, abandoning the idea of the intake worker as a jack of all trades and the client as an undifferentiated bundle of problems. These functional divisions would also afford greater choice to both clients and socialworkers and possibly lead to a more effective service to clients and to greater work satisfaction among socialworkers. Quasi-experimental action projects are badly needed in Britain now to test some of the hypotheses.

Chapter 10

Can Microinteraction Work as a Social Mechanism to Bridge the Gap Between Service Organizations and the Public Served?

*Friedhart Hegner**

FIRST STEPS TOWARD AN ANALYTICAL FRAME OF REFERENCE TO DEFINE THE GAP BETWEEN SERVICE DELIVERY ORGANIZATIONS AND THE CLIENTS

Speaking of "gaps" with regard to the relationships between service organizations and their public, we refer to the following problems:

To "social distances" that are such as to prevent an adequate delivery of services with regard to the social problems and personal needs clients have (Kadushin 1962; Sjoberg, Brymer, and Farris 1966; Walsh and Elling 1968; Grunow and Hegner 1979);

To those distances resulting from systematically biased processes of service production, distribution, and reception (Greenley and Kirk 1976; cf. Chapters 4 and 6); and

To the specific discrepancies between need (or demand) definitions on the side of the clients and administratively or politically defined clients' needs or demands (Kirk and Greenley 1974; Hegner 1978; Skarpelis-Sperk 1978).

These statements can be illustrated as shown in Figure 10-1.

*International Institute of Management, Science Center Berlin, and Research Group, Social Planning and Social Administration, Bielefeld, Federal Republic of Germany

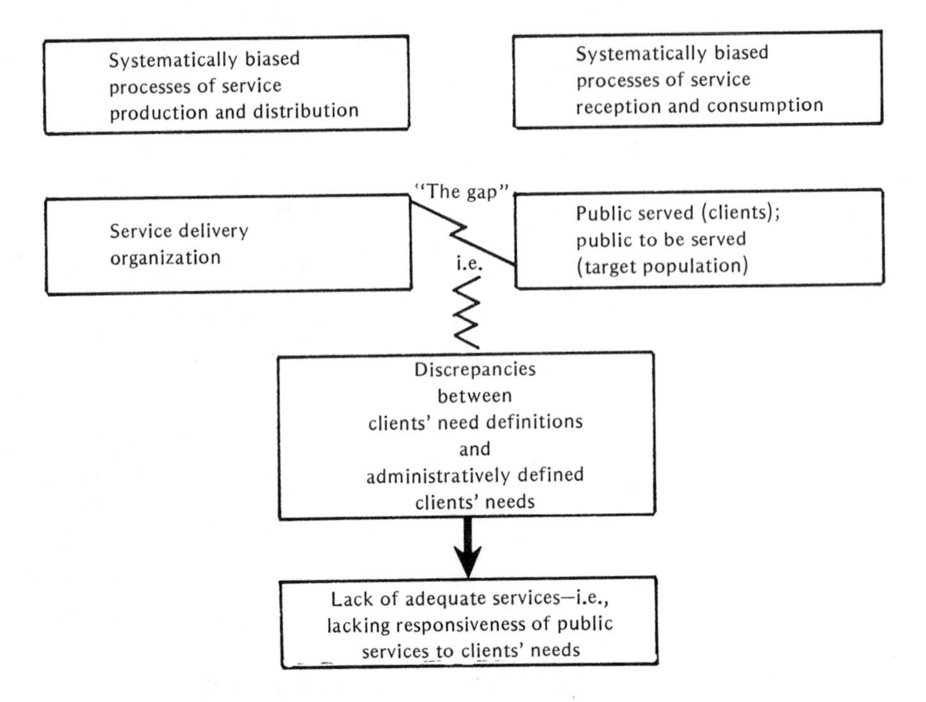

Figure 10-1. Main components of the gap between service organizations and the public served.

In everyday life there are many symptoms of this gap. Some people speak of a bad interaction climate; others point to the frustrating accompaniments of unreadable application forms and other attributes of "red tape"; still others refer to difficult access and business hours that form obstacles to easy service utilization; some people think of services that do not really fit the needs or problems of the clients; others refer to the nonuse or to the underutilization of services—that is, to services that do not reach the clients. Even at this level of everyday frictions and faults we can identify two main aspects of the gap (Katz and Danet 1973a, 1973b; Grunow and Hegner 1977a):

Discrepancies between the respective definitions of service organizations and the public with a view to sociopsychological aspects of the contact between clients and agencies; and

Discrepancies between the respective definitions of service organizations and the public with regard to the quantity and quality of services as related to the quantity and quality of clients' problems.

Catalogues of frictions and faults have only a descriptive and not an analytical value. One does not know from these lists exactly what the real problem or gap is, of which the frictions are nothing but symptoms. At the same time these catalogues do not offer criteria for weighing propositions and precepts with regard to more administrative responsiveness to clients' needs. Under the practical constraints of decisionmaking one has to realize that we are in need of a specific focus enabling us to say, first, what the needs of the clients are; second, what kind and degree of responsiveness to needs is necessary on the side of service delivery organizations; third, what kind and degree of frictions and distances can be tolerated without preventing an adequate responsiveness; and fourth, what kind and degree of responsiveness to administrative structures and dynamics is needed on the side of the clients to guarantee an optimal service delivery.

In trying to develop strategies for diminishing the discrepancies between clients' need definitions and administratively or professionally defined clients' needs, we have first to make clear what the term "need" really means. "Need is the main point of reference when one is dealing with the lack of responsiveness of public services to clients' problems (cf. Chapter 2). Within the terminology of psychologists, need refers to a "condition of lacking, wanting or requiring something which if present would benefit the organism by facilitating behavior or satisfying a tension" (Wolman 1973). Within a sociological frame of reference, individual needs result from social problems, a social problem consisting of "a substantial discrepancy between widely shared social standards and actual conditions of social life" (Merton 1971). Needs are at the same time consequences and reinforcing agents of natural or manmade discrepancies between social standards and social actuality (Ferber and Ferber 1978).

There has been, and still is, a more or less sophisticated discussion on the problem of identifying needs—especially true or basic human needs. One topic in this discussion deals with the question of who may be competent to define needs: the people involved in a social problem and feeling uneasy about it? Or the people offering help for those involved in a problem? Or the scientist engaged in analyzing social problems and the correlated conditions "of lacking, wanting or requiring something"? Instead of entering into this discussion, we simply state: needs are perceived and, at the same time, defined by those involved in a social problem as well as by those offering or denying help (cf. Figure 10-2). Thus, there can be found "clients' need definitions" as well as "administratively or professionally defined clients' needs." By definition (Berger and Pullberg 1966) of needs we implicitly refer to two analytical levels of defining reality: (1) the intraindividual processes of forming cognitive (and affective) "maps" with a view to social problems and other conditions of

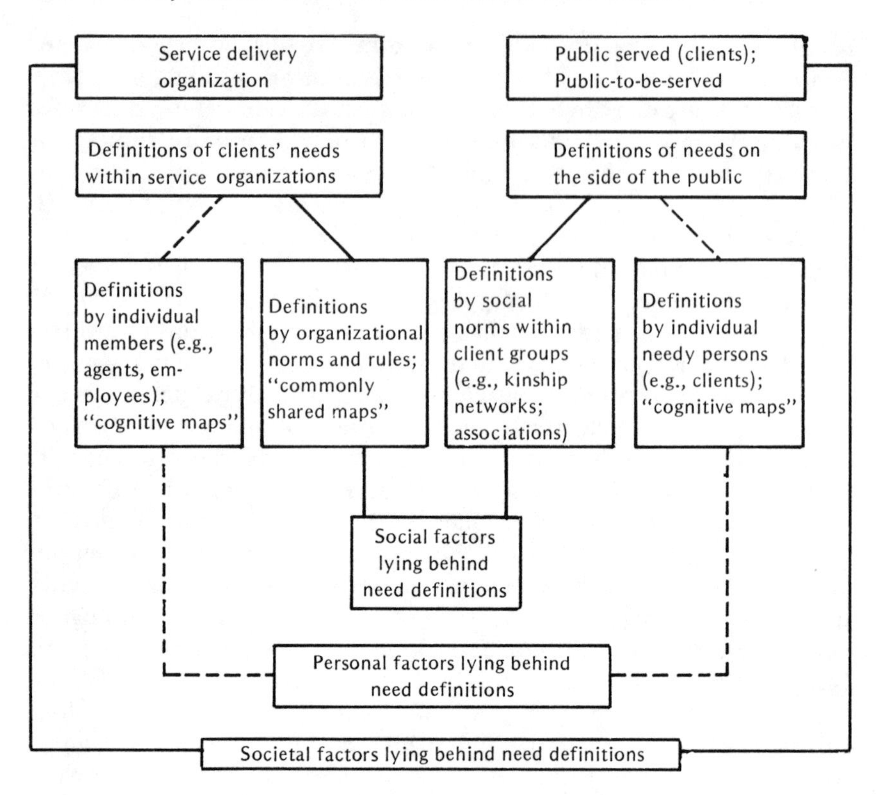

Figure 10-2. Societal, individual, organizational and social sources for definitions of needs.

lacking, wanting, or requiring something; and (2) the interindividual processes of developing commonly shared "social maps" with a view to standards of well-being, ill-being, and reducing the discrepancy between well-being and ill-being. Intra- and interindividual processes of need definition can be found on the side of the clients (as individuals and collectivities) as well as on the side of service delivery agencies (consisting of individual members and social norms).

Speaking of need definitions, one becomes conscious of the fact that needs are defined—that is limited—(1) in the actual intensity of lacking, wanting, or requiring, and (2) in the range of actually wanted objects. At the same time, each need definition constitutes a process of selection—that is, the constitution of a selective choice within a vast horizon of possible, individual as well as social, definitions of social problems and conditions of lacking, wanting, or requiring something. These general observations can help us to understand the rise of systematic biases within service production and consumption, which are based on social systems (e.g., service organizations or consumer associations) as well as on personal systems (e.g., public agents or needy clients). Some of those biased selection processes will now be sketched to bring out the bases of the gap between service delivery and service reception.

SOME PERSONAL AND SOCIAL BASES OF THE GAP BETWEEN CLIENTS' NEED DEFINITIONS AND ORGANIZATIONALLY DEFINED CLIENTS' NEEDS

Speaking of individual and social need definitions, we have already implicitly alluded to some of the factors that produce the gap—personal and social "maps" with regard to social problems and individual needs. Without entering into the traditional discussion on the relationships between personal, social, and societal structures and processes (see Israel 1977), we shall briefly describe some of the bases underlying the gap between service organizations and the public (served or to be served). In doing this, we implicitly identify the main factors that limit the possible effects of microinteraction in bridging the gap.

Intrapersonal Transformation Processes: From Needs to Felt Needs to Claims

Murray (1938) distinguishes "need" from "need felt," the latter referring to unsatisfying situations the individual is consciously aware of. Felt needs induce demands or interests while the dissatisfying situation continues and when the motivation to get rid of it continues, too. With a view to the utilization of public services by clients, it is necessary to rely on need felt and demand, because the awareness of lacking something is a precondition of looking for means or instruments to facilitate behavior or satisfy tensions. One of these means or instruments may be the contacting of a service delivery organization. When a need felt leads to a contact with a service organization it has become a claim, based on an interest or demand.

Once again we are confronted with the problem of selectivity: not all needs become needs felt, and not each need felt is transformed into an interest or demand. What kinds of factors or variables exercise an influence on the selectivity of transformation processes?

With regard to the step from need to need felt, there are at least two main sets of variables: (1) internal psychological structures and processes of perception, cognition, and motivation that result from general personality traits including internalized social norms and cultural values; and (2) sociopsychological structures and processes within the framework of social relations in family, neighborhood, workmate groups, and former experiences with means of need satisfaction. These sociopsychological structures and processes are embedded in general societal norms, values, income distribution, status differences, socialization institutions, and so forth.

With regard to the step from need felt to an articulated interest, demand, and claim, we can be more specific: the aforementioned variables constitute the general background of interest and demand formation. From this background two sets of variables are of dominant influence: (1) internal psychological structures and processes with a close connexion to experiences and actions resulting from former contacts with service delivery organizations—for example, from former experiences with public agencies as a means of need satisfaction; and (2) sociopsychological structures and processes connected with the experiences, assessments, and prejudices coming from members of relevant social networks and reference groups. Once again we have to note that these sociopsychological variables are embedded in the social and cultural framework of a specific society—especially in its political culture and in the norms and values concerning the relationship between public administration and the public. The intrapersonal process of transforming the perception of a social problem and the correlated needs into articulated interests and even claims can be summarized in Figure 10-3.

The aforementioned steps of the transformation process as well as the factors inducing the pursuit or breaking off of the process have important consequences for the use or nonuse of social services. At one extreme, there are needy persons—as seen from a medical, psychiatric, sociological, or economic point of view—who do not perceive "a substantial discrepancy between widely shared social standards and actual conditions of social life" (Merton 1971). Therefore they do not have feelings of lacking something or felt needs; as a consequence they do not articulate demands and claims. These people form the public to be served. At the other extreme, there are people who identify service delivery organizations as an adequate means of need satisfaction and problem solution. Therefore they contact these organizations—that is, they behave or act as claimants and applicants. These people constitute the public served.

Between these extremes, there are needy persons who may have feelings of lacking and needing something, but who do not approach the public services. In some cases the motivation to get rid of the unsatisfying situation is either too weak or sociopsychologically blocked, so that they do not articulate demands or interests. In other

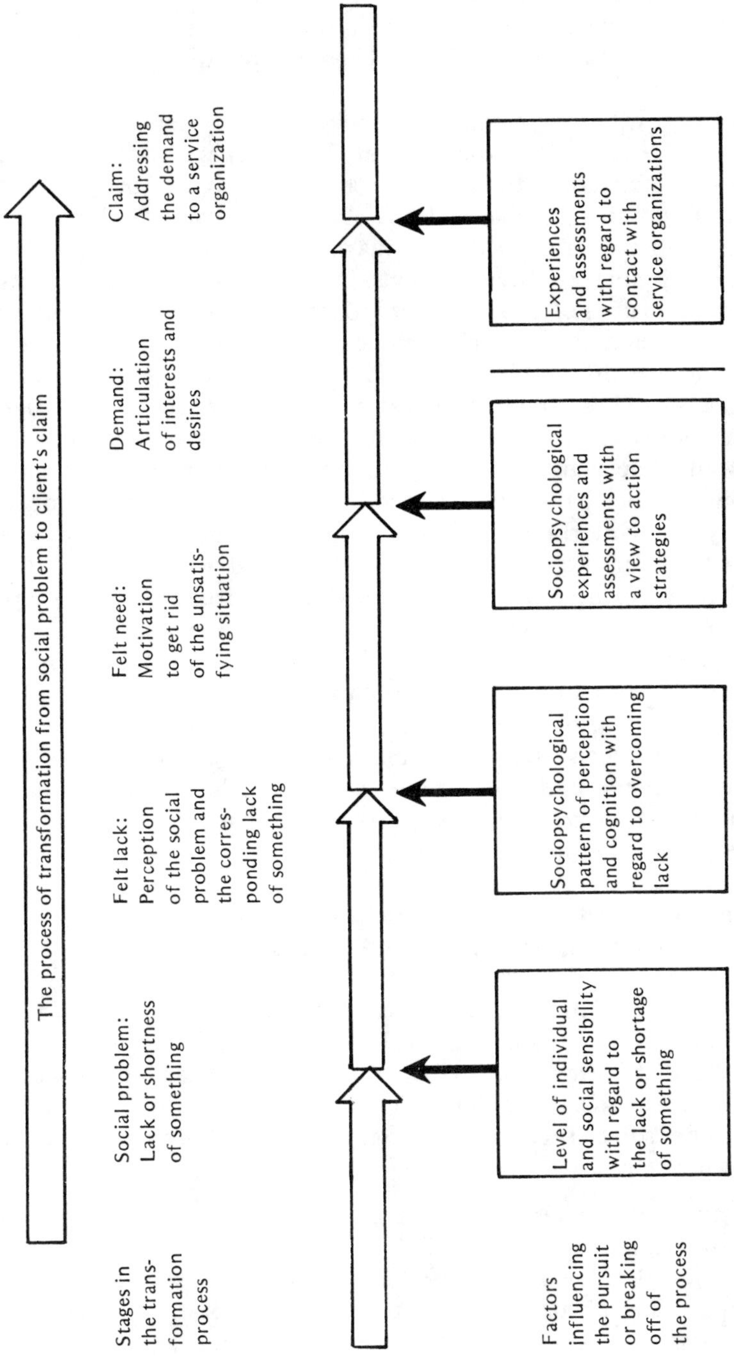

The process of transformation from social problem to client's claim

Stages in the transformation process	Social problem: Lack or shortness of something	Felt lack: Perception of the social problem and the corresponding lack of something	Felt need: Motivation to get rid of the unsatisfying situation	Demand: Articulation of interests and desires	Claim: Addressing the demand to a service organization
Factors influencing the pursuit or breaking off of the process	Level of individual and social sensibility with regard to the lack or shortage of something	Sociopsychological pattern of perception and cognition with regard to overcoming lack	Sociopsychological experiences and assessments with a view to action strategies		Experiences and assessments with regard to contact with service organizations

Figure 10–3. The process of transformation from social problem to client's claim.

cases there may be an articulation of demands, but these demands are not addressed to public service organizations—that is, no claims or applications are put forward. These people form part of the target population.

Until now, intrapersonal or sociopsychological bases of service utilization—or nonuse—have formed the main focus of attention. These variables have to be seen in the wider context of individual life situations. J.B. McKinlay (1972a, 1970) has elaborated some of the main properties that had been diagnosed in former studies. Demographic variables, spatial distance from delivery organizations, economic burdens of fees or other monetary contributions, and general sociocultural traits may have some influence on utilization behavior and interaction patterns, but they are less important then some former studies seemed to prove. Far more important are situational variables resulting from the interpenetration of individual personality traits and social networks. The shaping of individual behavior dispositions by social expectations and behavior patterns in the context of family, neighborhood, workmate groups, and the like exercise remarkable influences on the readiness and willingness to contact service organizations. Aspects of social life situations also shape the abilities to benefit from the services by interacting with different staff groups.

Here, we can draw a first conclusion with a view to the limited capacity of microinteraction as a possible social mechanism to bridge the gap between service organizations and the public served. This positive function—if there is one—can be fulfilled only with regard to those people who have passed through the whole transformation process from felt lack to claim.

Contingency and Selectivity in the Relationship Between Service Organizations and Clients

After having outlined some bases of the gap with a view to the target population and the clients, the focus of analysis has to be changed. There are at least three further sets of factors that induce discrepancies between social problems and clients' need definitions on the one hand and social services and organizationally defined needs on the other hand (Hegner 1978):

Structural properties of service organizations as well as characteristics of the personnel;

Structural problems in the relationship between social systems (e.g., service organizations as systems of cooperation) and personal systems (e.g., members and clients of service organizations); and

Societal structures and processes regulating the distribution and allocation of (power) statuses, goods, and services.

With regard to the first set of factors, we can be very brief, because other authors in this volume (Catrice-Lorey, Goldberg, Greenley, Grunow and Timms) have referred to the main variables of the context of staff-client interaction as seen with a view to organization and personnel:

Variables of organization structure—for example, characteristics of technology, type of goal and program, domain adjustment, selection and distribution of personnel, bureaucratization of communication and control processes, evaluation criteria for performance, and so forth;

Variables of organization culture—for example, links between general value conceptions and operative goals or norms, informal groups and group climate, incentive systems (material, solidary, and purposive incentives), conflicts of interest, bases and instruments of power or control (coercive, utilitarian, normative and social power), dominance of bureaucratic or professional orientations, and so forth;

Variables of personnel—for example, characteristics of individual perceptions, cognitions, motivations, needs, norms, and values resulting from personality structure as well as from vocational formation; and

Variables of space, time, and material resources—for example, spatial location and geographical distribution of offices, hours of opening, extensions or lapses of time, furniture, appointments, interior decoration, quantity and quality of application forms, and so forth.

These different sets of variables form the basis of definitions of clients' needs within service organizations. One must ask why these organizational definitions do not adequately fit the social problems and need definitions of the clients. Here, we have to go back to a general problem characterizing the relationships between social and personal systems—the problem of reciprocal contingency and selectivity (Luhmann 1971, 1976; Hondrich 1973; Hegner 1976, 1978).

Service organizations (as social systems) and persons (members as well as clients) form environments for one another. Each of them has its specific and—more or less—coherent patterns of identifying, selecting, and processing events (e.g., goods, services, symbols, persons). As seen from the perspective of one of the systems (organizations, members, clients), the other systems constitute unlimited possibilities of action and reaction. In this sense, they are perceived as contingent. If the different systems are dependent on one another—for example, in getting resources—they have to compete under the conditions of reciprocal, but not necessarily balanced, contingency.

This implies that the structures and action strategies of organizations depend on the way in which individual members and clients become relevant for the task fulfillment of the organization. Inversely, the personality structures and action strategies of individual members and clients depend on the way in which organizations become relevant for individual need satisfaction or purpose realization. The structures and dynamics of the two types of systems necessarily produce selectivities with regard to one another. These selectivities in terms of structural prerequisites for experience and action form the basis for coping with contingency and uncertainty: neither of the two sides is able to anticipate the range of possibilities resulting from experiences and actions of the other side; thus, both parties try to get along with contingency and uncertainty by means of selection mechanisms. The problem of reciprocal contingency and selectivity constitutes one of the main barriers to the responsiveness of service organizations to clients' needs. As long as individual needs, wants, and claims are addressed to formally and professionally organized service delivery systems, there will be structural obstacles to responsiveness. One could even state that selectivity and the correlated lack of responsiveness constitute a precondition of formally and professionally organized need satisfaction (cf. Luhmann 1964; Thompson 1975):

1. Service delivery organizations consist of two components (Silverman 1970): on the one hand, there are the "pattern systems" of norms, rules, and scientifically observable regularities, defining work programs, communication channels, scope and control, and ways for the selection and distribution of the labor force (Kuhn 1971). Within these pattern systems, rights and duties are fixed with a view to the personnel (staff) as well as to the clientele. On the other hand, there are the "action systems" of individual norm actualization and rule application (Kuhn 1971). Within these action systems, individual functionaries or groups of members with their personal perceptions, cognitions, and motives apply the rules to individual client cases. Only the reduction of needy clients to specific legitimate demands and interests makes it possible to confront the staff with the complexity of clients' experiences and actions. And only the reduction of needy persons to the specific role segments of clients—as claimants, applicants, complainants, and recipients—makes it possible to prevent the staff members from purely personal and arbitrary selection processes with regard to clients' needs felt.

2. At the same time, only the reduction of needy persons to specific clients. rights and duties makes it possible to define an organizational domain, which forms one of the preconditions for getting resources (Levine and White 1961; Thompson 1967).

Besides the two aforementioned bases of the gap—the sociopsychological transformation process from needs to claims and the reciprocal contingency and selectivity—there is a third type of factor impeding responsiveness of service delivery organizations to clients' needs—societal patterns of producing, distributing and allocating (power) statuses, goods, and services. These global patterns constitute the background of social problems and deficient individual life situations as well as of individual need definitions and organizational mechanisms to define legitimate claims (cf. Chapters 4 and 11).

In his *History of Economic Analysis*, J. A. Schumpeter (1954) indicates that all societies need and have social mechanisms to distribute scarce goods and statuses (i.e., rights and duties) and that one of the endeavors of economic analysis has always been to elaborate the adequate kind and degree of selectivity with respect to the interests of different groups. In modern societies public administration is one of the principal instruments or agents implementing the distribution of scarce goods and statuses (cf. Titmuss 1958; Robson 1976; Scharpf 1977). In this connection, "responsiveness" of service delivery organizations has always been limited by generally institutionalized and legally codified social selection processes (Achinger 1958; Skarpelis-Sperk 1978).

A further conclusion can be drawn with a view to the limited capacity of microinteraction as a possible social mechanism to bridge the gap between service organizations and the public served. Even if needy persons succeed in transforming felt needs into claims, there is no guarantee at all of being served adequately. Any attempt—on the side of the agents or the clients—to overcome discrepancies in the respective need definitions with the help of discussion, small talk, glances, and gestures is confronted with the limits set up by reciprocal selectivity and institutionalized social selection processes. Nevertheless, some interactive potentials may exist to diminish the gap.

THE LIMITED CAPACITY OF MICROINTERACTION TO REDUCE THE GAP AND INTERACTIVE ORIGINS OF NEW SELECTION PROCESSES

The participants in microinteraction (clients and members of service organizations) are confronted with two types of structural premises: (1) the results of sociopsychological selection during the transformation of perceived social problems into demands and claims, which function as latent or manifest barriers to learning and perception on the side of the individual clients and agents; and (2) the results of the legally, politically, organizationally, and professionally anchored processes of transforming needy persons into the well-defined role segments of applicants, claimants, or recipients, which function as legitimate guidelines within the socially defined interaction frame. There is only one possible escape from the limits set up by these structural premises: in interaction processes, the participants have to explain and explore their respective definitions of the situation (cf. Goffman 1959; Berger and Luckmann 1966). Even legally fixed claims or organizationally prescribed patterns of need articulation have to be interpreted and adapted with a view to specific situations and persons (Silverman 1970). Therefore microinteraction as a process of constructing or reconstructing social reality (Berger and Luckmann 1966) may open some ways for clients and members of service organizations to adapt their respective expectations and need definitions (cf. Grunow 1978; Scherer, Scherer, and Kliuh 1978).

Microinteraction: the Complementarity of Structural Selectivity with Situational Selectivity

Every service organization that has to rely on clients as one important sector of its task environment must guarantee that the general rules of the work program can be applied to individual cases (clients) by individual staff members (Blau 1955). As not all staff members have regular or constant contacts with clients, these specifications of the work program with regard to the handling of clients' demands can be limited to the incumbents of boundary positions and roles (Kahn, Wolfe, and Quinn 1964; Evan 1966). Thus there can be found, within the general work program, a specific work program that implies formal rules and social norms for the application of the work program to individual claimants and for the establishment and arrangement of contacts with clients.

The differences between these two types of rules and role expectations result in different patterns of perceiving and defining clients' problems, needs, and demands. The boundary personnel tends to have more specific and concrete orientations toward clients' interests than the staff members in higher echelons of the organization (Janowitz and Delany 1957; Francis and Stone 1956) and sometimes the boundary personnel even tends to define clients' needs in opposition to the general work program and to the definitions of superiors (Kahn, Wolfe, and Quinn 1964; Wassermann 1971). One of the main problems of client-centered organizations consists in combining an adequate responsiveness to the specificities of individual cases with the prevention of coalitions between clients and boundary personnel, distorting parts of the general work program (Thompson 1962; Macaulay 1967; Nagi 1974; Bush and Gordon 1978; Pesso 1978).

Service organizations that have to deal with complex, variable, and dynamic demands on the part of their clients must leave open areas of discretion to the incumbents of boundary positions (Bucher and Stelling 1969; Ruzek 1973; Robin and Wagenfeld 1977; Strong and Davis 1977). Administrative agencies and institutions that deliver personal or technical services on the basis of complex technologies have to rely on the capacities of their staff to handle areas of discretion adequately. Even service organizations with a high proportion of professionalized staff members cannot work without granting discretion to the boundary personnel. In this connection, administratively predefined demands and interests have to be seen as open to situational redefinition and reinterpretation. Most of these redefinitions take place during interaction processes with clients. Thus, they can be influenced by clients during verbal or nonverbal communication (Gordon 1975; Freidson 1975).

Interaction processes not only induce redefinitions of administratively predefined interests or demands, they also may affect the expectations and felt needs that clients bring to the situation. On the one hand, the interaction process can induce perceptions, cognitions, and motives that make the client aware of needs hitherto only unconsciously suspected. On the other hand, communication with staff members can help the client to conceive interests more precisely—needs that he or she had been aware of before the contact without knowing that it would be legitimate to articulate them as demands. Thus, communication processes between functionaries and clients may induce steps of transforming needs into felt needs and felt needs into claims. At the same time, they may give rise to more precise notions of legitimate demands on the side of the client, diminishing feelings of uncertainty and leading to clearer perceptions of public agencies as instruments to satisfy certain types of felt needs. This type of perception and notion is called adequately defined clients' demand or adequate need orientation. The aforementioned implications of interaction processes—redefinitions of organizationally defined clients' interests and induction of transformation processes from needs to claims—hint at the potential of microinteraction in bridging the gap between service organizations and the public served. Nevertheless, there are several reasons to question the positive functions of microinteraction:

Interaction processes not only suspend organizational and personal selectivities, they also create new ones. Interpersonal communication complements structural selectivities with situational selection processes. Even if there are interaction patterns of "reconstructing social reality" (Berger and Luckmann 1966), both sides cannot completely suspend the hitherto developed need definitions and formal procedures of claim treatment. They only can accentuate or neglect certain aspects of them—that is, they can produce a situational selection and shifting of normative aspects. Thus, structural mechanisms of contingency reduction are substituted or complemented by situational mechanisms of selection referring to experiences and actions of client and staff (Grunow 1978). They are based on a conscious or unconscious agreement that there should be some premises underlying the form and content of discourse and bargaining (cf. Herbst 1961; Luhmann 1972; Kroeger 1975).

This need for premises leads to the emergence of interpersonal selection patterns with regard to the definition of felt needs, demands, and claims (Mennerick 1974). If this assumption is correct, the question arises as to which of the two parties is able and willing to develop and to enforce the needed situational patterns of selection (Rhodes 1978). From an analytical point of view it may be interesting to find out if there are interaction systems with a completely balanced distribution of personal influence or if all interaction systems are characterized by unequal chances of carrying through personal selectivity patterns. There are good reasons to assume that this is an academic question, because there is always a difference with regard to social positions and roles, producing different abilities and competences to enforce one's personal selection patterns. From a pragmatic point of view it is more interesting to ask whether and to what degree these interpersonal patterns of selectivity increase or diminish the responsiveness of different groups of staff to the interests and demands of different groups of clients (Kroeger 1975; Scherer and Scherer 1977; Scherer, Scherer, and Kliuli 1978; McCleary 1978).

The answer to the latter question depends on two sets of factors—(1) on variables originating in the properties of specific types of interaction systems and processes; and (2) on variables resulting from the properties of the persons interacting. To answer the question as to whether social interaction can bridge the gap between public service organizations and their public, typologies of interaction systems and of interacting staff members must be developed.

In doing this we have to leave the general notion of service delivery organization as well as that of functionaries and clients. Only a differentiation of bureaucratic and professional organizations with their respective selection rules and standards will point out under which circumstances the substitution of generalized structural selectivities by situational selection processes really increases responsiveness of clients' needs. The differentiation of bureaucratic and professional functionaries will show if there are any vocational differences between them with regard to interaction competence and if both of them use their interaction competence primarily in favor of the client or in order to pursue their own interests.

Some Empirical Findings Illustrating the Limited Capacity of Microinteraction to Bridge the Gap

Public welfare agencies in the FRG—and similarly in other countries (see Chapters 9 and 12)—provide payments in cash and in kind as well as personal services (Liebfried 1976). Within the local offices, there are two types of departments or divisions: one, offering payments, that is organized bureaucratically and primarily concerned with the collection and processing of reliable information on family income and commitments (i.e., means testing); the other, providing personal services, that is, or should be, organized professionally and primarily concerned with counseling and doing casework (i.e., social work). Besides this general division of work, there are, or should be, some similarities and interdependencies between the two types of divisions. The Cash Benefit Division (*Leistungsabteilung*) is legally charged with giving advice to clients and referring needy persons to social workers, the home help service, or the housing office. The Social Service Division (*Allgemeiner Sozialdienst*) is administratively charged with providing detailed information on the client's family income and life situation to the Cash Benefit Division and with referring needy persons to social security officials or other local authorities.

To discover the specific problems within the relationships between clients and the divisions of public welfare agencies as well as between the two types of divisions, an empirical investigation in nine cities was carried out (Grunow and Hegner 1978b, 1979; Hegner and Schmidt 1979). Four hundred twelve public assistance officials and 344 social workers were interviewed; 3339 face-to-face contacts between clients and officials or socialworkers were systematically observed; 1411 files on welfare recipients were analyzed. The following observations are based on the data from this study.

About 79 percent of the officials and 84 percent of the socialworkers agree that the way services are transmitted to the public in contact is as important as the quantity and quality of payments and services. Only 17 percent of the officials and 9 percent of the socialworkers think that the way of transmitting payments and services is less important than their quantity and quality. When asked to select from a catalogue of thirteen measures those measures that are deemed to be most important for adequate satisfaction of clients' needs, officials and socialworkers primarily point to the following items: "there should be single rooms for contacts with clients"; "with a view to the selection and assignment of staff there should be better tests for skills in interacting with clients"; "the caseload should be reduced for officials and socialworkers."

This selection of interview answers—a lot of other items also point in this direction—makes clear that aspects of microinteraction are judged to be of great value for the responsiveness of service delivery organizations to clients' needs. At the same time, officials and socialworkers agree that microinteraction cannot work as a panacea. Forty-one percent of the caseworkers and 30 percent of the officials think that more than 10 percent of the public in contact do not receive all the payments and services provided for by law; only 6 percent of the socialworkers and 10 percent of the officials consider the proportion of the nonbeneficiaries to be smaller than 1 percent of all the claimants.

Asked for the reasons for this underutilization, caseworkers as well as officials tend to blame the victim. Most of them (more than 70 percent in both groups) do not mention deficiencies on the side of the agencies at all, but primarily point to sociopychological barriers on the side of the clients (e.g., "general anxieties with regard to authorities"; "being afraid of asking for administrative help"; "being in fear of getting stigmatized as a welfare recipient"). Less than 10 percent of the staff admit that "unfriendly and curt officials or socialworkers" or "lack of time on the side of the personnel" may also constitute sociopsychological barriers to the use of services.

Ninety-two percent of the officials and 64 percent of the socialworkers declare themselves competent to give advice to people who have become destitute or are in trouble. And more than 90 percent of both groups declare themselves willing to reveal further possibilities of getting benefits to clients who are unaware of them. Our systematic observation data show a clear-cut discrepancy between words and deeds—only in 17 percent of the observed contacts in the Cash Benefit Divisions did the officials point to further payments or services that had not yet been claimed by the clients. In the Social

Services Divisions—during office hours and home visits—only 38 percent of the observed interactions comprised special advice given by the socialworker with respect to benefits that had not yet been claimed by the client. Thus we can conclude that microinteraction processes do not necessarily help the clients to become conscious of needs or to transform felt needs into claims.

What are the reasons for these deficiencies? One answer could be actual lack of time on the side of the staff. This answer is favored by the staff. In contrast to this, our observation data reveal that there is neither permanent lack of time nor constant stress: officials as well as socialworkers are very rarely confronted with a queue during their office hours. A second answer could be inadequate offices and equipment. This fact is not only mentioned by the staff, but is also revealed by our observation data: when there is no single room for the contact with clients, the interaction climate is less favorable, the willingness of the staff to take positive measures is articulated less, and the length of conversation is shorter.

A third answer could be lack of interaction competence on the side of the clients. This answer is partly wrong: more than three-quarters of the contacts in the Cash Benefit Division are characterized by the observer as friendly and businesslike. This interpretation is clearly confirmed by the interview data. At the same time, this answer is partly right: 4 percent of the clients (observed) are not able to articulate their interests or claims in a way that could be understood by the observer (probably neither by the official), and 34 percent of the applicants give an unclear, long-winded, or fussy description of their problems and needs. The observation data show that claimants with a clear and precise description of interests and problems more often succeed in getting the help needed and in getting further advice with respect to benefits.

A fourth set of factors explaining the limited capacity of microinteraction to bridge the gap could be, and is, lack of interaction flexibility on the side of the staff as produced by the coincidence of structural and situational selectivity. This answer is confirmed by interview data and observation findings.

The officials in the Cash Benefit Departments mainly transmit money payments (means of subsistence), a benefit that is granted or refused on the basis of a highly standardized procedure of an income or means test. In less than 10 percent of the contacts are benefits in kind for specific life situations provided, a service that is granted or refused on social and/or medical grounds, substantiated or proved by records of socialworkers or physicians. The officials admit that they prefer clients who apply for money payments, submit clearly ordered documents, and give short and precise answers to the questions put. The officials also admit that they vary in the interpretation and use of their many discretionary powers, being generous toward clients who combine an open and precise presentation of their problems with a friendly and modest application for help. Our observation data confirm that clients with the following properties do have an outstanding chance of getting the benefits requested—being not too old and not too young (between twenty and forty years old); being already known to the official (having a file with documents on former means tests); being able to answer the questions of the official adequately; being clever in actively seeking help without being too demanding or even aggressive; and finally, not having too many problems or interests that do not easily fit the normal procedures of decisionmaking. In those cases, microinteraction processes tend to increase the responsiveness of service delivery to clients' interests (and, sometimes, even needs).

The socialworkers in the Social Service Divisions do not differ at all sharply from their colleagues in the Cash Benefit Divisions: they are distinct with respect to their words and beliefs, but not with regard to their deeds and behavior patterns. Although the great majority of the socialworkers (65 percent pretend to realize the professional goal of helping the client by giving advice, doing casework, and supporting applications for payments) in 60 percent of the interactions observed no concrete references to benefits or services not yet used were given. Twenty-eight percent of the interactions with clients were without any observable results; in 23 percent of the cases specific effects of the advice given can be observed, and in 5 percent of the cases the socialworker gives information on concrete results of former activities. Although 54 percent of the socialworkers declare that "comprehensive consideration of the clients' problems" and "openness to learning processes during contacts with clients" are the most important personality traits for people in the Social Service Division, the interaction behavior clearly reveals tendencies opposing this view: in 56 percent of the home visits the socialworkers predominantly make enquiries about the economic and social situation of the client; only in 12 percent of the home visits there are no investigations at all. In not more than 3 percent of the home visits, the client determines the interaction process by actively seeking help and advice; only in 20 percent of the cases is the client given more than one-fifth of the conversation time for a broad description of his or her experiences and problems. All things considered, the socialworkers have to be seen as the dominant and dominating partner in the interaction, whereas the client is reduced to the role of a more or less passive listener.

Therefore, the responsiveness of socialworkers to clients' needs seems to be dependent on the ability of the professional to identify those needs without listening to the client and without helping the client to transform his needs into demands. Undoubtedly, this one-sided interaction pattern is predefined by professional standards and by the fact that the socialworkers have been, and are, obliged to take part in the collection and processing of information on family income and commitments.

There are some remarkable differences of interaction patterns with clients between Cash Benefit and Social Service Departments. Whereas officials dominate interaction with clients by putting questions, socialworkers play the dominant role by combining questions with the monologue-like transmission of information (and very rarely with the transmission of emotional support and advisory dialogue).

In both divisions of public welfare agencies microinteraction can reduce the gap between service organizations and the public served if the clients are able and willing to adapt to the work program, the role expectations, and the professional standards defined within the organization. That is, responsiveness of public services to clients' needs presupposes responsiveness of clients to the public services' interests. This pattern is not suspended, but is confirmed by microinteraction.

PART IV

Emerging Developments in Social Service Delivery Systems

The contributions in Parts II and III have tried to show that there are still great possibilities for increasing the responsiveness of social service agencies. Both new and/or old methods are sought through changes in organizational structure, interorganizational coordination, or staff-client interaction. However promising these advances seem to be, they cannot obscure the fact that there are inherent limits of responsiveness in bureaucratic and professional social service delivery. Too often the possibilities have been exaggerated and the limitations of different social service provisions have been ignored. For the future we both expect and propose much more of an evaluative comparison between different strategies of service provision—for example, individual self-help, collective self-help, professional services, bureaucratic service provisions, and services offered by market economy. For each of these service strategies there should be a particular description and prognosis of the possibilities and limitations. Thus, an optimal social service delivery system will not be an extension of one strategy for all problems and client groups, but a thorough and differentiated combination of all of the strategies at hand. This flexible approach toward a design of service delivery systems—if any—should be adequate for a reduction of the well-known contraproductivity of many services provided nowadays.

The following three chapters try to point out some of the emerging trends in social service delivery and its scientific evaluation. Adrian Sinfield's study starts with a diagnosis of the failure of many important social programs. He asks whether adequate goals have yet been declared. Did the clients—or other people, or even the administrators—define the needs the social programs had to deal with? And in the same context, are the criteria of evaluation of services those that relate to need fulfillment of the clients—or just to the operation standards of the service delivery agencies? He argues that there is a need to observe and describe clients' need definitions as a continously changing process—not just as a standardized catalogue that seems to be dealt with quite effectively by formal or bureaucratic organizations. Thus, the author proposes to "let the client speak"—which implies that all persons engaged in social service delivery should "break down the predemocratic distinction between 'we the people—especially the planners, the providers and the experts' and 'they the recipients of the service.' "

Noel Timms's chapter starts with a critique of the traditional concepts of bureaucracy and profession hierarchy and team work and tries to explain why these concepts do not adequately describe working relationships and work processes in social service delivery. The main focus of illustration is the cooperation between social-workers and their seniors. The chapter concludes with some suggestions concerning the relationship between social development, social policy, and social work. This demands new and broader ways of theorizing as well as a closer connection with recent societal developments: "If welfare theory were developed and connected to social service activity, all the personnel concerned with the delivery of social service would find a means of understanding, improving, and justifying their activities."

One of the emerging aspects of social service provision is discussed in Bernhard Badura's study. He describes the rediscovery of the coproduction function of primary social networks in all kinds of service delivery systems. Individual and collective self-help is not just an additional productive factor, but in many cases an alternative to professional and bureaucratic service strategies. This does not mean, though, that the self-help movement is a step back into "the good old days"; it has to be seen as a new development that is a reaction to institutionalized service provisions as well as a new stage based on existing service delivery systems. "Only if we seek the causes of those social problems at least partly in the structure of sociopolitical regulations and institutions itself will the readiness to experiment with alternatives grow."

From this short overview of the following contributions it is quite clear that they point to just a few aspects of emerging trends in social service delivery systems. But even these selective arguments point out quite clearly the necessity of searching for a new theoretical and methodological approach to social service research. This topic will be taken up in chapter 14.

Chapter 11

Meeting Client Need: An Ambiguous and Precarious Value

*Adrian Sinfield**

INTRODUCTION

Administrators and planners in the social services tend to take it for granted in any account of their work that programs are created to meet need. The more able and imaginative among them and the energetic legislator and politician will wish to take initiatives in innovating and introducing new responses to a newly recognized or poorly met client need. In Britain less than fifteen years ago innovation in the social services was a much more certain and much less heavily loaded idea than today. In the first decade or so after the start of what is described as "the welfare state," those engaged in such innovation had a generally progressive and liberal image, concerned with measures that would help the reduction of inequalities and poverty as part of the incremental creation of a welfare society.
By the 1970s many people in Britain have become much more skeptical of that picture, and this includes many engaged in developing or assessing new schemes to ensure a better response to the needs of the client. Innovation has been devalued as a term—many would say debased. It is the short-term and deliberately limited expedient

*Department of Sociology, University of Essex, Great Britain

that is directed primarily to removing the demand, rather than the need, for radical reform. It is seen by program recipients or at least their pressure groups as an administrator's or political minister's word to camouflage cheap, hastily conceived, and temporary patching-up-innovation as the alternative to change that will meet need more fully and effectively. And this reaction is even more evident in the United States.

Why has this happened and what can be done? Obviously the answer is related to the lack of any evident success in very many of the best known innovations of recent years in terms of their own widely publicized goals or even more modest objectives. Perhaps the most celebrated, or notorious, is the American War on Poverty, which has been attacked as a betrayal of the poor, as political maneuvering for the vote of the inner-city black, or, quite simply, a cruel hoax (Rose, 1972; Piven, 1970; Higgins 1978). Certainly that war, when it was not diverted into skirmishes against the poor, ended in an early retreat before any significant triumphs had been scored.

But that campaign was by no means the only one to miss its target. In this chapter I want to indicate briefly some of the main reasons for the bad reputation of social policy innovations—and I am using this term widely, as we did at the seminar, and not in a very specific sense, contrasted for example to reform (e.g., Hall et al. 1975). Then I will examine the significance of external factors and the importance of the analysis of client need. In particular I want to outline the ways in which meeting client need is precarious in the original sense of the word—insecure and uncertain—in that it is dependent upon the willingness of others (see the thought-provoking analysis of "precarious values" by Clark [1956]). The vulnerability of the idea in action is increased by the considerable ambiguity that creeps into much policy-oriented discussion of client need.

Disillusionment and resistance are fostered by the many major policy changes that have turned out to be little more than substitutes for change. Murray Edelman has written of *The Symbolic Use of Politics* (1964), when the simple public visibility of programs reassures society that groups are being helped, however unsuccessful the schemes may be. The very existence of policy change can be dangerously lulling, not only for the general public, but for pressure groups who may themselves lose some impetus to push for more effective change or at least find wider support and sympathy disappearing—a point brought out in the title of Edelman's latest book, *Political Language: Words that Succeed and Policies that Fail* (1977). Many innovations might still have a better reputation if they had promised to achieve less at the outset, but the need to obtain support for any policy change from the appropriate power groups or relevant vested interests creates its own problems. Potential gains are magnified far beyond the possibility of the scheme at its most successful. Rising expectations and demands that can never be met are generated among the recipients or the funders; or limited resources are eventually spread too widely to obtain the necessary political support, so that what might have achieved something in a few districts disappears with little trace over many more. Alternatively, certain groups may feel so threatened that the proposal has its teeth drawn before it is put into effect; but such changes are often not publicized by either the losers or the victors, with the result that client or popular expectations are even more likely to be frustrated.

All or any of these problems may be exacerbated by the fact that the full extent, nature, or complexity of unmet needs is often not discovered until the new program begins. Unless further funds and initiatives are made available, the gap between professed intention and actual achievement is even greater and adds weight to the view of innovation as a cynical manipulation of the people. Finally, quite apart from any inherent flaws, many innovations fail in their original aims because they are quickly adapted for other purposes, if they are not abandoned.

HISTORICAL RECONSIDERATIONS: REACTIONS TO FRUSTRATING EXPERIENCES

The vulnerability of innovations to events outside the control of the innovators emerges clearly in this brief listing of the problems that tend to beset them. The ways in which the wider society may heavily influence outcome can be seen in an admittedly very simplified comparison of three attempts at policy change. The innovations of the British welfare state in the second half of the 1940s had considerable political, ideological, and popular momentum, even if discussion was fairly limited and diffuse. Although this was a period of economic austerity, there was at least some acceptance of, if not willingness for, increased public spending on social services. This may have been helped by the prevalent assumption that there was a finite level of need: once services had been brought up to a certain standard to maintain the reduction of basic inequalities, their expansion would cease and expenditure diminish.

The wider societal context was particularly important in terms of the pervasive influence of the British class structure, a significant determinant of outcome, irrespective of what was planned or at least intended. In retrospect we see that the welfare state was in many ways built more securely for the middle class and the securer of the working class than the very poor—in part a function of the social distance between the planners and those intended to benefit, in part a reflection of the ability of these groups to take better advantage of the services available. However valid these diagnoses, the basic point is that there is very little evidence of any attempt to take the nature of the class structure and its likely impact on planning into account at the time.

In many respects the ill-related motley of programs that were eventually packaged as the U.S. War on Poverty provides the model of innovation to meet client need that would best fit Burton Clark's (1956) analysis of precariousness—in particular, goals were impressive but vague or ambiguous, and means were often poorly related to the ends or inappropriately designed, especially taking account of the resources available. The War on Poverty may have collapsed because of a particular dependence on events and factors over which the innovators themselves had little or no control, but the poorness of its planning made it all the more vulnerable to the external pressures.

The limited attempts at change and innovation in the social services in Britain over the last ten years contrast sharply with both the previous examples. Innovation has been sought under the pressure of specific Treasury instructions to cut spending and the imposition of cash limits on annual budgets with no guarantee of adjustment for inflation. Although the exact extent to which expenditure has been actually cut rather than checked and reallocated among spending departments and within them is still being debated, the economic constraints have been explicit and dominant.

In all three instances there was a major failure to assess what was needed over time—in terms of economic resources, staffing, training, legislative development, and so forth—to ensure that any change made was maintained and developed in the required direction. The basic reason for this omission in the first two can probably be found in assumptions about the current structure of the society that encouraged simplistic explanations of the causes of poverty: optimism was sufficiently pervasive that any long-term planning was generally regarded as unnecessary. The British postwar legislation was believed to have brought about the structural changes that, allied with Keynesian economics, would ensure that we never again experienced the poverty, inequalities, and depression of the interwar years. The protagonists of the War on Poverty, by contrast, tended to see the measures as a nonstructural change, a one-time adjustment that enabled the underprivileged, especially poor blacks, to participate equally in a market society that was generally believed to be working fairly adequately (Marris and Rein 1974). In Britain in 1976-1977 the need to cut, or at least control, public spending at once was dominated by immediate economic priorities. In many places this destroyed or made a nonsense of previous planning. Most of the cutbacks in service were made by single departments concerned with their own cash limits on spending and apparently unaware of, or even indifferent to, costs created for public expenditure elsewhere, let alone costs borne privately by previous or would-be clients.

Finally, these three periods illustrate the importance of those involved in putting the changes into effect in determining the outcome of any intended policy innovations—and once again show how this activity is linked to the wider society. The bulk of the staff implementing the new National Assistance Act of 1948, for example, had learned their job and practiced under the more restrictive measures of the old Poor Law, which the new scheme was intended to supercede. The planning failed to take account of this and ensure that the spirit of the new act was explicitly incorporated into the regulations, the internal codes of practice, and the training to encourage the change of old well-sanctioned routines and values that remained supported "outside" in the society by views about the "deserving" and "undeserving" poor (a good example of Clark's thesis [1956]).

These examples have been extremely simplified for the purposes of comparison, although I hope not distorted. They were chosen to bring out the importance of the external setting, and it is useful to consider the two main reactions to frustration that have tended to emerge. One, current for many years, is to explain failures to reach the original client group of poor or disadvantaged in terms of Robert Merton's "unintended consequences" that happen to overtake a program. On many occasions, "unconsidered consequences" might be a more appropriate expression, indicating that the problems derive from the planners' failing to anticipate as much as the world suddenly and inexplicably failing to stand still. Indeed, with the benefit of hindsight, the paralyzing external forces have often appeared only too predictable, encouraging further skepticism and mistrust of those engaged in any innovation.

The other reaction—more recent, and in many ways a product of the recognition of the inadequacies of the welfare state, the War on Poverty, or the economic miracle of postwar Germany in creating significant change in capitalist societies—has been a more critical view of the role of the state. Presumptions of it as a neutral arbitrator between the underprivileged and the protected or powerful or as a

Robin Hood redistributing from the rich to the poor were seen to be the unquestioned inheritance of a period of relative political consensus, with its acceptance of a notion of effective pluralistic democracy. It has been argued that the state is part of the means by which the ruling classes maintain their position and that it plays a vital part in presenting, and bringing the rest of society to accept, these vested interests as "the public interest" (Cockburn 1977; NCDP 1977; and more generally, Miliband 1973). The argument has varied in its dependence on Marx's critiques of the bourgeois state and in the degree to which the process effectively excludes any form of innovation that might help the weaker groups without that becoming a further device of "regulating the poor" (Piven and Cloward 1972). But generally in the field of social policy and administration, a more searching appraisal of government intervention has been long overdue.

The language of welfare is no more a guarantee of benevolence to the weaker than any other rhetoric: as Titmuss has emphasized, "Welfare can serve different masters. A multitude of sins may be committed in its appealing name" (Titmuss 1965). In Britain the failures of the 1964–1970 Labour government to initiate significant reforms with a major reduction in poverty and inequality (Townsend and Bosanquet 1972) were followed by a Conservative government that introduced measures that often actively encouraged the widening of inequality and enacted schemes that in many ways trapped the poor in poverty even when they marginally eased their position (Townsend 1975). Planning, it is now better recognized, is neither a neutral, technical device nor, as many on the left seemed to believe, a natural ally of egalitarian engineering (Goldthorpe 1962). The control of market forces may take many forms with very different redistributive effects (Miller 1975). The redistribution of welfare can be upwards or sideways over a lifetime: it is by no means inevitably downwards.

In consequence, there is a tendency to see all innovations as doomed to reinforce or widen the inequalities of a capitalist society, and this view has been especially evident among many of the very people in Britain and the United States who only a few years ago would have provided the necessary determined and committed support to help the creation and development of innovation. Blaming the state in many forms and at many levels has become part of the politics of despair that in my view runs the great risk of establishing new deterministic sterotypes of change to replace previous ones; and would-be innovators and their supporters are seen as exploiters of the clients or, at best, well-meaning dupes of the system. This, I believe, overstates the degree to which change is determined by the economic and social structure of society and—admittedly at a very different level—understates the extent to which poor analysis and planning have handicapped innovations from the very start, especially in relation to the understanding of need, and outside government as well as within.

WHO IS THE CLIENT AND WHOSE ARE THE NEEDS?

The following section discusses ambiguities in the idea of innovating to meet client need because failure to allow for these and take them into account has contributed to the precariousness of many attempted changes. The analysis of need is not an "academic" exercise in the pejorative sense of that word, but an activity crucially linked to the formulation of policy goals; and so it is a vital part of any innovation to meet need. The ambiguities of assumptions about client need can be summarized baldly: to state the obvious but often neglected fact that there are many possible clients, many needs, and many different ways of meeting them.

Very often the client as the immediate recipient of the public service—the homeless, the disabled, or the unemployed person or family—becomes subordinated to the demands of other clients, in the sense of other potential, often unintended, beneficiaries of a service. These may include staff of the agency providing the service, the local government committees responsible for the service, and the local or central government bureaucracy. One or other of these may be seen as the contractual clients who approve or disapprove of present patterns of recognizing needs—and so increase or restrict resources and encourage innovation in some areas on some issues while resisting it elsewhere. The funders at local or central government level—especially the Treasury, who are more prepared to release resources for some programs than others whatever the requests made to them—may be among the less visible but more powerful controlling clients.

The client may be "the community"—a concept heavily overladen with ambiguity and fertile with moral and social connotations. Community workers may see a neighborhood of poor or underprivileged people as a generally united body to be defended and helped against the wider society; as an area that must learn to marshal its own resources and help itself; or as a district beset with problems including the divisions and conflicts of racial or religious differences. But, oversimplifying still, the community as client may be the local or national establishment, the representative of "the silent majority" through the press, television, or radio—in short, any of those indistinct but influential entities conjured up by such statements as "society demands action" when child abuse is revealed or an old woman is found, days after her death, in an isolated flat, neglected by neighbors and unknown to public or private agencies. On many occasions concern may be more control than welfare oriented in that there is more a demand that something needs to be done *to* "this type of parent," "juvenile delinquent," or "football hooligan" than *for* these people.

Needs may be infinite but, given even the mildest constraints on public policy of limited resources of money, staff, and time, there are a limited number of needs that can be newly or more fully met at any one time. There is likely to be a greater willingness to meet some needs for some groups than others. A new response that will save public resources, meet a government-defined urgent need, or recognize needs expressed by politically significant groups—those with "economic resisting power," to use Richard Tawney's (1913) phrase—seems likely to be given priority over the implementation of costly programs for the low status minority groups with low political support or salience who tend to be most dependent upon public services.

WHO DEFINES THE NEED?

That services should meet clients' needs is a belief deeply embedded in the professional ethic of personal service professions and in the traditions of public administration. In consequence, the conflicts, values, and controversies that obstruct the pursuit of such a goal often remain overlooked. Yet who defines the need has major implications for any service and any group or category of clients. I would suggest that there are at least these sources of definition of need—the client; the profession (and there any many of them); the service employer, including the various agencies and different levels of government; the wider establishment; or what can be subsumed under terms as vague as "the community" or "society at large." On most occasions the client, the receiver of the service, seems to be seen via professional, administrative, or political interpretation—often a combination of all three.

The "Indoor" Perception of Client and Need

"Indoor relief" was the term used to describe the support provided under the English Poor Law when the pauper and any dependents had to leave home and go to live inside the poorhouse or workhouse. Relief given to those who remained in their own homes while receiving financial aid was described as "outdoor." This thoroughly administrative-based perception of clients and their needs can still be found in both the organization and assessment of many innovations. Even now, remarkably little priority has been given to identifying and understanding the "normal" range of patterns of living and of the interchange of services inside and outside the family and how the existing distribution of public services fit or fail to fit the day-to-day pattern of people's lives. And not very much of what we do know seems to inform the design and evaluation of policies in the public social services, so great is the social distance between policymaker and service recipient in many programs, especially those that cater almost exclusively for the poor. People with difficulties they have been unable to resolve tend to be classified by the existing program category that the official or professional judges to approximate most closely his or her perception of their need. Often clients may carry out this translation themselves and so help to obscure the actual problems they have and the causes of their need. In this way the potential client as well as the staff helps to reinforce existing stereotypes of both need and service. Among the many examples, one can cite the number of old people who finish their lives in large institutions for the aged. They did not need attendants to look after them, and with sufficient resources or the right support in the community they could have managed by themselves—but in many districts a place in the old people's home was all that was available (Townsend 1962). Their needs were not so much consciously redefined as simply recognized in terms of what was seen as available.

Which needs are to be met is clearly conceptually distinct from how they are to be met: in practice, as the example of old people's homes shows, they interact upon each other, with the available means influencing the definition of need and program goals at general policy level as well as in its day-to-day implementation. We can reach the stage where unmet needs are discussed only in terms of existing services that embody definitions of need that may be long out of date, reflect more limited recognition of the extent of need, or embody a different understanding of the causes of dependence—particularly the degree to which clients are judged responsible for their plight

Evaluation by Whose Criteria of Need?

The ways in which the other clients' interests can come to dominate and moderate the meeting of the immediate clients' needs are equally evident when it comes to evaluating the success of any innovation. The criteria employed in any assessment are central to the evaluation. But in this apparently noncontroversial sentence lie quite basic problems, besetting both the innovation and its evaluation, which underline the importance of establishing clearly and explicitly "whose needs" and "who are the clients."

On many occasions there appears to be tunnel vision and/or a remarkable naivety on the part of administrators and evaluators about the criteria to be used. A new program is successful if the client does not go back to prison, does not reapply for income support, or does not get into arrears with the rent again. No further questions are asked about any significant improvement in the individual or family fortunes or experiences. What has happened, for example, after intensive official interviews of the client who is suspected of becoming too accustomed to state support and too little interested in finding work? Does such a client find a job when he or she ceases to claim benefit, and is the family income raised by it? Or has the spouse taken on part-time work but for a lower total family income? Is the client now in some institution, either mental hospital or prison?

There has often been little interest in these wider or client-centered criteria, and success has simply been measured by the drop in number of claimants or referrals or the reduction in the particular item of expenditure or the length of an official waiting list. The assessment by visible diminution of problems to officials or significant others (the press, politicians, police, etc.) can all too easily come to dominate where evident client-based criteria have not been publicly established. Later it may become evident that not only has the official success of one program change led to an increase in public expenditure elsewhere, but that it has also meant a deterioration in clients' lives. Meanwhile the other clients—the controllers, the politicians, or the wider community as taxpayers—are satisfied by the innovation because a politically volatile issue has been solved, removed, or at least defused.

The other type of problem is when the data used for monitoring progress bear little relation to the likely outcome, and so innovation becomes condemned to failure. The overall criteria used in the U.S. War on Poverty were the changes in the annual statistics of the percentage of the population, or of specific groups, below the officially defined poverty line. Yet most of its specific innovations were directed at changing people's behavior—by education or training, by preeducation or pretraining, and by community action neighborhood programs. Few of the programs would have raised people's income quickly even if they had been very successful. To avoid this dilemma and ensure further funding, there was a tendency for administrators to produce individual success stories, very often achieved by careful creaming of applicants in order to select those most easily trainable or educable. The result was a subversion of the original published aims to help the most disadvantaged and handicapped (Miller, Roby, and de vosvan Steenwijk 1970).

Let the Client Speak

Who assesses an innovation for whom and by what criteria provides a democratic challenge that so far seems to have received little attention beyond the generally abortive "maximum feasible participation" of the poor in some of the U.S. poverty programs of the 1960s. Of course some clients do succeed in having their views recognized by the providers and the controllers: education is one obvious instance where generally middle class, and often professional, parents have led to changes on practice and official policy, and other groups have had some success too. But these are more often the exceptions than the rule: medical care is a good example where even the most articulate class equal of the professional has been unable to influence the powerful professional-administrative complex much beyond changing appointment procedures and often not even that.

Not surprisingly, therefore, one solution that many see as cutting through these difficulties is to let the clients declare their own needs. Closer involvement and participation of clients may help to reduce, if not remove, the social distance between planner and planned, in which the detached language of "officialese" or, as insidiously, "professionalese," may flourish. But any real shift of power to the service recipient is notoriously hard to obtain. Far from steadily ascending what Sherry Arnstein (1969) has described as the "ladder of citizen participation," poor clients are likely to be submerged, taken over, or cooled out. For the rare exception to this, when some more militant black groups "mau-maued the flak-catchers," see Tom Wolfe's dramatic account, summarized in Higgins (1978).

In societies marked by differences of class, religion, or race that tend to separate planners and providers from the public service clients in greatest need, the sharing of power by the dominant groups is not likely to come about easily. When the traditions of liberal paternalism are so strongly embedded, "everything is viewed. . . through administrative spectacles—benevolently, no doubt, but always from the outside, at second hand. Only those who supply the various services, never those for whose benefit they are supplied, are fit to judge their quality. Be quiet, dear, Daddy knows best" (Wootton 1959). Where this administrative prerogative has been most seriously challenged, it has mostly been by the professions, including the various groups within the social sciences whom history may show to be among the greatest beneficiaries and clients of the welfare state. They have come to claim a right to speak with authority on the needs of clients, often in ways that have kept them quiet and inferior, and virtually disfranchised them from the political debate of whose needs are met and how.

In consequence, many external critics of government, as much as officials and professionals within, have tended to overlook the importance of letting the immediate client in. Many of us engaged in social policy debates have failed, in establishing our own legitimacy and validity as another group of experts deserving to be consulted and heeded, to recognize that we have often succeeded in removing the client-recipient one stage further away. This point made, however, involving the immediate client directly is itself no simple idea with precisely deducible programs for action, however much of a welcome relief—and salutary shock—it may be to our persistent welfare colonialism, supported by its ever growing family of professional and other experts and counsellors. It can only become one part of a process that involves deciding which clients and which needs are met in what form with what resources.

IDENTIFICATION OF PRIORITIES AND THE CONTRIBUTION OF RESEARCH

Priorities have to be decided. They do not resolve themselves or "make themselves evident" as one civil servant—maybe wryly—remarked. But the acceptance of past trends (Heclo and Wildavsky 1974) can simply mean that existing or more powerful demands are accepted. The importance of the correct identification, definition, and measurement of needs and the pitfalls involved in achieving these steps cannot be overemphasized. There is great value in obtaining knowledge of the operation of a service from the perspective of the client.

One limited example of what can be achieved easily and quickly is provided by a small piece of research carried out by students in the city of Norwich a few years ago. They found that one-third of the old people who received two cooked meals per week from the meals on wheels service had no other cooked meals. Such a finding obviously raises questions for allocating priority and for devising at-risk criteria.

On a larger scale, an assessment from the perspective of old people themselves would start with the question of how well do they eat, what meals and what arrangements do they prefer—for example, the help or exchange of services among families, friends, and neighbors, including the cooking and preparation of meals and shopping for food and the problems or constraints created. The contribution of external services would be assessed not simply in terms of already existing provision such as meals on wheels, but of others such as cooking aids and facilities, including insulation of cooked food; the role of transport or help in shopping or getting to relatives, friends, municipal restaurants or day centers; the costs of basic foods and fuel needed for cooking; and so on.

One vivid but relatively neglected example of the relation between family life and public services was a study, undertaken some twenty years ago, of *Living With Mental Illness* (Mills 1962). This showed the wide gulf between professional staff and administrators and the families of those judged to be mentally ill. Any planning appeared little informed by the considerable strain imposed on families by the location of hospitals on the opposite side of London from the areas they were supposed to serve or by the problems of maintaining visits with in-patient relatives and establishing any form of real contact with staff. The value of this work can be greatly strengthened by the comparative approach that examines how people fare with similar needs but with differences in resources, status, or power. The deprivation and extent of need of elderly people in some ex-workhouses were brought out all the more starkly when they were compared with others retired and living in small private "homes" (Townsend 1962).

The comparative analysis of the lives of old people in Denmark, the United States, and Britain shows the value of setting the assumptions of need in one industrial society against others' and encourages the questioning of established means of meeting need (Shanas et al. 1968). Even within one country, much could be gained from repeating *Living with Mental Illness* on a broader, more comparative basis, examining how those in different areas and of different class, age, or sex cope with mental illness when it affects them or their families. These analyses help to reveal what Richard Titmuss (1958) identified as "the social division of welfare," where distinct systems of welfare separate from the public services may operate privately or through the occupational structure, often aided by fiscal concessions from the state. The neglect of these systems by public planners may foster the provision of public services that are separate and unequal for those excluded from these other benefits and services. Public services may become second class at best, labeling and stigmatizing the recipient. In consequence they may fall short of the basic requirement that Florence Nightingale set for the hospital—"that it should do the sick no harm" (quoted in Titmuss 1958; for recent discussion of the three systems of welfare, see Sinfield 1978).

More and better research can be of very limited value alone, but the part it can play has in my view been both oversold and overdismissed. In particular much too little regard has been paid to the ways that research may help us to a fuller understanding of needs and to a greater questioning of judgements "too much in terms of objectives already defined than of those which have yet to be defined, too much in terms of needs already recognized, subjectively and socially, than of those which have still to be recognized" (Townsend 1975, 1970). The stranglehold on the planning imagination of what is already there is part of the neglected study of the social construction of need. We have to analyze the role of past pressure groups, already established administrative agencies, professionals, and other vested interests that have come to determine not only how we recognize and meet needs, but also the very language that we use to discuss the subject, thus imprisoning ourselves in yesterday's innovations.

The resistance to innovation created by the perpetuation of old forms of recognizing certain needs for certain limited groups goes deeper than has often been realized. "Chronic social problems, recurring beliefs about them and recurring language forms that justify their acceptance reinforce each other. Only rarely can there be direct observations of events, and even then language forms shape that meaning of what the general public and government officials see" (Edelman 1977). This emphasizes the importance of those that influence the perception of needs, the ways they can be met, and the very words we use to discuss these issues. The professionals' part in this is an important one where, for example, the demarcation disputes, often assumed to be an irrationality peculiar to strike-prone manual workers, exercise a significant effect on who determines needs. Doctors and lawyers are past masters in establishing their legitimacy over certain defined services and areas of territory.

Recently in Britain the term "needology" has been used in attacks on sociologists' use of the concept of need by those economists and others who have emphasized "that need can only be a useful concept if it is equated to a demand by governments or individuals for goods and services. So long as prices and quantities are omitted from estimations of 'need,' the concept can have neither theoretical nor empirical value, and it properly belongs not to the social sciences but to the vocabulary of political rhetoric" (Nevitt 1977: 125-6 particularly critical of Townsend 1975: ch. 14, or 1970: 7-22). This thesis overlooks the horizon-narrowing effects of speaking only of needs that are sufficiently recognized and formally established to have a market value, as well as giving little weight to the differences in values underlying the sociological and economic interpretations (see also Reddin 1970).

We need to take more account of Eliot Friedson's analysis of how professional dominance involves "a way of organising work" and so of working relationships in the social division of labor, as well as "an orientation toward work or a body of knowledge" (Friedson 1970a). Professional arguments over how to talk of client need therefore are part of the social construction of needs—and eventually of policy goals—that links the second part of this chapter with the first. Despite the hopes so prevalent in the 1960s, and still to be found today, the delineation of needs and policy goals cannot be a matter of technical expertise untainted by political and other values and concerns.

WHAT IS TO BE DONE?

The basic argument of this chapter has been that innovations in meeting client need have been precarious in that programs tended to be dominated, diverted, and often distorted by external and more powerful influences or events. The dependence of success on others not within the control of the innovators has been made yet more precarious by the uncertain and ambiguous nature of the concept of client need—which clients, which needs, in what way, and with what priority?

I have paid particular attention to the maintenance and reinforcement of what I have called the "indoor perception" of clients and their needs. However difficult their original establishment, past innovations may have become embodied as conventional wisdom in the very language we use and maintained not just by the existence of institutions and services but actively defended by their supporters, administrators, professionals, established pressure groups, and by a whole range of other bodies that have an interest in maintaining certain perceptions of needs and clients against competing claims. The lessons of earlier measures should help us to move toward more effective initiatives with a greater break from social administration as "the regulatory reproduction of the status quo" (Nizard 1975). Although wider societal constraints are likely to be the major blocks to successful innovation, the realization of need in the form of a service is intimately related to these developments and not a separate technical apolitical exercise in analysis and policy formulation. We must learn therefore to identify more clearly and precisely:

1. The nature and extent of needs to be met in terms that do not reproduce established patterns of service with their own earlier discoveries of need;
2. The clear formulation of goals related to these needs;
3. The structural constraints that threaten or limit the aims;
4. The range of possible strategies open to the planners;
5. The implications for recipients of meeting a need in one way rather then another; and
6. The establishment of relevant and public criteria for assessing the changes in practice as successful and the means by which these are to be measured and publicly reported.

In engaging in this work care must be taken to break down the predemocratic distinction between "we the people"—especially the planners, the providers and the experts—and "they the recipients of the service." New ways of assessing needs and innovations in the public social services must be developed—with the clients themselves and on client-based criteria—and, as I have argued above, the value of external and comparative analyses must not be neglected.

The needs to be met must be given priority in order to escape the force of a criticism made by an assistant secretary in the U.S. Department of Health, Education and Welfare: "Quite often. . . specialists are quick to exchange whatever expertise they normally have for alleged political expertise. They tell us what is feasible, but they do not tell us what we ought to be trying to do or how we ought to be trying to do it" (Carter 1968).

"Without vision the people perish and without continued restatement and redefinition of the vision we will have forgotten not only where we want to go but why we want to get there" (Reddin 1970). To avoid the vision becoming the substitute for the change or its redefinition leading to acquiescence in the fifth best, then the objectives must be stated and planned with a clear time perspective that indicates the allocation of resources over the length of time needed to establish the required program. There is no ineluctable logic that decrees that all change is totally determined by the establishment—admittedly a tempting reaction to the depressing history of many innovations simplistically conceived and launched in a spirit of apolitical and technical enthusiasm that often left potential beneficiaries more victimized and blamed for the program's failure (Ryan 1970). As Miller (1968) has insisted, we must ask "does the increment lead to pinpointing the issue and building further action, or does it lead to institutional structures which will block further action?" The challenge facing those who wish to contribute to social planning that leads to a more equal recognition and meeting of need is to learn from the experiences of the past, however limited or counterproductive they have been, and not to repeat them.

Chapter 12

The Social Worker and His Senior

*Noel Timms**

INTRODUCTION

In my contribution to problems of responsiveness of service organizations to clients' needs I shall argue that social services and social work have been insufficiently studied within the work or industrial context and thus cannot be adequately related to their outcome and impact on the client. I shall start my argument with the hypothesis that what happens in service delivery is heavily influenced by what happens within the organization and that within the organization relations between two particular levels in the staff hierarchy (basic socialworker and senior) are quite crucial.

This study therefore consists of a further statement of the significance of the subject, an indication of the main ways in which practitioners and academics have tried to understand it, and a criticism of the way in which the major concepts have been used to work on the problems. Finally, the chapter indicates briefly a possibly more fruitful approach to the problems revealed by a consideration of the relations between the socialworker and his or her senior. The study tries to encompass such empirical research as I know, but its main emphasis will be conceptual. The chapter should be seen as a preliminary

*University of Newcastle, Great Britain

study of some of the major concepts used to promote understanding of the relations between the socialworker and his or her immediate senior seen in the context of social work as work.

Significance of the Subject

Social work seen as work has not been systematically studied, but work problems currently emphasized clearly concern the senior grade socialworker directly, for they revolve around questions of staff morale and sense of direction and the adequacies of seniors in relation to supervision. So a relatively recent British article on the reality of work in an area team states that

> Four years after reorganisation of the social services, some of us are seriously wondering how long we can continue to provide a service to clients in the face of ever-increasing public demand for (and dissatisfaction with) social work help and services, at a time when persistent overwork and inadequate resources of all kinds, including manpower, are reflected in low morale, poor work satisfaction and high staff turnover. (Pickering 1975).

Jordan (1974) has sketched a similar picture, drawing on some of the concepts with which this chapter is concerned, of a social services department as "a large organisation. . . staffed by young, disaffected and relatively inexperienced workers under close administrative control of a large hierarchy of well-organised bureaucrats and confused, alienated, senior professionals bemoaning their lack of contact with clients."

Wasserman's small American study of new entrants to social work found that most "of the new workers viewed their supervisors as insecure and frightened people who were unsure of their authority and power, conforming, lacking courage, unwilling to take a stand on critical issues. . . and more sensitized and attuned to organizational demands and needs than to those of their clients" (Wasserman 1971). Part, at least, of the reason for such a picture may be found in the relatively speedy promotion to the status of senior or supervisor in both Britain and America. Kadushin (1974), in one of the very few empirical studies of supervision, reports on a study that found "that many professionally trained workers assumed positions as administrators, supervisors, or consultants within two years of graduation." It is also worth noting what this promotion entails: "the promotion of the M.S.W. social worker from practitioner to supervisor often involves a move from a private to a public agency; from a smaller to a larger agency; and from a psychiatric-mental health, medical, or school social work setting to a public assistance or child welfare setting."

Second, the relationship of senior to basic grade socialworker raises questions about the nature of social work practice—Is it or can it become autonomous; can professional social work survive in a large state bureaucracy; and so on? If it is true that (to accept at face value for the moment some recent formulations) socialworkers carry three roles—as helper, as member of an organization, and as bureaucrat—or if it is the case that the professional socialworker in a public welfare bureaucracy serves two masters—the professional self and the employing organization—then the relationship between socialworker and supervisor becomes of crucial importance. The supervisor is another socialworker to whom the socialworker is accountable and is, therefore, the socialworker's main link with the organization. (As we shall see, it is not always clear quite how the socialworker relates to the senior nor how the senior relates to the organization.)

Third, it is becoming increasingly apparent that one of the key factors in the implementation of social policy (and in its change) is the person who actually provides (or refuses to provide) social service. Such a person does not, however, act alone. Donnison (1975) in a study of small-scale innovation in the social services drew attention to three essential participants: "the providers of the service, those who controlled the resources they needed for the job, and their customers." The socialworker's senior assumes importance in this context for several reasons. The senior may control certain resources and certainly can exert influence over the ways in which they are distributed. It is also worth entertaining the hypothesis that certain features of the relations between seniors and their socialworkers influence the socialworker's work with his or her clients. I mean by this not simply that the senior can make certain decisions (in whatever style of decisionmaking) that affect the client directly. I refer also to the effect of one set of superior-subordinate relationships on another. In brief, how the socialworker "belongs" to the organization may affect the client's mode of "belonging" (as well as the senior's). It is not without significance that the concept "member" is one of the least developed notions in social work literature, though there are signs of a convergence on this and associated ideas. Marxists and other radicals are now arguing that the social services should belong to those they serve, while writers such as Talcott Parsons see membership as a special feature of service organizations (Parsons 1970a). His first approach to such organizations was to see them operating in a market for professional services in a fee-for-service context, but later he found that a more fruitful approach was to treat the service agency and those who receive service as fellow members of a collectivity.

Previous Treatments

It is difficult to differentiate between previous treatments of the subject of social work as work (and such is the background against which the particular set of relationships of senior and basic grade socialworker can most usefully be seen). However, for present purposes four broad strands of interest may be identified: (1) work based on the concept of professional supervision; (2) studies, often but not invariably of an exhortatory kind, using the concepts of bureaucracy, professionalism and, to a lesser extent, the team; (3) studies of an empirical nature or of an impressionistic-qualitative kind into the work socialworkers actually do; and (4) most recently, the radical emphasis on the socialworker as worker belonging to a trade union, using a nonrestrictive notion of his or her occupation, working in what *Case Con* (a radical social work journal) would describe as Seebohm factories, and seeking political alliance and solidarity with all the other workers there employed. The last two approaches will not be discussed further. Good examples of empirical work that takes problems of measurement with appropriate seriousness can be found in Goldberg, Mortimer, and Williams (1970). A three-year project by Stevenson (1977) and Parsloe (1977) promises a large amount of impressionistic-qualitative data on the social work task. This has been briefly reported, but the final report will show how successful the authors have been in avoiding the danger that the interminable stories socialworkers used to tell about their clients are now told about the workers themselves. Useful accounts of the radical position can be found in Statham (1978) and in Corrigan and Leonard (1978).

TWO THEMES IN THE STUDY OF THE SOCIALWORKER AND THE SENIOR

Some Inadequacies in the Main Concepts Dealing with Problems of Social Work: Bureaucracy, Profession, and Team

A great many statements about social work use one or more of the concepts of bureaucracy, profession, and team, and much contemporary literature in social work is concerned with the dilemmas or strains arising from professional practice in a bureaucratic setting. Socialworkers are encouraged to become good bureaucrats (Pruger 1973) or to foster debureaucratization (Green 1966); they are persuaded that one way forward is to become members of a radical profession; they are urged to stand up for the profession against the bureaucracy or to appreciate that "professionalism can, in effect, be allied with bureaucracy against the interests of the welfare client" (Corrigan and Leonard 1978). Statements like this abound, but closer attention to the major concepts would have increased the return on them.

Bureaucracy: The use of this term by participants as well as by commentators has been characterized by two main tendencies—a failure to see that this rich and manifold concept conveys a number of distinct meanings and a negative evaluation of bureaucratic behavior. Socialworkers and commentators on social work may well wish to refer to one or all of these, but in using the same term to cross so many boundaries, it would be an advantage to specify which particular aspect is being emphasized. Otherwise we cannot be sure precisely what is being stated.

One thing, of course, is clear from most discussions, and that is that acting professionally is always good, while the actions of a bureaucrat are, at the very best, always suspect. Such assumptions ignore the reasons for the growth of bureaucracy in contemporary Western society (and this growth is different from bureaucratization, which refers to the parasitic and illegitimate extension of a bureaucracy's sphere of activity and power in its own interests or those of a power elite). Bureaucracy is growing largely because of an increasing distrust of personal or charismatic authority. The tendency is increasing for authority to be vested in rules. It is this tendency that leads sympathetic critics of social work to pose as a question the possibility that unless the socialworker's power is regulated by law in accordance with the principles of justice, the socialworkers themselves may constitute a significant obstacle to the implementation of welfare rights (Campbell 1978). Professionals—and especially those striving for professional status—characteristically reject any idea of rules, though in doing so, they neglect the extent to which their own behavior is rule governed.

Profession. Hence I would like to make just two points. First, that occupational groups called professions often behave in ways that are described as bureaucratic; this is one instance that questions the general assumption in social work that behaving in a professional manner is always good. Second, it is not easy to find agreement on precisely which features of professional behavior are supposed to be incompatible or in tension with bureaucracy.

Social work teachers seem often to see the criteria for judging an occupation to be professional as series of virtues. Freidson, in a study of a particular group of professions (dominant professions), has drawn attention to the fact that "by virtually all writers, expertise and professions are equated with a flexible, creative and equalitarian way of organising work, while bureaucracy is associated with rigidity, and with mechanical and authoritarian ways" (Freidson 1970c). However, he goes on to argue that much of the rigidity and authoritarian behavior said to characterize the health services may stem more from its professional organization than from its bureaucratic features. "The expertise of the professional is institutionalized into something similar to bureaucratic office."

If we accept that tensions can arise between bureaucrat and professional, there are obviously a number of ways in which this tension may be expressed. Studies of bureaucracy and professionalism (sometimes described as bureaucracy versus professionalism) need to specify what kinds of difficulty are envisaged. Is it that socialworkers cannot work with effectiveness in a bureaucracy or that some kind of integrity or autonomy are at risk? Do the difficulties arise from differences between the orientations of the professional and of the bureaucrat, and if so, is this because the two groups work with different systems of authority, or respond to different reference groups, or hold different attitudes to the service of clients?

The Team. Ever since the early days of the Child Guidance Movement, the concept of the team has played an important part in social work. It has often seemed in social work that where two or three are gathered together there is a team. In England since the Seebohm reorganization, the team has become more dominant: socialworkers belong to generic teams, seniors lead teams, area directors run area teams, whilst the director and his management team work in a team-like manner. Yet socialworkers have shown little tendency to question the emphasis on team or even its meaning. No one has recently repeated the question once asked by Fritz Redl: Must working together be called a team?

At least three problems require further study. First, the boundaries that mark off particular teams need to be ascertained for analytical as well as practical reasons. Past discussion of social work as work has sometimes been frustrating because insufficient attention has been given to the different collectivities to which most socialworkers belong—the organization, the occupation, the work groups, and groups of workers.

Second, socialworkers for all their reverence for the team seem often to work as independent practitioners, sometimes of a distinctly entrepreneural kind. If, however, team practice (contrasted with practice in a team) is to become a reality, we need to change not simply socialworker attitudes but also the ways in which social work is organized. As Leonard has pointed out

> The organizational structure which must be developed in the future as a pre-requisite for effective team practice should emphasise functional complementarity rather than hierarchy. This complementarity of parts in relation to a whole should characterise the relation of individuals within a team, where joint policy-making and the sharing of knowledge and skills is an essential means by which the complexities of client system and environment can be comprehended and appropriate interventions developed. (Leonard 1975).

Third, we should attend to the actual positive returns from working in team terms. Just as we need to be sure of the returns in increased understanding of the use of "profession" and "bureaucracy," so we should be clear both about the problems "team" is supposed to clarify and solve and also its relative success in solving them. We could, for example, assume that the concept team is used to solve two distinct though related problems—namely, more effective delivery of service and the resolution of hierarchical problems that would otherwise interfere with service delivery. As a matter of fact it is extremely difficult to know the extent to which we are solving either of these problems. Kane has reviewed well over 200 accounts of interprofessional teamwork and found that "the interprofessional team is. . . an entrenched modality and yet remains relatively untested" (Kane 1975). In the teams reviewed, in 65 percent of the cases formal leadership was in the hands of physicians or psychiatrists and in 12 percent in the hands of socialworkers. As far as intraprofessional teams are concerned, coordinate as opposed to collegial membership seems at least as popular and successful as groups based on an idea of democratic, nonhierarchical participation.

As we have seen, the general concepts discussed in this first part of the chapter leave open many questions about social work and its effect on the clients. Common reasons are the often very abstract formulations and unproven hypotheses. One step toward a more precise and praxis-oriented discussion can be taken by dealing with the relationship between the socialworker and his or her supervisor. Here again we have to acknowledge aspects of bureaucracy, professionalism, and teamwork in their effect on the solution of clients' problems. But now it can be done in the context of a more detailed analysis of a working situation—despite any inadequacies we might observe in the relevant contributions.

Professional Supervision as a Crucial Process for Explaining Different Modes of Social Work and Their Impact on Clients

The main way in which the work relationship with which we are concerned has been treated has been through a consideration of a social work process called supervision. A supervisor, to whom one or a small group of socialworkers is accountable, carries, according to the literature, three roles—as administrator, as helper or support, and as teacher or person concerned with the socialworker's professional development. Texts on supervision have appeared over the last ten years or so, but the subject is treated in a relatively uniform manner and without significant development. Discussion of the subject is often characterized by a degree of abstractness and by lack of any reference to the possibility let alone desirability of testing any of the crucial statements made. Two quotations from a recently published British guide to staff supervision can be used to illustrate these general criticisms (Westheimer 1977).

> The supervisor needs to remind herself that when social workers are allocated too large a volume of work, they will define problems as less than they are. She also needs to remain alert to idiosyncratic selection and enable the worker to keep this within reasonable bounds, this she can do by helping the worker acquire the kind of self-awareness that moderates personal needs and prevents unnecessary sense of failure or disillusionment.

This does seem somewhat remote from the acute problems of, for example, the principles upon which cases are allocated—by worker's personality fit with the client, by worker's specialist preferences, by worker's style—or how far allocations can "fairly" represent the distribution of need in any particular area or between kinds of client (e.g., the physically handicapped adult compared to the neglected child).

> Caseload management can only be satisfactory when it is part of ongoing supervision, is carried on over a substantial period of time, and when both supervisor and social worker apply their diagnostic skills to the category of clients.

What seems to be presented as a definition of successful caseload management is in fact a set of three conditions for such management that require empirical investigation.

It is possible, however, to derive from the literature on supervision (American and British) and the few research studies four relatively distinct sets of information—some indication of the job description of the senior, a description of the main guiding functions of the senior, some idea of different models of supervision, and some idea of the different kinds of power exercised by supervisors. Each item raises complex issues that have not always been firmly grasped. Some of these will become clear in the course of the discussion, but it is important to recognize that most treatments of supervision mark an advance on previous impressionistic and largely psychological discussions of social work as work. Such discussions were usually set on a plane of high abstraction.

For a clear indication of the usual job description of the senior as supervisor we can use Pettes (1979). She lists seven tasks usually assigned: (1) giving leadership to a team of workers, (2) ensuring that statutory requirements are met and records and statistics kept, (3) maintaining professional standards, (4) allocating work, (5) standby duty as required, (6) carrying a small caseload, and (7) special duties as required. Each of these duties could be discussed at length, but for illustrative purposes attention will be drawn only to the last two tasks named.

There is no general agreement among those who have written on supervision that the supervisor should carry a caseload, though Kadushin (1974) reported that half of his sample of over 450 supervisors carried a caseload in addition to their supervisory responsibilities. This is in fact one of the few acknowledged controversies, but it is usually settled by what is virtually an assertive definition rather than explored in anything like an experimental manner. "Special duties" is obviously an open-ended phrase, but seniors in a particular kind of working group sometimes take on routinely tasks of a planning or management nature. I refer to seniors in what are called "intake teams" (groups who specialize in intake and short-term work). Intake teams often acquire information that is crucial for any assessment of the whole work of their department. The senior, responsible for building a network of relations in the community often represents or is seen to represent the higher management of the department.

These roles, carried usually by seniors in intake teams, raise an important question about the nature of the senior's task. He or she is described in the texts on supervision as the main link between socialworker and the management, but the tasks as usually listed emphasize the orientation toward the socialworker. The senior is a socialworker to whom other socialworkers are accountable. Yet, at least in the case of intake seniors, it seems that some supervisors carry by default or by design certain management responsibilities. Some writers accept and emphasize the senior as manager, while others stress the importance of distinguishing between the managerial and the supervisory roles.

One basis for such a distinction can be found in the different degrees of authority connected with management and with supervision. Hey and Rowbottom (1971) describe the management role as carrying the fullest degree of accountability for the work of others. Therefore, in their view, it requires the following authority—to approve or veto the appointment of others, to be able to prescribe the work of subordinates, to be able to assess the performance of subordinates from his or her teams. The authority of the supervisor is more limited—to assist in inducting new workers into their duties, to allocate and prescribe work within the manager's policy, to help and advise on a day to day basis, and to carry out checks in work.

The second set of information that can be derived from the supervision literature concerns the description of the three main elements in supervision—namely, education, support, and administration. This trinity, under these or similar terms, is hallowed in all the texts on supervision, even though it is quite possible to separate the work of education or staff development from that of administrative oversight. Indeed Pettes (1979) points out that such a division seems to be working well in Switzerland. One major problem, of course, concerns the extent to which administrative and teaching functions or professional development can be combined. Stevenson suggests that such a combination is not always even attempted:

> The attitude of some seniors towards their supervisory role was ambivalent. Consultation, support, discussion—all these were "O.K. terms", but the element of control and checking seemed to be reluctantly accepted by some seniors. . . . In relatively few instances. . . did the seniors' assumption of accountability extend to a review of all his social workers' caseload, whether through discussions or reading of records. This must mean that in many teams the seniors' accountability can only be a formality. (Stevenson 1977)

Kadushin (1974) found that 60 percent of the supervisees saw their relationship with their supervisors as one of colleague-collaborator, but only 30 percent of the supervisors saw it in this way.

Other problems with this categorization of the three main aspects of professional supervision concern the extent to which supervisors can actually be responsible for overseeing work that is hardly even directly seen by them, and questions about social work accountability. I will take just two of these questions for purposes of illustration. First, How does the socialworker relate his orientation to individual clients to agency policy and to the law? Pearson (1975) has recently drawn attention to the fact that "the social worker sometimes serves the function of a Lilliputian Robin Hood who, if he is not actually robbing the rich to feed the poor, is aiding and abetting the offence" in fairly systematic ways. He suggests that many socialworkers, for example, "ignore the illegal fiddling of some of their clients against the Department of Health and Social Security . . . ." Socialworkers, in his view, do and should act as deviants in the industry of welfare.

Second, Britain has recently witnessed a series of inquiries into social work practice in particular cases concerned with the injury and death of children. These raise questions about the achievements or lack of achievements for which socialworkers should be held accountable, as well as to whom. Is there some kind of general accountability "to society," since socialworkers are not infrequently described as "keeping society's conscience," as well as accountability to senior and to higher management? Has the socialworker a sufficient technology and a system of values of such a kind that he or she can be held accountable for the actual outcome of a case (a battered child dies) rather than for acting appropriately according to his or her professional knowledge and principles?

I will discuss the third and fourth sets of information together, partly because of limitations of space but mainly because they present the same difficulty—How adequately do their major concepts encompass the extremely varied work relations that come to be established between socialworkers and their seniors? Epstein (1973) has suggested four possible models of supervision, depending on where the emphasis is placed—on growth, on group supervision, on quasi-autonomous supervision where the educational functions and the administration are located in different people, and on autonomous practice. Such a categorization enables the variety of actual practice to be seen more clearly, but it seems doubtful whether autonomous practice is a model of supervision. Also, group supervision could be undertaken with an emphasis on growth. In other words, the categorization does not take us very far.

Similarly, Levy's (1973) categorization of the kinds of power a supervisor may exercise is helpful in breaking down rather global descriptions of the weight of the supervisor's power. However, it is doubtful how far such a categorization captures each kind of social work. Take, for example, the case of community work. A recent study of such workers in a social services department by Thomas and Warburton (1977) found that none of Levy's seven categories applied. Let me cite two examples:

1. The supervisor has power because " he represents and interprets the supervisee to those in high authority and in turn determines whether and how the agency will be represented and interpreted to the supervisee." To which Thomas and Warburton reply: "In

Exshire, supervisors only partially mediated. Not only did the Community Work Adviser offer an alternative point of mediation but the workers and those in higher authority were not totally dependent on the supervisor for the way in which they were represented and interpreted to each other."

2. None of the supervisors or community workers shared Levy's view that the supervisor expects and often requires the supervisee to reveal much about himself in the supervisory relationship.

CONCLUSION

Speaking as a commentator and as someone convinced of the importance of attending to the experience of practitioners in its most detailed aspects, I would argue that practitioners and academics would benefit from a simple vacation from the set of illuminating concepts they both use—bureaucracy, profession, team, and so on. This is not because I welcome a little quiet darkness; I suggest a spell of abstinence simply because, in this way, we may more nearly approach the actual problems.

But, of itself, this is a defective remedy. We cannot just face the problems without benefit of concepts. How should we proceed? I believe that the most immediately fruitful approach is to consider social work and social service delivery jointly within a social policy framework. Warham has pointed to some of the benefits to be gained:

> social services, like other social institutions, including social work, are best to be understood both as processes and as open systems. Social policy incorporates processes of continuous change in a changing society and the formal organisations through which publicly sponsored services are implemented cannot be tidily separated off from other systems with which they interact. Nor can the role of the social worker even be defined exclusively by social workers. The cords which tie social work to the network of social processes and systems through which statutory social services are sponsored, developed and maintained, can never be cut. (Warham 1977)

A social policy framework emphasizes the limitations to an hierarchical approach either to an analysis of levels of action or to relationships between clients and the service delivery system. It can easily be assumed that social policy is a matter of high level concern—and so it is—but only to an extent. Policy is both interpreted and made at the lowest levels. In terms of the relationship between clients and service delivery systems, it seems important that we recognize that socialworkers are but one of the occupational groups involved in service delivery and that the majority of them are probably not professionally trained. Yet we need also to see their work within the general context of welfare and theorizing about welfare. Until now social work theorizing and social work have characteristically been developed without connection with a slowly developing body of theorizing that seeks to describe and justify welfare activity. (I have in mind notions like that of the gift relationship developed by Professor Titmuss or of altruism now being studied by, among others, Professor Pinker [Titmuss 1970; Pinker 1974]).

If welfare theory were developed and connected to social service activity, all the personnel concerned with the delivery of social service would find a means of understanding, improving, and justifying their activities. Until this is done, it seems that neither observers nor participants can cope with such otherwise insoluble problems as the rationing of services. Such problems cannot be satisfactorily met by what are seen as professional or bureaucratic measures.

Chapter 13

Self-help Groups as an Alternative to Bureaucratic Regulation and Professional Dominance of the Human Services

*Bernhard Badura**

> For most people much of "the good life" is found in small groups. Family life, the rearing of children, love, friendship, respect, kindness, pity, neighborliness, charity: these are hardly possible except in small groups. . . The nation-state can only provide the framework within which "the good life" is possible; it cannot fulfill the functions of the small groups. . . .
> Dahl and Lindblom 1963

> Modern socail welfare has really to be thought of as help given to the stranger, not to the person who by reason of personal bond commands it without asking. It assumes a degree of social distance between helped and
> Wilensky and Lebeaux 1958

> The main limits on the use of an integrative method are set, not by the existence of integrative problems, but by the availability of knowledge and emotional resources.
> Diesing 1962

This chapter presents a brief discussion of a number of structural problems that strain the relationship between the "management" of social services and socialworkers engaged "in the field," problems in the theoretical conceptualization and analysis of social services, and finally the tasks, types, and problems of self-help groups as alternatives to institutionalized assistance.

*University of Konstanz, Federal Republic of Germany

Table 13-1. Dimensions of Efficient Forms of Service Delivery and Social Problem Treatment

	Traditional Regulatory Administration	*Social Service Administration*	*Self-help Groups*[a]
Tasks	Supervision	Production of human services	Mutual help
Criteria of rationality	Legality; orientation toward "essential official duties"	Effectiveness and efficiency	Meeting social and individual needs through working in groups
Knowledge relative to function	Legal knowledge; procedural knowledge	Social-scientific knowledge; familiarity with local conditions	Personal experience; lay knowledge
Type of social policy	Regulatory intervention of the state	Income distribution; social investments (advice, education, etc.)	Mobilization of the consumer; deprofessionalization of the satisfaction of nonmaterial needs

[a]The options for the solution of social problems mark a social policy alternative in the field of psychosocial and medical care to be more fully treated later in the chapter.

A CONFLICT OF PRIORITIES WITHIN THE INSTITUTIONS

There are ministries for social affairs at federal as well as at state (*bundeslander*) level whose traditional function is not the provision of social services to citizens, but the exercise of authority over them. The delivery of services is the responsibility of (1) local government (e.g., welfare agencies, health offices) and (2) corporations of public law (e.g., self-governing sickness funds). All three branches are organized as bureaucracies. Originally developed as an instrument for carrying out quite different functions, bureaucracy has shown itself to be ill-suited to the task of providing the social services more recently demanded of it. (see Table 13–1).

It has become apparent to many observers that the legalistic outlook of the administration and the nature of its organizational structure hinder the efficient, humanistic delivery of the services required by an industrial society. The clash between societal needs and the capacity of the administration to cope with them is especially virulent within the providing organizations themselves—that is between the traditional managerial professionals at the upper, or administrative, levels and the new groups of professionals in the field.

The former are primarily oriented toward bureaucratic and legalistic goals, whereas socialworkers and other new providers of services are client-oriented, humanistically disposed, and consider themselves social scientists. The latter model themselves on a professional image that is anything but legalistic and is perhaps even antibureaucratic in nature. They have difficulty in conforming to traditional bureaucracy's methods of performing tasks and its particularly legalistic, depersonalized bent. A further source of discord is the high degree of regulation in this field of work: the body of German social legislation, as well as tax regulation, is a model of complexity. In questions of procedure, every socialworker "at the front" is systematically disadvantaged by lacking—and his or her superior is rewarded by possessing—an extensive knowledge of the law.

Under these circumstances a certain "emancipation" of social administration from the constraints and operating principles of the classical German bureaucracy, combined with a greater clarity of legal provisions and procedural regulations, could well result in a better performance in the administration of social services—to the benefit of its clients. Thus, one can only concur with Noel Timms (see chapter 12), who (in reference to Friedson) warns against making analytically vague distinctions between "professional" and "bureaucrat." But an array of considerations and distinctions well-founded in theory must provide the background for any meaningful discussion of the analytical and practical problems of providing human services. Though the significance of the conflicts between bureaucrats and professionals cannot be denied, those conflicts cannot be the point of departure for a theory of social services. Instead, such a theory must first consider the present, concrete state of the provision of social services, its characteristics, and the requirements generated by its working dynamic as well as its consequences.

HUMAN SERVICES: CHARACTERISTICS AND REQUIREMENTS

Human services have two particular characteristics that differentiate them from other types of socioeconomic activity. They are "human" due to their vital concern for people and the fact that the consumer-client is essential to their production. Thus, the providing of human services is quite different from the production of physical goods, which is primarily concerned with transforming material things and not with the consumer-client as such. Moreover, they are "social" because, as a rule, they are produced outside the private sector and the market system. The services may be rendered for a fee, but their production is not guided by effective demand—namely, the ability to pay—as are other types of goods and services, but by the societal demand for them (Badura and Gross 1976; Gartner and Riessman 1977, 1978).

Complexity of Evaluating

An accurate assessment of the effects and benefits of a particular social service provided—be it counseling, instruction, assistance, or treatment—is beset with many problems. We might subsume them under the heading "multifariousness of goals and norms." The evaluation of the benefits of such a service rendered to a client may be impossible, not only at the time it is provided, but even in the long run. This ambiguity in assessing the effects of a particular activity is a general problem in the psychosocial areas of human experience, where concrete goals and objective criteria are often very fuzzy or lacking completely.

The problem does not lie in the technical complexity of the human service itself. The multifariousness of goals and norms and the objectifiability of the criteria of evaluation are the chief factors inhibiting assessment. The problem of evaluating the consequences of a social service affects not only the consumer-client, but also the direct producers of the service and the planners and managers in the administration. As long as the experts cannot agree upon criteria for "successful intervention," one can hardly expect a consensus among those affected to rest upon more than a theoretical or practical ad hoc basis (Steiner 1966).

Importance of the Consumer

The prevailing social policies of Western capitalist societies are based on a principle whereby individuals apply to providers of social services rather than on a principle of distributing or apportioning services among the general population. As a rule, consumers can seek access to the appropriate institution only when they have first defined themselves as being in need of help. When the consumer sits together with a socialworker or doctor, the performance and direct result of the counseling or treatment he or she will receive are highly dependent on his or her own input—the information given, his or her credibility and demeanor, and so forth—that is, dependent on the client's ability to deal with professional dispensers of social services.

The "contribution of the client-patient" entails, then, much more than his or her mere respect for the "technical competence of the helper," belief in the moral integrity of the professional, and gratitude, as Erving Goffman acknowledged in his work on asylums (Goffman 1961, 1972). The postconsultative behavior of the assistance seeker is also frequently vital to the success of the service rendered. It is here that sociologists need to supplement and revise their understanding of social service (Fuchs 1966). Only when the consumer is seen as a co-producer of human service—and this is the basic assumption of my considerations—can avenues be opened to a more comprehensive theory of, as well as practical changes in, social service as we know it.

Intensity of Interaction

Jean Fourastie (1963) advanced the view that the growth of the tertiary sector, especially in comparison with that of the industrial sector, is attributable to the lesser possibilities for engineering rationality into the productive process. We have come to regard rationality, understood as the application of technology, to be directed not by the needs of the consumers alone, but by the purveyors of social services—an arrangement that is presently counterproductive. I do not take the Fourastie thesis to be a prognosis of a development by natural necessity as it were, but as an indication of a contemporary characteristic of the provision of social services that distinguishes it from the production of material goods. At least within the realm of human services, the quality of the final result appears to depend on the quality of the interaction that takes place between the provider and the consumer—in many cases to a wholly significant, decisive, and irreducible degree. Certainly, research on this aspect of client-provider interaction is in its primal stages, if it can be said that it has even begun. We are dealing here with basic issues of the welfare state—assumptions about the possibilities and limits of its organizational forms, its dominant professions, and procedures and patterns of intervention (Badura and Gross 1976).

A possible response to the aforementioned theoretical and practical challenges can be found in the large number of studies that are concerned with transforming existing welfare organizations into more "people-oriented" or "humane" bodies (Kaufmann 1977b; Howard and Strauss 1975). The main thrust of these works, which are rather ambitious in their theory and method, is toward a critique of the modern welfare state. Within the Federal Republic of Germany, a second approach is gaining interest; it maintains that a dual system of social assistance exists in the modern welfare state, one institutionalized and the other preinstitutional. It also takes the view—considering changing social conditions and with regard to the manifold problems endemic to bureaucratized or professionalized assistance—that preinstitutionalized forms constitute an equally appealing or even more favorable alternative. This is the case especially where (1) psychosocial problems are to be overcome, (2) problem-solving takes intensive forms of interaction, (3) little or no professional qualifications are required, (4) sufficient knowledge (of personal problems and ways to cope with them) is easily accessible to the layperson, and (5) necessary personal experience is provided through participation in self-help groups themselves. There has been a recent profusion of pertinent literature (Caplan and Killilea 1976; Levin, Katz and Holst 1976; Gartner and Riessman 1977), and we now have the first empirical studies on the proliferation, growth in membership, organizational forms, and successes of self-help groups at our disposal (J.A.B.S. 1976). The need for further research in this area remains, however, considerable. At the same time, there are frequent theoretical and empirical indications that in the intensification of self-help lies a significant potential for raising the level of effectiveness and democratization of a social assistance system now dominated by professionals.

SELF-HELP GROUPS: ORIGINS, TYPES, POTENTIALS

Self-help groups have developed and gained in importance in part because of definable trends specific to a society—for instance, a tradition of active self help—and in part because of general conditions and developments found in all Western societies. In particular these include: (1) a growing distrust of science and technology and of experts, whose increasing political and social influence shows up the limits of professional assistance—for instance, in fighting poverty, unemployment, and illnesses whose incidence has grown with the advance of civilization; (2) a growing dissatisfaction with centralized and bureaucratized decisionmaking processes and care-providing institutions, as well as an increasingly positive view of informal, controllable, flexible, and egalitarian forms of mutual help; (3) the overburdening and weakening of traditional help systems such as the family, circles of close friends, and community or neighborhood organizations by the problems and expectations of modern society; and finally (4) inadequate and inefficient service systems in education and in the field of social and medical services.

At present there are probably more than half a million self-help groups worldwide with millions of members. In the Federal Republic self-help groups meet with growing interest as alternatives to bureaucratic or professional arrangements for the provision of care.

Among the most important problems that self-help groups deal with are alcoholism, drug abuse, mental and physical disabilities, psychosocial problems of the aged and the unemployed, coping with chronic diseases, and rehabilitation after medical treatment. Gussow and Tracy (1976) assume that self-help organizations in the United States deal with nearly all of the seventeen categories of illness established by the WHO. According to their suggestions, self-help groups can be divided into two main categories. Type I includes groups that see their main duty as providing service and care to their own members (thus offering a narrow definition of self-help groups). Type II includes organizations that concentrate on influencing public opinion, the media, political parties, and representatives in government; they are mainly interested in heightening awareness and in enlightening people, in procuring or augmenting material support for their problems groups, and in influencing the political process.

The best-known examples of Type I organizations are Alcoholics Anonymous, Synanon, and Recovery Inc. Examples of Type II organizations in the Federal Republic are the *Burgerinitiativen* (grassroots organizations) and other associations of the sick and disabled, such as the *Deutsche Krebshilfe* (German Cancer Aid) and the umbrella organization *Hilfe für die Behinderten* (Aid to the Disabled). More narrowly defined self-help groups are involved in providing mutual help and services (Type I); as a rule they try to maintain political and financial independence. Their members face problems either personally or in their immediate social surroundings and feel unable to cope with them alone. Among other things, self-help groups are attractive because they are in a position to avoid some of the characteristic weaknesses of bureaucratic and professional organizations:

1. Members of self-help groups know each other personally and strive to deal with their problems by informal means; help is not given by a stranger, but by someone who is known and trusted.
2. Self-help groups make a great effort to steer clear of hidden forms of specialization and social inequality by constantly exchanging roles; they seek to develop symmetrical relationships between members and to avoid dependencies and social distance, which seem to be almost unavoidable in the physician-patient, teacher-pupil, and socialworker-client relationships.
3. The impetus to join a self-help group arises from personally experienced feelings of helplessness and despair. Personal involvement makes the provision of aid more authentic and credible than assistance from lay persons motivated by a sense of altruism or services from experts or members of the social bureaucracy whose motivations are economic and frequently paternalistic (Badura 1978).

THREE SELECTED FIELDS OF ACTIVITY OF SELF-HELP GROUPS

Self-help groups have proved practicable and effective in the following three central fields of social service—ageing, unemployment, and illness. Here, some specific examples are instructive. In England a self-help organization by the name of Link Opportunity organizes the exchange of services and temporary assistance between senior citizens, and also for the youth population. Link Opportunity "is a job-exchange scheme for retired people. . . . Run by volunteers, its aim is to put to good use, in the interest of members themselves, the vast accumulation of 'know-how' they have built up during their working years" (Modes 1978). For each service rendered, the senior citizen receives a bonus that entitles him or her to other services within the scope of Link Opportunity.

In the United States senior citizens offer services to children under the auspices of the Foster Grandparents Program in "hospital pediatric wards, institutions for the mentally retarded and emotionally disturbed, correctional facilities, homes for dependent and neglected children, and more recently in public school classrooms for exceptional children, day-care centers and private homes" (Modes 1978). In the Federal Republic there are comparable senior citizen self-help groups—for example the Sozialwerk e.V. (Social Work, a nonprofit organization) in Berlin, initiated by senior citizens themselves. The group concentrates its efforts on homes for the aged. "Aside from occupational facilities and therapy, our work concentrates on organizing a contact-person who adopts an inhabitant of a home for the aged; today some 245 members care for approximately 4,200 people a year" (Modes 1978).

Perhaps the largest field of activity in which self-help groups are engaged is health care. In order to define better the responsibilities that go beyond those of existing self-help activities, the inadequacies and inefficiencies of medical care must first be analyzed. A diagnosis of those shortcomings will allow an investigation to ascertain which of them could be eliminated through changes within institutionalized care and which through changes in the lay care system. Encouragement and support for self-help could be an important alternative to present health policy, in part supplementary, in part corrective.

Apart from its other deficiencies, six particular aspects of scientific medicine are repeatedly criticized:

1. It is too strongly oriented toward curative approaches and concentrates too little on preventive measures.
2. It concentrates too heavily on somatic disturbances, thereby neglecting psychosocial causes of disease and the interdependence of physical, psychological, and social stress and problems.
3. Apart from problems of preventive health care, those of follow-up care after medical treatment or surgery point up a grave omission by present practitioners of medical care. The infirm, as a rule, may receive adequate medical treatment, but are left on their own during rehabilitation or left to the "invisible hand" of the lay system.
4. An exaggerated commitment to technical apparatuses and the fact that doctors are often too pressed for time has led to considerable restrictions in and formalization of doctor-patient interaction; too little attention is paid to the psychosocial dimensions, health education is neglected, and patients are denied an explanation of their illnesses.
5. Although exact numbers are lacking and the existing figures

must be treated with caution, there are increasingly numerous indications that the growth of medical care has been accompanied by an even faster growth of iatrogenic damages (misdiagnoses, errors in administering medication, and surgical errors).

6. Finally, the explosive rise in cost of modern medicine in the last ten to fifteen years has been a growing burden to the general population and has forced politicians to intervene in the health care field.

Self-help groups in the health care field could contribute to rectifying the above faults and inadequacies in institutionalized medical care. For example, numerous women's self-help clinics have been founded in the United States. Canada, and Europe (in the Federal Republic in Berlin); these are self-help organizations that see their main goals as health education and preventive health care. The first detailed analysis of the work of a women's self-help clinic, the Vancouver Health Collective, has been summarized in a comprehensive research report financed by the Canadian government (Kleiber and Light 1978).

Psychotherapeutic self-help groups seek to overcome neurotic disturbances and other psychosocial problems (Moller 1978). Meanwhile, thousands of groups fight drug and alcohol dependency. The same is true of disabilities and chronic diseases. Self-help groups have also begun work in the field of rehabilitation. In January 1978, for example, twenty-two groups in the Federal Republic concerned with cancer treatment followup care formed a women's self-help group after cancer. Their membership has since been estimated at over 2000.

In the rise of the German Workers' movement various forms of self-help—such as associations and co-ops—played an important role. Especially after World War II, steady economic growth and a qualitative expansion of publicly provided social services in the Federal Republic and other developed industrial societies gave the impression that self-help, especially among those capable of earning a living, was an outdated, superfluous form of care. The recent economic crisis and the high rate of unemployment, especially among youth, has forced policymakers and the general public to rethink traditional providing procedures. Social services for the unemployed are often inadequate and inefficient; in this field self-help groups could help to eliminate these shortcomings and defects. Material support alone will not overcome the psychosocial side effects of permanent unemployment, and the public employment service often finds it impossible to counsel adequately the enormous number of unemployed.

In the winter of 1975, when youth unemployment in the Federal Republic soared for the first time, a large number of self-help initiatives for the unemployed were founded (Lehmann 1978). Some of these groups have been supported—at least in part—by public funding or by already existing organizations and receive help from socialworkers; other groups, which have been initiated by students and the unemployed, endeavor to remain financially and politically independent. The groups receiving public funds are primarily engaged in advising and attending to the problems of unemployed youth, in addition or complementary to the efforts of the public employment service, and in trying to reintegrate them into the labor force. The independent groups concentrate on creating alternative forms of working and living. Both types of self-help groups try to contact unemployed youths and to motivate them to take charge of their situation collectively. Self-help groups are often more successful in establishing such a contact with unemployed youth than is the public employment service or any other institution, for the social distance is less marked, and the unemployed individual's psychological barriers against cooperation are either less pronounced or more easily overcome.

MUTUAL AID AND THE PROFESSIONS

Self-help groups in the realm of social service deserve an intensive investigation that looks at their formation, development, activities, potentialities, and limitations. Further research needs to be conducted on the relationship of self-help groups to their environment: (1) to the phenomenon of self-help within the family and neighborhood; (2) to the work environment; (3) to the centers of political decisionmaking; and (4) to the institutions of professional care. In the current literature on the relationship between self-help groups and professionalized care, four distinct positions are evident:

Self-help as an Instrument for Disseminating Professional Knowledge and for Alleviating the Caseload Borne by Institutionalized Care

Here self-help is still seen wholly from the perspective of the classical, professionalized services and is supposed to serve an increase in the efficiency and effectiveness of institutionalized care, without—and this the decisive point—calling into question, much less undermining, the purposes and measures of the existing institutions of professionalized care (Moller 1977). The goal of the activities of self-help groups seen in this light is, for instance, to help its participants become more conscious of their general health needs and, when immediately in need, to accommodate themselves better to the maxims, regulations, and advice of professionals and other providers—in other words, to help the care seeker to become, in the eyes of the care-dispensing institutions, a fully socialized and, accordingly, a "well-functioning" client-patient.

Thus, self-help becomes an extension of the professional provision of social care, as it is carried on in harmony with professional standards and as the members of self-help groups attach a great importance to consensus with the respective professionals. This concept of self-help is most often evidenced where (1) professionals participate in or have initiated the activities of the self-help group; (2) the group serves to relieve institutionalized care of either "petty cases" or of those cases that cannot be readily solved within the scope of institutionalized care; or (3) the prevailing opinion is that self-help can be practiced with success similar to professionalized care and at considerably less expense.

Self-help as an Instrument for Activating Clients and Encouraging Them to Perceive and Act Better in Their Own Interests, Within the Framework of Institutionalized Care

Here self-help is seen from the vantage point of those immediately in need of care and is purported to contribute to greater efficiency and effectiveness of care through reform of the existing care-providing structures (Gartner and Riessman 1977). Self-help groups engage in diagnostic, therapeutic, counseling, or fostering activities, again primarily in accordance with professional standards; beyond that, however, they enlighten their members as to the deficiencies and flaws within institutionalized care and also to the societal causes of being in need of care. Though groups operating in accordance with this concept of self-help do not deny that professional care may be competent, they cannot agree politically—that is on the ends, means, and structures—with the operation of existing care institutions. An example of this position might be seen in the somewhat liberal women's self-help groups engaged in health care activities.

Self-help as an Alternative Care System, as a Substitute for Existing Institutions and Professions

Advocates of this concept either consider institutionalized care the main cause of the need for care or maintain that institutionalized care serves not to provide clients with "care" per se, but to impose surveillance, punishment, control, or mere custodial care upon them. This is the standpoint of "democratic psychiatry" or, in more radical form, the standpoint of "antipsychiatry." They either believe that problems of care boil down to structural problems that can be solved by structural change alone or partake of a general skepticism toward all forms of organized assistance and believe that either paraprofessionals or laypersons are equally or even better able to handle a large proportion of existing care problems. Examples of the above would be more radical women's self-help groups or the work of those groups engaged in what the Italian psychiatrist Basaglia and others have designated "democratic psychiatry."

Self-help as an Alternative Form of Living and Caring, Disinterested in the Politics of Public Assistance

Here self-help is carried on in relative isolation from the rest of society and its professions, but without questioning the validity of established societal norms or institutions. Personal growth alone is the essential goal of these groups, which exist alongside institutionalized care, whose additional goals (e.g., rehabilitation or cure of addiction) they otherwise fundamentally share. Yet in pursuing those goals they employ more group-specific—in part more highly spiritualized, and in any case more interaction-intensive—forms, or modes, of operation. Examples of the above would be the "anonymous" organizations, such as Alcoholics Anonymous.

To advocates of the self-help idea, the considerable inadequacies and ineffectiveness of care that is bureaucratically controlled or dominated by professionals cannot—and this is the vital point—be remedied through reform of the system of offering aid in itself, because of a hitherto inevitable social distance between organized providers and consumers, because of the hitherto unavoidable degradation of consumer needs vis-à-vis those of the purveyor, and because of the hitherto unavoidable dominance of professional orientations and bureaucratic imperatives. The structural limitations of existing social services can only be surmounted if (1) the consumer of social services is no longer viewed merely as passive recipient, but as active co-producer; (2) his or her opportunities for consultation and co-determination within social and political institutions (when feasible) are improved; and (3) the possibilities of self-production of non-material goods outside the sociopolitical system are facilitated and encouraged (and more heavily researched).

What we need is a new rethinking of social policy. Only if we first revise the outdated view that political regulation, as it has been applied, and political institutions, as they have developed, are essentially practicable instruments for overcoming social problems and if we then seek the causes of those social problems at least partly in the structure of sociopolitical regulation and institutions itself will the readiness to experiment with alternatives grow and will our chances of overcoming pressing structural problems improve.

Chapter 14

Conclusion: Do We Need New Theoretical and Methodological Approaches for Future Analyses of Social Service Delivery?

*Dieter Grunow**

The answer to this question was "yes" before, during and at the end of the conference. In fact, the main reason for organizing this meeting of scientists and practitioners was the idea that we need new approaches to social service delivery and for its scientific analysis. This idea could only be realized, we thought, by inviting social scientists from many different countries, with different experiences and different "spirits" and opinions. On the other hand, we sought to structure the contributions somewhat in advance in order to have this international team of experts think and discuss a common frame of questions and problems. This frame of topics is summarized in Figure 14-1.

As the chapters of the volume indicate, the discussion was concentrated on the formulation of the relationship between clients and social service networks. This focus is illustrated by many different terms and concepts, depending on the level of analysis chosen:

Social Rationing,
Organizational selectivity,
Needs of clients versus need definition of elites,

*Research Group, Social Planning and Social Administration, Bielefeld, and Project Group, Administration and the Public, University of Bielefeld, Federal Republic of Germany

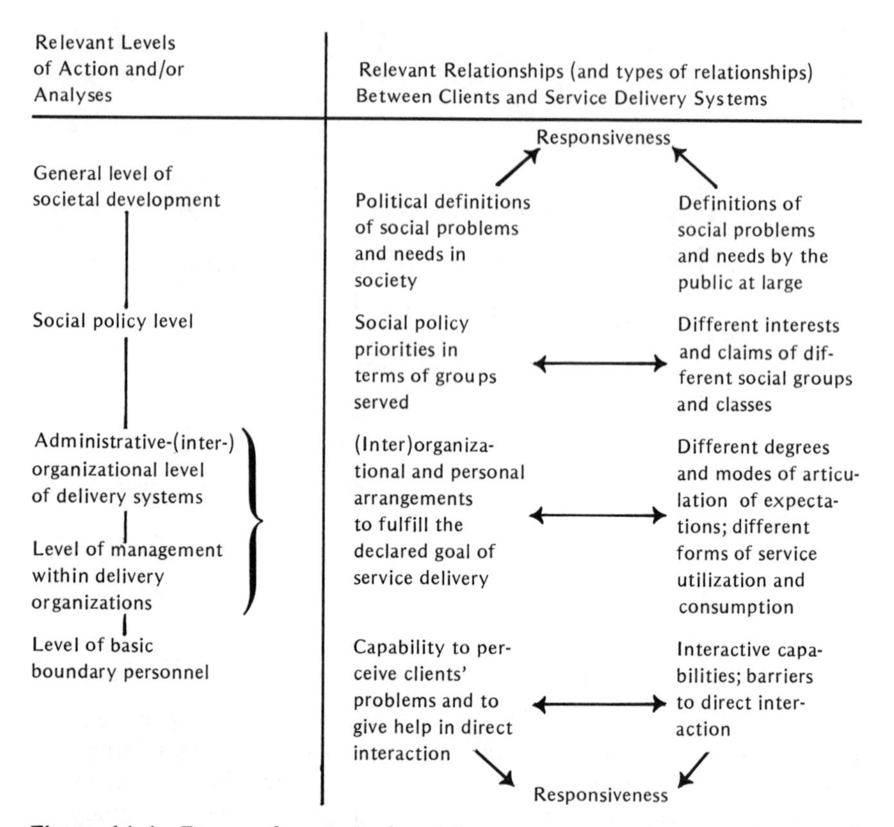

Figure 14-1. Frame of analysis for doing research on the responsiveness of service delivery to clients' needs.

consensual and conflicting definitions of the helping relationship by clients and by professionals,
utilization of services and their barriers, and
interaction processes.

By focusing on the simultaneous analysis of the perspectives of clients, on the one hand, and of officials-professionals-organizations, on the other (multiperspective approach), we had to take into account that each contribution would tend to remain on one level of analysis—on the societal level (Chapter 2), on the organizational level (Chapter 6), on the interaction level (Chapter 10). This unintended but unavoidable fact draws attention to a major defect and problem of social service analysis: the theoretical concepts and empirical approaches are themselves very selective. Therefore, they might "produce" or at least legitimate as much selectivity as the practical service delivery does.

If this holds true, we should be able to draw sound conclusions in analyzing this field. Among other things, our discussions in Berlin indicated:

1. There are many scientific domains that relate themselves to social service analysis; one of the main bases of domain competition is disciplinary differentiation. Social psychology, demography, sociology, and economics are just a few global fields of scientific interest and activity. All of them, and especially their subfields (in terms of applied social sciences), show a large discrepancy between de facto and claimed domains; they assert a much greater competence in dealing with problems of service delivery then they really have. Thus, it is quite likely that these gaps between de facto and claimed domains explain some gaps in the empirical knowledge, theoretical sophistication, and practical relevance we have recognized in our discussions.
2. Social science is very often used "to cool out clients" by showing "scientifically" that they have false needs, or that service provisions cannot meet these needs, or that they have themselves to blame for being in the trouble they are in,
3. Social scientists can gain many more rewards by taking perspective of the agencies, institutions, or professional and union interests. By this they tend to support and strengthen inadequate perceptions of clients' problems and needs, false client selections, or one-sided causal analyses,
4. Social scientists might support "rationing mechanisms" in society by raising only few out of many possible research questions and applying only few out of many theoretical concepts and empirical research devices,
5. Social scientists might be as little responsive to clients' problem definitions and needs as social service personnel. They accept the definitions of those in power rather than of those without power.

These considerations lead to the conclusion that we have to reorganize our modes of scientific division of labor with regard to social service analysis. Moreover, we will have to describe the selectivity of our approaches much more intensively and acknowledge the consequences of this selectivity in theoretical, empirical, and practical terms.

It is not just accidental that we invited an international and interdisciplinary group of social scientists to this conference. It is almost a commonplace that we have to be confronted with practical experiences and scientific work from other countries to recognize the selectivity of individual approaches and concepts and to be stimulated to innovative scientific activity in the field of social service analysis and evaluation.

The division of labor of social sciences does not only result in separation and domain competition among different disciplines, but it also very often separates methodologists, social theorists, empirical researchers, and practitioners with interest in applying research results. This division of labor has even more negative consequences for the quality and relevance of social service analysis than disciplinary differentiations might have. Thus, within the discussions it could be observed that the number of theory-oriented and empirically based analyses of social service delivery systems and their impact on clients' problems and needs is still very small. Very often empirical data are plainly demanded and used for practical purposes—a purely empiricist procedure; on the other hand, many so-called theoretical contributions lack any data basis. They facilitate "innovations" that do not change things but adhere to the symbolic use of social policies. In addition, the number of valid, reliable, and relevant evaluative studies is small. Thus, many descriptions of the problems of service delivery systems are at hand, but only a few explanations can be presented; many practical suggestions are at our disposal but only a few of them include a solid prognosis of consequences and impacts.

Summarizing and expanding some of the results of the discussion in Berlin, I want to answer the initial question of this Conclusion with, Yes, we do need new theoretical and methodological approaches for future analyses of social service delivery. My general proposition here is that we should be aware of the special selectivities in our approaches to social service analysis, and we should continually try to reduce them.

1. We are in need of theoretical concepts and empirical studies that combine different perspectives of different actors in the field of service delivery (individuals, client groups, private enterprises, local authorities, service institutions). They should be preferred and supported—instead of singling out small aspects or just one perspective from many relevant ones.
2. We should stimulate studies that try to relate macro-, meso-, and microprocesses of social service delivery—instead of discouraging interdisciplinary work. One of the main handicaps and fallacies of recent social service analysis is the fact that the analyses of societal rationing processes, of the barriers of bureaucratic service institutions, and of the analysis of power relationships in client-professional interaction are separated. They should be related and integrated.
3. We should be much more interested in the causation and rise

3. We should be much more interested in the causation and rise of social problems—instead of limiting the analyses to the service delivery systems. This demands an open view of the relationship between individual and structural conditions of problem origin, as well as the acknowledgement of social, economic, legal, and political conditions of problem development and problem solution.
4. Instead of looking to one type of solution to social service delivery (e.g., through professional counseling), we should stimulate empirical analyses and evaluations of different types of solutions on behalf of the same problem. This might include bureaucratic institutions, professions, self-help in primary social networks, special self-help groups (e.g., A.A.), solidary action on the basis of a cooperative, market economy provisions, and others. Each of these "solutions" is de facto no solution but just a contribution to a solution; each has its fundamental, built-in limitations. Instead of the attempt to maximize one type of strategy of service delivery—which almost inevitably leads toward contraproductivity of the services—a combination of different types is a much more relevant practical and scientific question.
5. To be able to compare these alternative approaches we will have to support public political action that gives different approaches (including financial support) and not just one type of a chance for development. For a scientific analysis this implies that we should stimulate studies that relate social service delivery and social policy development. Or, in a more generalized formulation, we need longitudinal studies that are a systematized description and evaluation of the whole process of problem development, political problem definition, and program formulation; administrative initial implementation; and day-to-day operations of service preparation and delivery as well as impact evaluation.
6. If the problems of social service delivery, its preconditions, and its impact or lack of it are seen in the context of the development of the welfare society and the welfare state and its dynamics, it can be expected that theory-oriented empirical research of the type proposed here will always be slow in comparison with developments in society. Thus, in future it will be most important to have relevant social agencies keeping their own evaluating records that are almost "real time" descriptions of social processes. Among the tasks of the social scientist there will be the development of descriptive and evaluative measures as well as of adequate techniques of analysis and interpretation of these data.

7. Last but not least, this indicates the importance of innovations and greater precision in the use of the range of empirical research instruments. The types and procedures of data collection belong probably to the aspects of our topic with the smallest amount of innovative action. We still have almost the same array of tools as at the beginning of this century. But before looking for new, innovative ways of empirical research, we still have to use the existing tools more effectively and comprehensively. Thus, research projects should always apply different types of research methods to obtain different types of data from different sources. At the same time—although there are still problems to solve with multimethod studies—we should stop spending so much money on routine survey research.

If I reflect on the studies presented at the conference in Berlin and included as chapters in this volume, I would admit that some of the propositions formulated seem to be utopian. Although the volume and our discussions may not demonstrate a very promising point of departure, they still show the progress that can be made if we put together the experiences, theoretical frameworks, methodological skills, and empirical results developed in different countries. However much this might achieve, it seems self-evident to me that social scientists cannot propose new strategies for social service delivery systems because the old ones did not succeed and at the same time go on doing research with the same selective and only partially effective conceptual and empirical tools. If we ask practitioners to stop paying ever more money to a family instead of giving necessary psychosocial support, we in turn should be willing to stop research procedures that have proven their ineffectiveness to explain social change, the development of social problems, the structural and personal problems of service delivery, and the negative or positive impacts of services on clients' living conditions and needs.

Bibliography

Achinger, H. 1958. *Sozialpolitik als Gesellschaftspolitik: Von der Arbeiterfrage zum Wohlfahrtsstaat.* Reinbek.

Anderson, R., and J.F. Newman. 1973. "Societal and Individual Determinants of Medical Care Utilization in the United States." *Milbank Memorial Fund Quarterly* 51 (1): 95-124.

Anshen, M., ed. 1974. *Managing the Socially Responsible Corporation.* New York.

Arnstein, S. 1969. "A Ladder of Citizen Participation." *Journal of the American Institute of Planners* (July): 216-32.

Badura, B. 1978. "Volksmedizin und Gesundheitsvorsorge." *WSI-Mittei-lung* 10.

Badura, B., and P. Gross. 1976. *Sozialpolitische Perspectiven. Eine Einfuhrung in Grundlagen und Probleme sozialer Dienstleistung.* Munich.

Baekeland, F., and L. Lundwall. 1975. "Dropping out of treatment: A critical review." *Psychological Bulletin* 82(5): 738-83.

Baier, H. 1977. "Herrschaft in Sozialstaat." In C.V. Ferber and F.-X. Kaufman, eds., *Soziologie und Sozialpolitik.* Opladen.

Barber, B. et al. 1973. *Human Experimentation.* New York.

Bar-Yosef, R. 1968. "Desocialization and Re-Socialization: The Adjustment Process of Immigrants." *International Migration Review* 2:6.

——. 1977. "Egalitarianism, Participation and Policy in Israel." In I.L. Horowitz, ed., *Equity, Income and Policy: A comparative Developmental Context,* 106-45. New York.

Bar-Yosef, R., and E.O. Schild. 1966. "Pressures and Defenses in Bureaucratic Roles." *American Journal of Sociology* 81:6.

Bar-Yosef, R.; G. Schild; and J. Varsher. 1974a. *Unemployed Professionals.* Jerusalem. (In Hebrew.)

____ . 1974b. *The Economic Situation of Large Families during the Yom Kippur War.* Jerusalem. (In Hebrew.)

Beck, B. 1967. "Welfare as a moral category." *Social Problems* 14 (Winter): 258-77.

Beck, D.F. 1962. *Patterns in the Use of Family Agency Service.* New York.

Becker, H. 1956. "Some problems of professionalization." *Adult Education* 6 (Winter):101-105.

____. 1962. "The nature of a profession." *Sixty-first Year Book of the National Society for the Study of Education*, pt. 2, Education for the Professions, pp. 27-46. Chicago.

____. 1967. "Whose side are we on?" *Social Problems* 14 (Winter):239-47.

Bell, D. 1960. *The End of Ideology.* New York.

Ben-David, J. 1958. "The professional role of the physician in bureaucratized medicine." *Human Relations* 11 (August):255-74.

Bensman, J., and A.J. Vidich. 1971. *The New American Society.* Chicago.

Berger, P.L., and T. Luckmann. 1966. *The social construction of reality.* Garden City, N.Y.

Berger, P., and S. Pullberg. 1966. "Reification and the sociological critique of consciousness." *New Left Review* 35(1):56-71.

Bidwell, C.E. 1970. "Students and schools: Some observations on client trust in client-serving organizations." In M. Lefton, ed., *Organizations and Clients* pp. 37-69. Columbus.

Blau, P.M. 1955. *The Dynamics of Bureaucracy.* Chicago.

Blau, P.M., and W.R. Scott. 1962. *Formal Organizations.* San Francisco.

Blum, A.F., and L. Rosenberg. 1968. "Some problems involved in professionalizing social interaction." *Journal of Health and Social Behavior* 9:72-86.

Blum, H.L. 1975. "Utilization in the Health Care Delivery System." *Social Welfare Forum*, 102d Annual Forum, pp. 96-114.

Bohnsack, R.; F. Schliehe; and S. Schneider. 1977. "Modelleinrichtungen in der Sozialpolitik: Experimentelle Reformverfahren im Rahmen der Jugendhilfe." See Kaufmann (1977b:150-93).

Booth, T., ed. 1977. *Effectiveness and Priorities: Research Strategies for the Social Services.* Proceedings of the Annual Workshop of the Social Services Research Group, Loughborough University of Technology, March-April.

Bramness, G., and V. Christiansen. 1976. *Koer som rasjoneringsmetode*, ch. 1. Oslo.

Bredermeier, H.C. 1964. "The socially handicapped and the agencies: A market analysis." In F. Riessman; J. Cohen; and A. Pearl, eds., *Mental Health of the Poor*, pp. 88-109. New York.

Brown, M., ed. 1974. *Social issues and the social services.* London.

Bucher, R., and J. Stelling. 1969. "Characteristics of professional organizations." *Journal of Health and Social Behavior* 10:3-15.

Bujard, O., and U. Lange. 1978. *Theorie und Praxis der Sozialhilfe.* Zur Situation der einkommensschwachen alten Menschen. Weinheim.
Bunker, D.R. 1972. "Policy sciences perspectives on implementation processes." *Policy Sciences* 3:71-80.
Burchard, W.W. 1954. "Role conflicts of military chaplains." *American Sociological Review* 19:528-35.
Bush, M., and A.C. Gordon. 1978. "Client choice and bureaucratic accountability: Possibilities for responsiveness in a social welfare bureaucracy." *Journal of Social Issues* 34:22-43.
Campbell, T.D. 1978. "Discretionary Rights." In N. Timms and D. Watson, eds., *Philosophy in Social Work.* London.
Campenhausen, A.V., ed. 1976. *Kann der Staat fur alles sorgen?* Dusseldorf.
Caplan, G., and M. Killilea, eds. 1976. *Support Systems and Mutual Help.* New York.
Caplowitz, D. 1963. *The Poor Pay More.* New York.
Carlson, R.O. 1964. "Environmental constraints and organizational consequences: The public school and its clients." In *Behavioral Sciences and Educational Administration,* pp. 262-76. Chicago.
Carr-Saunders, A.M., and P.A. Wilson. 1933. *The Professions.* Oxford.
Carter, L.C. 1968. "The Perspective from Washington." In M. Burns, ed., *Children's Allowances and the Economic Welfare of Children.* New York.
Catrice-Lorey, A. 1976. "Inegalités d'acces aux systemes de protection sociale et pauvreté culturelle." *Revue française des affaires sociales* No 4.
____. 1978. *Dynamique interne de la Securité sociale: du système de pouvoir à la fonction Peronnel.* Paris.
Clark, B.R. 1956. "Organizational Adaptation and Precarious Values." *American Sociological Review* 327-36.
_____. 1960. "The 'cooling-out' function in higher education." *American Journal of Sociology* 65 (May):569-76.
Cloward, R., and I. Epstein. 1965. "Private social welfare's disengagement from the poor. The case of family adjustment agencies." In M.N. Zald, ed., *Social Welfare Institutions,* pp. 623-44. New York.
Cockburn, C. 1977. *The Local State.* London.
Cogan, M.L. 1953. "Toward a definition of profession." *Harvard Education Record* 25:902-14.
Coleman, J.S. 1972. *Policy Research in the Social Sciences.* Morristown.
Coleman, J.; R. Janowicz; S. Fleck; and N. Norton. 1957. "A comparative study of a psychiatric clinic and a family agency." *Social Casework* 38:3-8, 74-80.
Converse, P. 1963. *Attitudes and Non-Attitudes; Continuation of a Dialogue.* Washington, D.C.
Corrigan, P., and P. Leonard. 1978. *Social Work Practice under Capitalism: A Marxist Approach.* London.
Coser, L.A. 1969. "Some unanticipated conservative consequences of liberal theorizing." *Social Problems* 16 (Winter):263-72.
Crozier, C. et al. 1974. *Ou va l'Administration Française?* Paris.

Dachler, H.P., and B. Wilpert. 1978. "Conceptual dimensions and boundaries of participation in organizations: a critical evaluation." *Administrative Science Quarterly*, March.

Dahl, R.A., and C.E. Lindblom. 1963. *Politics, Economics and Welfare.* New York.

Danet, B., and H. Hartman. 1972. "Coping with bureaucracy: The Israeli case." *Social Focus* 51 (September):7-22.

Daniels, A.K. 1969. "The captive professional: bureaucratic limitations in the practice of military psychiatry." *Journal of Health and Social Behavior* 10: 255-65.

——. 1975. "Professionalism in Formal Organizations." See McKinlay (1975: 301-38).

Deisher, R.W. et. al. 1965. "Mothers' opinions of their pediatric care." *Pediatrics* 35 (January):82-90.

Diesing, P. 1962. *Reason in Society.* Urbana.

Domscheit, S., and F.X. Kaufmann. 1977. *Elternarbeit im Kindergarten*—Zur Implementation des Nordrhein-Westfalischen Kindergartengesetzes, Erster Zwischenbericht, Universitat Bielefeld, (vervielfaltigt).

Donnison, D. et al. 1975. *Social Policy Revisited.* London.

Dye, T.R. 1972. *Understanding public policy.* Englewood Cliffs, N.J.

Easton, D. 1965. *A Systems Analysis of Political Life.* New York.

Edelman, M. 1964. *The Symbolic Uses of Politics.* Urbana.

——. 1977. *Political Language: Words that Succeed and Policies that Fail.* New York.

Elliot, J.L. 1972. "Cultural barriers to the utilization of health services." *Inquiry* IX, 4 (December):28-35.

Engel, G.V. 1969. "The effect of bureaucracy on the professional autonomy of the physician." *Journal of Health and Social Behavior* 10 (March):30-41.

Epstein, I. 1973. "Is Autonomous Practice Possible?" *Social Work* 18:5-12.

Eskeland, S., and J. Finne. 1973. *Rettshjelp.* Oslo.

Estes, C.L. 1974. "Community planning for the elderly: A study of goal displacement." *Journal of Gerontology* 29:648-91.

Etzioni, A. 1964. *Modern Organizations.* Englewood Cliffs, N.J.

Evan, W.M. 1966. "The organization-set: Toward a theory of interorganizational relations." In J.D. Thompson, ed., *Approaches to organizational design*, pp. 174-91. Pittsburgh.

Ferber, Chr. v., and L.v. Ferber. 1978. *Der kranke Mensch in der Gesellschaft.* Reinbek.

Ferber, C.v., and F.X. Kaufmann, eds. 1977. *Soziologie und Sozialpolitik.* Sonderheft 19 der Kolner Zeitschrift fur Soziologie und Sozialpsychologie. Opladen.

Festinger, L. 1964. "Behavioral support for opinion change." *Public Opinion Quarterly* 28 (Fall):404-17.

Fisher, B.M. 1969. "Claims and credibility: A discussion of occupational identity and the agent-client relationship." *Social Problems* 16 (Spring): 423-33.

Flora, P.; J. Alber; and J. Kohl. 1977. "Zur Entwicklung der westeuropaischen Wohlfahrtsstaaten." *Politische Vierteljahresschrift* 18(4):707-72.

Fourastie, J. 1963. Le grand espoir du XXe siècle. Paris.

Francis, R.G., and R.C. Stone. 1956. *Service and procedure in bureaucracy: A case study*. Minneapolis.

Francis, V.; B.M. Korsch; and M. Morris. 1969. "Gaps in doctor-patient communication: Patients' responses to medical advice." *New England Journal of Medicine* 280:535-40.

Freidson, E. 1961. *Patients' Views of Medical Practice.* New York.

_____. 1970a. *Professional Dominance: The Social Structure of Medical Care.* Chicago.

_____. 1970b. *Profession of Medicine.* New York.

_____. 1970c. "Dominant Professions, Bureaucracy and Client Services." In W. Rosengren, and M. Lefton, eds., *Organizations and Clients.* Columbus.

_____. 1975. "Dilemmas in the doctor-patient relationship." In C. Cox, ed., *A sociology of medical practice*, pp. 285-98. London.

Fritschler, A.L., and M. Segal. 1971. "Intergovernmental relations and contemporary political science: developing an integrative typology." *Publius* 1:96-122.

Fuchs, V. 1966. *The Growing Importance of the Service Industries.* New York.

Galbraith, J.K. 1973. *Economics and the Public Purpose.* Boston.

Gans, H.J. 1962. *The Urban Villagers.* New York.

_____. 1971. "Social Science for Social Policy." In I.L. Horowitz, ed., *The Use and Abuse of Social Science.* New Brunswick, N.J.

Gans, S., and G. Horton. 1975. *Integration of human services.* New York.

Garfinkel, H. 1956. "Conditions of successful degradation ceremonies." *American Journal of Sociology* 61 (March):420-24.

Gartner, A., and F. Riessman. 1977. *Self Help in the Human Services.* San Francisco.

_____. 1978. *Der aktive Konsument in der Dienstleistungsgesellschaft. Zur politische Okonomie des tertiaren Sektors.* Frankfurt. (Eng. 1974.)

Gilbert, N. 1977. "The transformation of social services." *Social Services Review* 624-41.

Glampson, A., and E.M. Goldberg. 1976. "Post-Seebohm Social Services: The Consumer's Viewpoint." *Social Work Today* 8:6.

Goffman, E. 1952. "On cooling the mark out: some aspects of adaptation to failure." *Psychiatry* 15:451-63.

_____. 1959. *The Presentation of Self in Everyday Life.* New York.

_____. 1961. *Encounters.* Indianapolis.

_____. 1963. *Stigma.* Engelwood Cliffs, N.J.

_____. 1972. *Asyle. Uber die Situation psychiatrischer Patienten und anderer Insassen.* Frankfurt. (Eng. 1961.)

Goldberg, E.M., and D.J. Fruin. 1976. "Towards Accountability in Social Work: A Case Review System for Social Workers." *British Journal of Social Work* 6:1.

Goldberg, E.M., and R.W. Warburton. 1978. *Ends and Means in Social Work.* "The development and outcome of a case review system for social workers" (in press).

Goldberg, E.M.; A. Mortimer; and B.T. Williams. 1970. *Helping the Aged: A Field Experiment in Social Work.* London.

Goldberg, E.M.; R.W. Warburton; B. McGuinness; and J.H. Rowlands. 1977. "Towards Accountability in Social Work: One Year's Intake to an Area Office." *British Journal of Social Work* 7:3.

Goldner, F.H., and R.R. Ritti. 1967. "Professionalization as career immobility." *American Journal of Sociology* 72 (March):489-502.

Goldthorpe, J.H. 1962. "The Development of Social Policy in England, 1800-1914." *Transactions of the Fifth World Congress of Sociology* IV.

Goode, W.J. 1961. "The Librarian: from occupation to profession." *Library Quarterly* 31 (October):306-20.

Gordon, L.K. 1975. "Bureaucratic competence and success in dealing with public bureaucracies." *Social Problems* 23:197-208.

Gore, W.J., and J.W. Dyson. 1964. *The Making of Decisions: A Reader in Administrative Behavior.* New York.

Goss, M.E.W. 1970. "Organizational goals and quality of medical care: evidence from comparative research on hospitals." *Journal of Health and Social Behavior* 11 (December):255-69.

Green, A.D. 1966. "The Professional Worker in the Bureaucracy." *Social Service Review* 40:71-83.

Greenley, J.R., and S.A. Kirk. 1973. "Organizational characteristics of agencies and the distribution of services to applicants." *Journal of Health and Social Behavior* 14 (March):70-79.

———. 1976. "Organizational influences on access to health care." *Social Science and Medicine* 10 (June):317-22.

Greenley, J.R., and R.A. Schoenherr. 1975a. *Encounters with Help-Delivery Organizations: Patient and Client Experiences.* Madison.

———. 1975b. "Patient satisfaction and organizational processes." Presented at the annual meeting of the American Sociological Association, San Francisco.

———. 1978. "Patient-client satisfaction and organizational processes." Manuscript.

Greenwood, E. 1957. "Attributes of a profession." *Social Work* 2 (July):44-45.

Groell, R. 1972. *Organisationsmodelle im Bereich der kommunalen Sozialund Jugendhilfe.* Frankfurt.

Gross, P., and B. Badura. 1977. "Sozialpolitik und soziale Dienste: Entwurf einer Theorie personbezogener Dienstleistungen." In C.v. Ferber and F. -X. Kaufmann, eds., *Soziologie und Sozilpolitik.* Opladen.

Grottian, P., and A. Murswieck, eds. 1974. *Handlungsspielraume der Staatsadministration.* Hamburg.

Grunow, D. 1977. "Problemsyndrome alterer Menschen und die Selektivitat organisierter Hilfe: zur Analyse des Angebots organisierter Hilfe durch Sozialamter and soziale Dienste." *Archiv für Wissenschaft und Praxis der sozialen Arbeit,* pp. 165-95.

_____. 1978. *Alltagskontakte mit der Verwaltung.* Frankfurt and New York.

Grunow, D., and F. Hegner. 1977a. "Moglichkeiten und Grenzen organisierter Hilfe fur Alte und psychisch Gestorte auf ortlicher Ebene." In F. -X. Kaufmann, ed., *Burgernahe Gestaltung der sozialen Umwelt,* pp. 194-236. Meisenheim am Glan.

_____. 1977b. "Von der Burokratiekritik zur Analyse des Netzes burokratischer Organisationen." In T. Leuenberger and K.H. Ruffmann, eds., *Bürokratie,* pp. 45-79. Bern and Las Vegas.

____. 1978a. "Burgernahe der Verwaltung: Moglichkeiten und Grenzen." In F. Laux, ed., *Das Dilemma des offentlichen Dienstes,* pp. 51-100. Bonn.

____. 1978b. *Die Gewahrung personlicher und wirtschaftlicher Sozialhilfe: Untersuchungen zur Burgernahe der kommunalen Sozialverwaltung.* Bielefeld.

_____. 1979. "Organisatorische Rahmenbedingungen der Gewahrung personlicher und wirtschaftlicher Sozialhilfe und ihre Auswirkungen auf 'Burgernahe'." F.X. Kaufmann, ed., *Burgernahe Sozialpolitik.* Frankfurt.

Grunow, D.; F. Hegner; and J. Lempert. 1979. *Sozialstationen: Analysen und Materialien zur Neuorganisation ambulanter Sozial- und Gesund-heitsdienste.* Bielefeld.

Gurin, G.; J. Veroff; and S. Feld. 1960. *Americans View their Mental Health.* New York.

Gussow, Z., and G.S. Tracy. 1976. "The Role of Self-Help Clubs in Adaptation to Chronic Illness and Disability." *Social Science and Medicine* 10: 407-14.

Hall, P. 1965. *The Social Services of Modern England.* London.

Hall, P.; H. Land; R. Parker; and A. Webb. 1975. *Change, Choice and Conflict in Social Policy.* London.

Hall, R.H. et al. 1977. "Patterns of interorganizational relationships." *Administrative Science Quarterly* 22:457-74.

Hasenfeld, Y. 1972. "People processing organizations: An exchange approach." *American Sociological Review* 37 (June):256-63.

Haug, M.R., and M.B. Sussman. 1969. "Professional autonomy and the revolt of the client." *Social Problems* 17:153-61.

Heclo, H., and A. Wildavsky. 1974. *The Private Government of Public Money.* London.

Hegel, G.F.W. 1821. *Grundlinien der Philosophie des Rechts.* Berlin.

Hegner, F. 1976. "Strukturelemente formal organisierter Handlungssysteme." In H. Buschges, ed., *Organisation und Herrschaft,* pp. 228-50. Reinbek.

_____. 1978. *Das burokratische Dilemma: Zu einigen unaufloslichen Widerspruchen in den Beziehungen zwischen Organisation. Personal und Publikum.* Frankfort and New York.

_____. 1979. "Inwieweit sind Sozialstationen geeignet, die nicht-professionelle Erbringung soziales Leistungen zu fordern?" *Soziales Fortschrift* 2.

Hegner, F., and E.H. Schmidt. 1979. "Organisatorische Probleme der horizontalen Politiksegmentierung und Verwaltungsfragmentierung." In F.X. Kaufmann, ed., *Burgernahe Sozialpolitik*. Frankfurt.

Heimann, E. 1929. *Soziale Theorie des Kapitalismus—Theorie der Sozialpolitik*. Tubingen.

Hellstern, G.M., and H. Wollmann. 1977. "Methodische Vorstudie fur die Analyse der stadtebaulichen und stadtstrukturellen Wirkungen ausgewahlter Sanierungs-massnahmen nach dem Stadtebauforderungsgesetz (Endbericht)." Berlin.

Hentschel, V. 1978. "Das System der sozialen Sicherung in historischer Sicht 1880-1975." *Archiv fur Sozialgeschichte* XVIII:307-52.

Herbst, P.G. 1961. "A theory of simple behavior systems, I and II." *Human Relations* 14:71-83, 193-239.

Herlth, A.; F.X. Kaufmann; and K.P. Strohmeier. 1976. "Offentliche Sozialleistungen und familiale Sozialisation—Zur Analyse der Wirkungen familienpolitischer Massnahmen." In K. Hurrelmann, ed., *Sozialisation und Lebenslauf: Empirie und Methodik sozialwissenschaftlicher Personlichkeitsforschung*, pp. 243-59. Reinbek.

Hey, A., and R. Rowbottom. 1971. "Task and Supervision in Area Social Work." *British Journal of Social Work* 1:435-53.

Higgins, J. 1978. *The Poverty Business: Britain and America*. Oxford.

Hogan, D.P. 1977. "Racial Stratification and Socioeconomic Change in the American North and South." *American Journal of Sociology* 1 (July).

Hollingshead, A.B., and F.C. Redlich. 1958. *Social Class and Mental Illness*. New York.

Homans, G.C. 1961. *Social Behavior: Its Elementary Forms*. New York.

____. 1964. "Bringing Men Back In." *American Sociological Review* XXIX:5 (December).

Hondrich, K.O. 1973. "Bedurfnisorientierungen und soziale Konflikte. Zur theoretischen Begrundung eines Forschungsprogramms." *Zeitschrift fur Soziologie* 2:263-81.

Howard, D.S. 1969. *Social Welfare, Values, Means and Ends*. Philadelphia.

Howard, J., and A. Strauss, eds. 1975. *Humanizing Health Care*. New York.

Hughes, E.C. 1966. "Comment to J. Roach." *American Journal of Sociology* 71 (July):75-76.

Hulka, B.; S. Thompson; J. Cassel; and S. Zyzanski. 1971. "Satisfaction with medical care in a low-income population." *Journal of Chronic Diseases* 23: 661-73.

Hunt, R.G.; O. Gurrslin; and J.L. Roach. 1958. "Social status and psychiatric service in a child guidance clinic." *American Sociological Review* 23 (February):81-83.

Innes, I.M. 1977. "Does the professional know what the client wants?" *Social Science and Medicine* 11:635-38.

Israel, J. 1977. *Die sozialen Beziehungen*. Reinbek.

J.A.B.S. 1976. Special Issue on Self-Help Groups. *Journal of Applied Behavioral Science* 12:3.

Janowitz, M., and W. Delany. 1957. "The bureaucrat and the public: A study of informational perspectives." *Administrative Science Quarterly* 2:141-62.
Jordan, W. 1974. *Poor Parents.* London.
Kadushin, A. 1974. "Supervisor-supervisee: a survey." *Social Work* 19:288-97.
Kadushin, C. 1962. "Social distance between client and professional." *American Journal of Sociology* 67:517-31.
——. 1969. *Why People Go to Psychiatrists.* New York.
Kahn, A.J., and S.B. Kamerman. 1976. *Social Services in International Perspective: The Emergence of the Sixth System.* Washington, D.C.
Kahn, R.L.; D.M. Wolfe; and R.P. Quinn. 1964. *Organizational stress: Studies in role conflict and ambiguity.* New York.
Kamerman, S.B., and A.J. Kahn. 1976. *Social Services in the United States.* Philadelphia.
Kane, R. 1975. *Interprofessional Teamwork.* Syracuse, N.Y.
Katz, E., and B. Danet. 1973a. "Bureaucracy as a problem for sociology and society." In E. Katz and B. Danet, eds., *Bureaucracy and the public*, pp. 3-27. New York.
——. 1973b. "Communication between bureaucracy and the public." In I.d.S. Pool et al., eds., *Handbook of communication.* pp. 666-705. Chicago.
Kaufmann, F.X. 1970. *Sicherheit als soziologisches und sozialpolitisches Problem*—Untersuchungen zu einer Wertidee hochdifferenzierter Gesellschaften. Stuttgart (2nd. ed. 1973).
——. 1977a. "Sozialpolitisches Erkenntnisinteresse und Soziologie: Ein Beitrag zur Pragmatik der Sozialwissenschaften." In Ferber and Kaufmann (1977).
——. ed. 1977b: *Burgernahe Gestaltung der sozialen Umwelt:* Probleme und theoretische Perspektiven eines Forschungsverbundes. Meisenheim.
Kaufmann, F.X., and P. Schaefer. 1977. "Burgernahe Gestaltung der sozialen Umwelt: Ein Bezugsrahmen zur Problemposition." In Kaufmann (1977b: 1-44).
Kaufmann, F.X.; F. Hegner; L. Hoffmann; and J. Kruger. 1971. *Zum Verhaltnis zwischen Sozialversiche-rungstragern und Versicherten:* Gutachten fur das Bundesministerium fur Arbeit und Sozialordnung. Bielefeld (vervielfaltight).
Kaufmann, F.X.; A. Herlth; H.J. Schulze; and K.P. Strohmeier. 1978. *Sozialpolitik und familiale Sozialisation:* Abschlussbericht des Forschungs-projekts "Wirkungen offentlicher Sozialleistungen auf den Sozialisations—prozess." Universitat Bielefeld.
——. 1979. "Wirkungen offentlicher Sozialleistungen auf den familialen Sozialisationsprozess." In K. Luscher, ed., *Sozialpolitik fur Kinder.* Stuttgart.
Kaufmann, M.-Th. 1965. "Europaisches Seminar uber die Beziehungen zwischen sozialer Sicherheit und sozialen Einrichtungen." *Pro Infirmis* 24:9 (Zurich).
Kegeles, S.S. 1967. "Attitudes and behavior of the public regarding cervical cytology: Current findings and new directions for research." *Journal of Chronic Diseases* 20 (December):911-22.
Kirk, S.A., and J.R. Greenley. 1974. "Denying or delivering services?" *Social Work* 19:4 (July):439-47.

Kjønstad, A. 1975. "Sosialretten." In *Knophs oversikt over Norges rett*, p. 723. 7th ed. Oslo.

Kleiber, N., and L. Light. 1978. *Caring for Ourselves. An Alternative Structure for Health Care.* Vancouver.

Kolberg, J.E. 1976. "*Hvorfor kom sa mange pa trygd—og flere enn man forventet?*" University of Tromso. Mimeo.

Konglan, G. et al. 1976. "Interorganizational measurement in the social service sector: differences by hierarchical level." *Administrative Science Quarterly* 21:675-87.

Kornhauser, W. 1962. *Scientists in Industry: Conflicts and Accommodations.* Berkeley.

Kosa, J.; J.J. Alpert; and R.J. Haggerty. 1967. "On the reliability of family health information: A comparative study of mothers' reports on illness and related behavior." *Social Science & Medicine* 1 (July):165-81.

Kramer, R.M. 1969. *Participation of the Poor.* New Jersey.

Krause, E.A. 1968. "Functions of a bureaucratic ideology: 'Citizen Participation.'" *Social Problems* 16:129-43.

Kroeger, N. 1975. "Bureaucracy, social exchange, and benefits received in a public assistance agency." *Social Problems* 23:182-96.

Kuhn, A. 1966. *The Study of Society: A Multidisciplinary Approach.* London.

———. 1971. "Types of social systems and system controls." In M.D. Rubin, ed. *Man in systems.* New York.

Ladinsky, J. 1976. "The traffic in legal services: Lawyer-seeking behavior and the channeling of clients." *Law and Society Review* 11:2 (Special Issue): 207-23.

Laslett, H., and W.G. Runciman, eds. 1967. *Neutrality in Political Science.* Oxford.

Lehmann, H.L. 1978. "Probleme aktiver Sozialpolitik am Beispiel der Bekampfung der Jungendarbeitslosigkeit durch die Arbeitsverwaltung." Masters thesis. Koustanz.

Leibfried, S. 1976. "Armutspotential und Sozialhilfe in der Bundesrepublik." *Kritische Justiz*, pp. 377-93.

———. "General Assistance in the Federal Republic of Germany—Towards an Explanation of the Submerged Majority of Non-Recipients." ISA Research Committee on Poverty, Social Welfare and Social Policy seminar, Geneva.

Leonard, P. 1975. "Policy and Priorities: the Role of the Team Leader." In R. Olsen, ed., *Management in the Social Services.* Bangor.

Levin, L.S.; A. Katz; and E. Holst. 1976. *Self-Care: Lay Initiatives in Health.* London.

Levine, M., and A. Levine. 1970. "The more things change: A case history of child guidance clinics." *Journal of Social Issues* 26:3 (Summer):19-34.

Levine, S., and P.E. White. 1961. "Exchange as a conceptual framework for the study of interorganizational relationships." *Administrative Science Quarterly* 5:583-601.

Levine, S.; P.E. White; and B.D. Paul. 1963. "Community interorganizational problems in providing medical care and social services." *American Journal of Public Health* 53 (August):1183-95.

Levy, C.S. 1973. "The Ethics of Supervision." *Social Work* 18:14-21.

Levy, F.; A.J. Meltsner; and A. Wildavsky. 1974. *Urban Outcomes: Schools, Streets, and Libraries.* Berkeley.

Linden, V. 1972. "I hvilken utstrekning nar informasjonen om de sosiale trygder frem?" *Tidsskrift for den norske laegeforening* 23.

Luhmann, N. 1964. *Funktionen und Folgen formaler Organisation.* Berlin.

____. 1971. "Sinn als Grundbegriff der Soziologie." In J. Habermas et al. *Theorie der Gesellschaft oder Sozialtechnologie.* Frankfurt.

_____. 1972. "Einfache Sozialsysteme." *Zeitschrift fur Soziologie* 1:51-65.

_____. 1976. "A general theory of organized social systems." In M.S. Kassem and G. Hofstede, eds., *European contributions to organization theory.* Amsterdam.

Lundberg, G.A. 1953. *Foundations of Sociology.* New York.

Lyngstad, R. 1974. "Driv trygdeetaten god nok informasjon?" *Sosial Trygd* 4.

Maas, H.S. 1955. "Sociocultural factors in psychiatric clinic service for children." *Smith College Studies in Social Work* 25 (February):1-90.

Macaulay, S. 1967. "Non-contractual relations in business. A preliminary study." *American Sociological Review* 32:55-67.

Madison, B. 1970. "The Welfare State—Some Unanswered Questions for the 1970's." *Social Service Review* 44 (December):434-51.

Majone, G., and A. Wildavsky. 1978. "Implementation as evolution: exorcising the ghosts in the implementation machine." *Policy Analysis.*

Marret, C.B. 1971. "On the specification of interorganizational dimensions." *Sociology and Social Research* pp. 83-99.

Marris, P., and M. Rein. 1974. *Dilemmas of Social Reform.* Rev. ed. Harmondsworth.

Marx, K. 1952. *Das Kapital.* Berlin. (First published 1887.)

Mayer, J., and N. Timms. 1970. *The Client Speaks.* London.

Mayntz, R. 1977. "Die Implementation politischer Programme: theoretische Uberlegungen zu einem neuen Forschungsgebiet." *Die Verwaltung - Zeitschrift fur Verwaltungswissenschaft* 10:51-66.

McCleary, R. 1978. "On becoming a client." *Journal of Social Issues* 34(4): 57-75.

McKay, A.; E.M. Goldberg; and D.J. Fruin. 1973. "Consumers and a Social Services Department." *Social Work Today* 4 (16).

McKinlay, J.B. 1970. "Some Aspects of Lower Working Class Utilization Behaviour." Doctoral Dissertation, Aberdeen.

_____. 1972a. "Some approaches and problems in the study of the use of services: An overview." *Journal of Health and Social Behaviour* 13 (June): 115-52.

_____. 1972b. "The sick role-illness and pregnancy." *Social Science and Medicine* 6:561-72.

_____. 1975. "Clients & Organizations." In J.B. McKinlay, ed., *Processing People—A Study of Organizational Behaviour.* London.

_____. 1977. "The Business of Good Doctoring or Doctoring as Good Business, Reflections on Freidson's View of the Medical Game." *International Journal of Health Service* 7.

Mechanic, D. 1976. *The Growth of Bureaucratic Medicine.* New York.

Mennerick, L.A. 1974. "Client typologies. A method of coping with conflict in the service worker-client relationship." *Sociology of Work Occupations* 1:396-418.

Merriam, I.C. 1963. "Social Services Provided by Social Security Agencies Members of ISSA." Preliminary Draft, September 1963.

Merton, R.K. 1940. "Bureaucratic Structure and Personality." *Social Forces* 18:560-68.

———. 1958. *Social Theory and Social Structure.* Rev. ed. New York.

———. 1971. "Social problems and sociological theory." In R.K. Merton and R. Nisbet, eds., *Contemporary social problems.* 3rd ed. New York.

Metcalfe, J.L. 1976. "Organizational strategies and interorganizational networks." *Human Relations* pp. 327-44.

Meyer, J.W., and B. Rowan. 1977. "Institutionalized organizations: Formal structure as myth and ceremony." *American Journal of Sociology* 83:2 (September):340-63.

Meyer, M.W. 1975. "Organizational domains." *American Sociological Review* 40 (October):599-615.

Meyer,-Cronemeyer, H. 1969. *Kibbutzim Geschichte, Geist und Gestalt.* Verlag fur Literatur, Zeitgeschehen, Geschichte.

Miliband, R. 1973. *The State in Capitalist Society.* London.

Miller, S.M. 1968. "Criteria for Anti-Poverty Policies: A Paradigm for Choice." *Poverty and Human Resources Abstracts* III (5):3-11.

———. 1975. "Planning: Can It Make a Difference in Capitalist America?" *Social Policy* (September-October):12-22.

Miller, S.M.; P. Roby; and A. de vos van Steenwijk. 1970. "Creaming The Poor." *Trans-Action* (July).

Mills, C.W. 1951. *White Collar: The American Middle Class.* New York.

Mills, E. 1962. *Living with Mental Illness.* London.

Modes, H.J. 1978. "Die gesellschaftliche Ausgliederung der alten Menschen in der BRD—und einige Alternativen zur aktiven Reintegration." Masters thesis, Konstanz.

Moller, M.L. 1977. "Zur Bildung von Selbsthilfegruppen: Ein Erfahrungsbericht fur Teilnehmer und Experten." *Psychiatrische Praxis* 4:197-212.

———. 1978. *Selbsthilfegruppen.* Reinbek.

Muller, W. 1973. "Die Relativierung des burokratischen Modells und die situative Organisation." *KZfSS* 25:719-49.

Murray, H.A. 1938. *Explorations in personality.* 3rd ed. New York.

Murswieck, A., ed. 1976. *Staatliche Politik im Sozialsektor.* Munich.

Musgrave, R.A. 1959. *The Theory of Public Finance: a Study in Public Economy.* New York.

Nagi, S.Z. 1974. "Gate-keeping decisions in service organizations: When validity fails." *Human Organization* (Spring):47-58.

NCDP (National Community Development Project). 1977. *Gilding the Ghetto: The State and the Poverty Experiment.* London.

Neghandi, A., ed. 1971. *Organization theory in an interorganizational perspective.* Kent, Ohio.

Neill, J.E.; R.W. Warburton; and B. McGuinness. 1976. "Post-Seebohm Social Services: The Social Worker's Viewpoint." *Social Work Today* 8 (6).

Neill, J.E.; D.J. Fruin; E.M. Goldberg; and R.W. Warburton. 1973. "Reactions to Integration." *Social Work Today* 4 (15).

Nevitt, D.A. 1977. "Demand and Need." In H. Heisler, ed., *Foundations of Social Administration.* London.

Nisbet, R. 1975. *Twilight of Authority.* New York.

Nizard, L. 1975. "Planning as the Regulatory Reproduction of the Status-Quo." In J. Hayward, and M. Watson, eds., *Planning, Politics and Public Policy: The French, British and Italian Experience.* Cambridge, England.

NOU. 1976. *Anke til Trygderetten* 56:12, 22.

O'Connor, J. 1973. *The Fiscal Crisis of the State.* New York.

Odland, M. 1977. "Svaksyn og blindhet i Bergen og Hordaland. En medisinsk og sosialmedisinsk undersokelse." Thesis, Faculty of Medicine, Bergen.

OECD. 1976. "Analytical Report." In "Policies for Innovation in the Service Sector." pp. 209-21. Paris. Manuscript.

Offe, C. 1972. *Strukturprobleme des kapitalistischen Staates.* Frankfurt.

____. 1974. "Rationalitatskriterien und Funktionsprobleme politisch-administrativen Handelns." *Leviathan* 2:333-45.

Øyen, E. 1974. *Sosialomsorgen og dens forvaltere.* Oslo.

____. ed. 1976. *Sosiologi og ulikhet* (Sociology and Inequality). Oslo.

____. 1978. "Taushetspliktens sosiale konsekvenser" (Some Consequences of Professional Secrecy). Memorandum prepared for the Committee on Ethics, The Norwegian Research Council, Oslo, April.

Pankoke, E. 1970. *Sociale Bewegung—Sociale Frage—Sociale Politik:* Grundfragen der Deutschen "Socialwissenschaft" im 19. Jahrhundert. Stuttgart.

____. 1971. "Kommunale Beteiligung als Problem der Verwaltungs—organisation." *Die Verwaltung* 4:395-422.

Pareto, V. 1963. *Treatise on General Sociology.* New York.

Parker, R.A. 1970. "The Future of the Personal Social Services." In W.A. Robson and B. Crick, *The Future of the Social Services*, pp. 105-16. Harmondsworth.

Parsloe, P. 1977. "How training may 'unfit' people." *Social Work Today* 9: 15-18.

Parsons, T. 1951. *The Social System.* Glencoe, Illinois.

____. 1970a. "How Are Clients Integrated into Service Organisations." In W. Rosengren and M. Lefton, eds., *Organisations and Clients.* Columbus.

____. 1970b. "Some Problems of General Theory in Sociology." In J.C. McKinney and E.A. Tiryakian, eds., *Theoretical Sociology, Perspectives and Developments.* New York.

Pearson, G. 1975. "The politics of uncertainty." In H. Jones, ed., *Towards a New Social Work.* London.

Perrow, C. 1961. "The analysis of goals in complex organizations." *American Sociological Review* 26:6 (December):855.

Pesso, T. 1978. "Local welfare offices: Managing the intake process." *Public Policy* 26:305-30.

Pettes, D. 1979. *Staff and Student Supervision: A Task Centred Approach.* London.

Peyser, D. 1951. *The Strong and the Weak: A Sociological Study*. Sydney.

Pickering, M. 1975. "Realities of work in an area team." *Social Work Today* 6:397-98.

Pinker, R. 1971. *Social Theory and Social Policy*. London.

——. 1974. "Social Policy and Social Justice." *Journal of Social Policy* 3:1.

Piven, F.F., and R. Cloward. 1971 and 1972. *Regulating the Poor.* New York *Forum* XIII:2 (Summer):17-22.

Piven, F.F., and R. Cloward. 1971 and 1972. *Regulating The Poor.* New York and London.

Ponsioen, J.A., ed. 1962. *Social Welfare Policy*. The Hague.

Pruger, R. 1973. "The good bureaucrat." *Social Work* pp. 26-32.

Rainwater, L. 1967. *Behind Ghetto Walls: Black Families in a Federal Slum.* Baltimore.

Randall, R. 1973. "Influence of environmental support and policy space on organizational behavior." *Administrative Science Quarterly* 18:2 (June): 236-47.

——. *Rapport om enkelte sider av folketrygdens utforming og virkninger.* 1971. 62-74.

Rapport om enkelte sider av folketrygdens utforming og virkninger. 1971. Report presented by a committee appointed by the Ministry for Social Affairs, December 30.

Raskoff, S.H., and G.T. Schaefer. 1970. "Politics, Policy and Political Science: Theoretical Alternatives." *Politics and Society* 1:51-77.

Reader, C.G.; L. Pratt; and M.C. Mudd. 1967. "What patients expect from their doctors." *Modern Hospital* 89 (July):88-94.

Reddin, M. 1970. "Utopia and Social Planning." Department of Social Science and Administration, London School of Economics. Mimeo.

Reid, W.J., and L. Epstein. 1972. *Task-Centred Casework.* New York.

Rhodes, S.L. 1978. "Communication and interaction in the worker-client dyad." *Social Service Review* 52:122-31.

Robin, S.S., and M.O. Wagenfeld. 1977. "The community mental health worker: Organizational and personal sources of role discrepancy." *Journal of Health and Social Behavior* 18:16-27.

Robson, W.A. 1976. *Welfare state and welfare society*. London.

Rogers, D.L. 1974. "Toward a scale of interorganisational relations among public agencies." *Sociology and Social Research*, pp. 61-74.

Romanyshyn, J.M. 1971. *Social Welfare. Charity or Justice.* New York.

Rosengren, W.R. 1970. "The careers of clients and organizations." In W.R. Rosengren and M. Lefton, eds. (1970).

Rosengren, W.R., and M. Lefton, eds. 1970. *Organizations and clients.* Columbus.

Rowbottom, R. et al. 1974. *Social Services Departments.* London.

Rose, S.M. 1972. *The Betrayal of the Poor.* Cambridge.

Ruzek, S.K. 1973. "Making social work accountable." In E. Freidson, ed., *The professions and their prospects*, pp. 217-43. Beverly Hills.

Ryan, W. 1971. *Blaming the Victim.* London.

Sainsbury, E. 1977. *The Personal Social Services.* London.

Schaffer, B., and W. Huang. 1975. "Distribution and the Theory of Access." *Development and Change* 2 (April).

Scharpf, F.W. 1977. "Public Organization and the Waning of the Welfare State: A Research Perspective." *European Journal of Political Research* 5:339-62.

Scherer, K.R., and U. Scherer. 1977. "Burgernahe im Publikumsverkehr." In F.X. Kaufmann, ed. *Burgernahe Gestaltung der sozialen Umwelt,* pp. 237-72. Meisenheim.

Scherer, K.R.; U. Scherer; and M. Klink. 1978. "Burgernahe im Publikumsverkehr: Sozialpsychologische Untersuchungen von Bediensteten-Burger-Interaktionen." Giessen. Mimeo.

Schluchter, W. 1972. *Aspekte burokratischer Herrschaft.* Munich.

Schumpeter, J.A. 1942. *Capitalism, Socialism and Democracy.* New York.

———. 1954. *History of economic analysis.* London.

Scott, R.A. 1961. *The Making of Blind Men.* New York.

———. 1969.

Scott, W.R. 1966. "Professionals in Bureaucracies—Areas of Conflict." In W.M. Vollmer, and D.L. Mills, eds., *Professionalization.* Englewood Cliffs, N.J.

Seebohm, F., Chairman. 1968. *Report of the Committee on Local Authority and Allied Personal Social Services.* Cmnd. 3703. London.

Selznick, P. 1957. *Leadership in administration: a sociological interpretation.* New York.

Sethi, P.S. 1974. *The Unstable Ground: Corporate Social Policy in a Dynamic Society.* Los Angeles.

Shanas, E. et al. 1968. *Old People in Three Industrial Societies.* London.

Sheriff, P. 1976. "Sociology of Public Bureaucracies 1965-1975." *Current Sociology* 24:2.

Siegal, N.H.; and R.L. Kahn; H. Pollack; and H. Fink. 1962. "Social class, diagnosis, and treatment in three psychiatric hospitals." *Social Problems* 10:191-96.

Silverman, D. 1970. *The theory of organizations. A sociological framework.* London.

Sinfield, A. 1978. "Analyses in the Social Division of Welfare." *Journal of Social Policy* 7:2 (April):129-56.

Sjoberg, G.; R.A. Brymer; and B. Farris. 1966. "Bureaucracy and the lower class." *Sociology and Social Research* 50:325-37.

Skarpelis-Sperk, S. 1978. *Soziale Rationierung offentlicher Leinstungen.* Frankfurt and New York.

Sleeman, J.F. 1973. *The Welfare State—Its Aims, Benefits and Costs.* London.

Smith, A. 1976. *An Inquiry into the Nature and Causes of the Wealth of Nations.* Oxford.

Sozialbericht. 1976. Edited by Bundesminister fur Arbeit und Sozialordnung. Bonn.

Spiro, M.E. 1956. *Kibbutz: Venture in Utopia.* Cambridge, England.

Stanton, E. 1970. *Clients Come Last.* Beverly Hills.

Statham, D. 1978. *Radicals in Social Work.* London.

Steiner, G.Y. 1966. "The Social Work Syndrome." In *Social Insecurity: The Politics of Welfare*. New York.

Stevens, S. 1954. "An ecological study of child guidance intake." *Smith College Studies in Social Work* 25 (October):73-84.

Stevenson, O. 1977. "Focus on the task of the local authority social worker." *Social Work Today* 9:11-14.

Stevenson, O. et al. 1978. *Social Service Teams: The Practitioner's View*. London.

Strauss, A.; L. Schatzman; R. Ehrlick; R. Bucher; and M. Sabshin. 1963. "The hospital and its negotiated order." In E. Freidson, ed., *The Hospital in Modern Society*. New York.

Strong, P.M., and A.G. Davis. 1977. "Roles, role formats and medical encounters. A cross-cultural analysis of staff-client relationships in children's clinics." *Sociological Review* 25:775-800.

Suchman, E.A. 1964. "Sociological variations among ethnic groups." *American Journal of Sociology* 70:319-31.

———. 1965. "Social patterns of illness and medical care." *Journal of Health and Human Behavior* 6 (Spring):2-16.

Sykes, G. 1958. *The society of captives*. Princeton.

Szasz, T.S. 1967. "The psychiatrist as a double agent." *Transaction* 4 (October): 16-25.

Talmon, Y.G. 1970. *The Individual and the Group in the Kibbutz*. Jerusalem. (In Hebrew.)

Tawney, R. 1913. "Poverty as an Industrial Problem." *Memoranda on Problems of Poverty* (London) II:9-20.

Taylor, C. 1967. "Neutrality in Political Science." In H. Laslett, and W.G. Runciman, eds., *Philosophy, Politics and Society*. Oxford.

Tennstedt, F. 1976. "Sozialgeschichte der Sozialversicherung." In M. Blohmke et. al., ed., *Handbuch der Sozialmedizin* III:385-492. Stuttgart.

———. 1977. *Geschichte der Selbstverwaltung in der Krankenversicherung:* von der Mitte des 19. Jahrhunderts bis zur Grundung der Bundesrepublik Deutschland. Bonn.

Thomas, D., and W. Warburton. 1977. *Community Workers in a Social Services Department: A Case Study*. London.

Thompson, J.D. 1962. "Organizations and output transactions." *American Journal of Sociology* 68:3 (November):309-24.

———. 1967. *Organizations in action. Social science bases of administration theory*. New York.

Thompson, V.A. 1975. *Without sympathy and enthusiasm*. Alabama.

Titmuss, R.M. 1958. *Essays on "The Welfare State."* London.

———. 1965. "Poverty versus Inequality: Diagnosis." *Nation* (February):130-33.

———. 1970. *The Gift Relationship*. London.

Touraine, A. 1969. *La societe post-industrielle*. Paris.

Townsend, P. 1962. "The Last Refuge." In P. Townsend and N. Bosanquet 1972. London.

———. 1970. "The Objectives of the New Social Service." In *The Fifth Social*

Service. London.

——. 1975. *Sociology and Social Policy*. London.

Townsend, P., and N. Bosanquet, eds. 1972. *Labour and Inequality*. London.

Tuite, M. et. al., eds. 1972. *Interorganizational decision making*. Chicago.

Utredning. 1973. *Utredning om sporsmal som knytter seg til misbruk og overforbruk av Folketrygdens midler—spesielt om sykefravaer og sykepenger m.v.* Report presented by a committee appointed by the local social security offices, September 24.

Utting, B. 1977. "The Future of the Personal Social Services." *Social Work Service*, May.

Vinter, R.D. 1963. "Analysis of treatment organizations." *Social Work* 8 (July): 3-15.

Walsh, J.L., and R.H. Elling. 1968. "Professionalism and the poor: Structural effects and professional behaviour." *Journal of Health and Social Behaviour* 9 (March):16-28.

Ware, J.E.; M.K. Snyder; and W.R. Wright. 1976. *Development and Validation of Scales to Measure Patient Satisfaction with Health Care Services*. Vol. I of a Final Report. Carbondale, Ill.

Warham, J. 1977. *An Open Case: The Organisational Context of Social Work*. London.

Warner, W.K., and A.E. Havens. 1968. "Goal displacement and intangibility of organizational goals." *Administrative Science Quarterly* 12:4 (March): 539-55.

Warren, R.L. 1967-68. "The Interorganizational field as a focus for investigation." *Administrative Science Quarterly*, pp. 396-419.

Wasserman, H. 1971. "The professional social worker in a bureaucracy." *Social Work* 16 (January):89-95.

Weirich, T.W. et al. 1977. "Interorganizational behavior patterns of line staff and services integration." *Social Service Review*, pp. 674-89.

Weller, L. 1974. *Sociology in Israel*. Connecticut.

Westheimer, I. 1977. *The Practice of Supervision in Social Work: A Guide for Staff Supervision*. London.

Wickenden, E. 1976. "A Perspective on Social Services: An Essay Review." *Social Services Review* 50 (December):570-85.

Widmaier, H.P. 1976. *Sozialpolitik im Wohlfahrtsstaat. Zur Theorie politischer Guter*. Reinbek.

Wilensky, H.L. 1964. "The professionalization of everyone?" *American Journal of Sociology* 70 (September):137-58.

——. 1975. *The Welfare State and Equality*. Berkeley.

Wilensky, H.L., and C.N. Lebeaux. 1958. *Industrial Society and Social Welfare*. New York.

Williams, W. 1971. *Social Policy Research and Analysis: The Experience in the Federal Social Agencies*. New York.

Wirth, W. 1978. "Soziale Dienste: Analyse der Bedingungen ihrer Inanspruchnahme." Diplomarbeit, Universitat Bielefeld.

Wolman, B.B. ed. 1973. *Dictionary of behavioral science*. New York.

Wootton, B. 1959. "Daddy Knows Best." *Twentieth Century* (October): 248-61.

Index

About the Editors

Dieter Grunow studied sociology, economics, psychology, and German in Tuebingen, Jackson (in the United States), and Muenster. Since 1980, he has been director of the project group "Verwaltung und Publikum" ("Administration and the Public") at the University of Bielefeld. Dr. Grunow is involved in research, teaching, and publishing in the fields of empirical organizational and administrative sociology, social and health care policies, and social gerontology.

Friedhart Hegner studied sociology, psychology, history, and political science at the Universities of Saarbruecken and Muenster. The project director and senior research fellow for the research team on "Social Planning and Social Administration" at the University of Bielefeld, in 1980 he joined the staff of the International Institute of Management at the Science Center Berlin. Dr. Hegner is involved in research, teaching, and publishing in the fields of the history of sociology, organizational theory, social and health care policies, and citizens' action committees and other similar movements.

About the Science Center Berlin

The Wissenschaftszentrum Berlin (Science Center Berlin), a non-profit corporation, serves as a parent institution for institutes conducting social science research in areas of significant social concern.

The following institutes are currently operating within the Science Center Berlin:

1. The International Institute of Management,
2. The International Institute for Environment and Society,
3. The International Institute for Comparative Social Research.

They share the following structural elements: a multinational professional and supporting staff, multidisciplinary project teams, a focus on international comparative studies, a policy orientation in the selection of research topics and the diffusion of results.